MW00586322

10/7

10/7

100 HUMAN STORIES

LEE YARON

Afterword by
JOSHUA COHEN

ST. MARTIN'S PRESS
NEW YORK

First published in the United States by St. Martin's Press,
an imprint of St. Martin's Publishing Group

10/7. Copyright © 2024 by Lee Yaron. Afterword © 2024 by
Joshua Cohen. All rights reserved. Printed in the United States
of America. For information, address St. Martin's Publishing
Group, 120 Broadway, New York, NY 10271.

www.stmartins.com

Design by Meryl Sussman Levavi

Map by Jeffery L. Ward

The Library of Congress Cataloging-in-Publication Data is
available upon request.

ISBN 978-1-250-36628-3 (hardcover)
ISBN 978-1-250-36629-0 (ebook)

Our books may be purchased in bulk for promotional,
educational, or business use. Please contact your local
bookseller or the Macmillan Corporate and Premium Sales
Department at 1-800-221-7945, extension 5442, or by email at
MacmillanSpecialMarkets@macmillan.com.

First Edition: 2024

1   3   5   7   9   10   8   6   4   2

To Gal,

A man of peace who did not come back from war

October 7, 2023

© 2024 Jeffrey L. Ward

Contents

10/7

Mourning

AN INTRODUCTION

The Jewish tradition of "sitting shiva"—of observing a ritual mourning period following a death—is derived from the Hebrew word *sheva*, meaning "seven."

In the book of Genesis, Joseph, after burying his father, Jacob, "mourned with a great and very sore lamentation" for seven days. In the prophetic book of Job, Job loses his wife, his seven sons, and his three daughters, following which his companions sit him down on the ground—down in the dust—and attempt to comfort him for seven nights and seven days.

Millennia later, in the lands of the Bible as among Jewish communities worldwide, the ritual still follows the ancient formula:

The seven days of mourning commence with the day of burial, as the immediate family members are compelled to "sit." During this time, any semblance of daily routine is forbidden: A mourner may neither work nor cook, clean the house nor bathe. They must remain in the home of the deceased, sitting as close to the ground as possible, embodying the lowness of their sorrow. The door must be left open to any comforters who wish to visit; their role is to help to carry out the family's everyday tasks. Throughout this period, the mourners must abstain from pleasure. They must tear their clothes, to demonstrate the rip in their souls and to show the unimportance of terrestrial trappings. They must also cover their mirrors, so as not to be distracted by appearances as they turn their gaze inward. Greeting mourners with any word involving the root *shin-lamed-mem*, the Semitic origin of the Hebrew *shalom* (and of the Arabic *salām*) is forbidden; no peace should be sought during the mourning period. On the seventh and final day, those who came to offer condolences are asked to "wake" the mourners and help them rise; grief, that most controlling of emotions, must have a formal end.

Seven full days, the span it took God to create the world and all living things, is barely enough for us humans to mourn one single life, to rise above our lamentation.

Judaism, which has commandments that govern every aspect of human experience from birth to death, offers little guidance on how to hold the kind of shiva required following a massacre such as the one that occurred on October 7, 2023—*shiva b'October* in Hebrew—or the war that came in its wake.

If one has lost one's son, daughter, mother, and husband, all on the same day, should they be mourned collectively, or is there a certain order? Should one sit seven days of shiva for each individual or sit collectively for one weeklong stretch? What does one do without a body to bury? Or if the body is held in captivity—should one start mourning without a burial or wait for the corpse's return? Or if the body is in fragments—should one bury the fragment, mourning a single limb or tooth? What is the role of the comforters if they themselves are in mourning? And how to mark shiva's end, without a routine, or even a home, to return to, especially in the midst of war?

Writing this book, interviewing hundreds of bereaved parents and children, along with survivors and first responders, I searched for answers to such questions—for a way to mourn and a way to rise, for a way once again to say "shalom."

On October 7, 2023—which was the Sabbath, and the holiday of Simchat Torah, itself the final day of the holiday of Sukkot—members of Hamas along with allies in Palestinian Islamic Jihad and eight other groups launched an operation for which they'd been training for at least three years. Crashing through the Gaza border, they attacked from land, sea, and air, indiscriminately massacring civilians in what became one of the worst terror attacks in modern history, and, in the words of President Biden, "the deadliest day for Jews since the Holocaust."

In fewer than twenty-four hours, approximately 3,000 terrorists managed to claim the lives of over 1,200 individuals and abduct around 250—most of them Israeli citizens, but others hailing from more than thirty countries. Civilians ranging in age from infants to the elderly, who'd just woken up that morning, were gunned down, stabbed, and burned alive; they were tortured, raped, and purposefully amputated, in hellish scenes that many of the terrorists documented and posted globally. Entire communities were destroyed, and hundreds of thousands of Israelis were forced to leave their homes, becoming refugees within their own country.

Following the massacre, Israel went to war, striking Gaza with unprecedented fury with the aim of destroying Hamas—a terrorist organization that has vowed to annihilate Israel and ruled Gaza for almost twenty years, ingraining itself into the heart of the civilian population.

At the time of this writing, over thirty thousand Gazans have been killed in this war according to the Gaza Ministry of Health. Many of those killed have been innocent civilians, including thousands of children. According to the United Nations, nearly two million Gazans have been displaced from their homes, and about 70 percent of the territory's homes have been destroyed, along with most of its hospitals, markets, schools, and mosques. The price paid by ordinary Gazans has been unimaginable: dispossessed, with many crowded into makeshift, crowded tent cities close to the Egyptian border, they face hunger and dehydration and illnesses caused by lack of healthcare and lack of access to utilities and basic sanitation services. Men, women, and children who had nothing to do with the crimes of Hamas have wound up paying the heaviest price. For them, even the commandment to mourn has turned into a privilege under fire. The death and suffering of so many innocents are unconscionable.

I am the daughter and granddaughter of refugees and survivors of the Holocaust. I am a Jew; I am an Israeli; I am also a woman, a feminist, a journalist, and a proud adherent of the camp that supports the rights of all peoples between the Jordan River and the Mediterranean Sea, the camp that still believes in the dream of two states for two peoples, ensuring democracy and human rights for Jews and Arabs, Israelis and Palestinians alike.

For nearly a decade, I have worked as a journalist for *Haaretz*, Israel's oldest and most respected newspaper—and the only Hebrew-language newspaper that has consistently covered Arab and Palestinian life and defended the civil liberties of Israeli minorities. Before I became the paper's climate correspondent—trying to awaken the Middle East to its most severe existential threat—I served as its social-welfare reporter. This meant that I tended to enter people's lives during moments of acute pain: victims of prejudice, domestic abuse, and sexual violence. I wrote about asylum seekers contending with discriminatory schooling and housing policies; I wrote about LGBTQ people resisting biased marriage policies and pursuing the right of adoption; I wrote about major polluters, climate change deniers, and state agencies that were denying Holocaust survivors state benefits that were rightfully theirs.

Some of these investigations resulted in policy changes, and even in new legislation, and I came to regard my work as a type of public advocacy: when the state's victims rose into the headlines, they became harder to ignore. Over the course of my career, I came to know nearly every vector of Israeli society: Jewish, Arab, Bedouin, Ethiopian, Eritrean, Sudanese, Chinese, with a special focus on those at the margins, the people whom majoritarian Israel tended to denigrate if not pass over.

In my experience, most journalism, and consequently most history, recounts the exploits of the powerful from the perspective of the powerful: reporting on politics is all too often anchored by quotes from politicians, not from the people most affected by their governance; reporting on the military is usually anchored by quotes from generals and military spokespeople, not from rank-and-file soldiers, and certainly not from the enemy. In writing this book, I sought to present the 10/7 massacre through the type of reporting I was raised on: reporting "from the bottom up," in which the victims and the victimized communities are allowed, as much as possible, to relate their own experiences, their own tragedies, sometimes in their own words, at all times from their own perspectives.

Anchored in the traditions of both investigative journalism and oral history, I along with my researchers conducted hundreds of interviews and supplemented that material with reams of phone and email message transcripts and official documentation. The result is what you hold in your hands: a book that tells the stories of over one hundred people—over one hundred civilians, humans, who lived and died on the Gaza border.

From left-wing kibbutzniks and Burning Man–esque partiers to Bedouins and Israeli Arabs, peace activists and organizers, Holocaust survivors, refugees from Ukraine and Russia—many of whom have endured nearly two decades of Hamas's rocket barrages and yet still managed to believe that a day would come when they and their neighbors would live in peace. Others among the people I've written about lost hope for peace a long time ago, voting for Israeli prime minister Benjamin Netanyahu time and again, believing that through him and only through him they could ensure at least a modicum of security—a simulacrum of peace—for their children. Then there are those in this book such as the Thai and Nepalese guest workers—temporary laborers at farms along the border—as well as tourists from Europe and South America who were in the midst of their vacation, people who had limited experience with the Israeli-Palestinian conflict and did not even know the difference between Hebrew and Arabic when they were slaughtered.

Many of the local border communities that fell victim to this modern pogrom—including Sderot, Ofakim, and Ashkelon—rank among Israel's poorest cities. They are home to significant populations of Jews who were forced to flee their homes in Arab countries such as Morocco, Tunisia, Algeria, Yemen, and Egypt following the midcentury massacres and persecutions that attended Israel's establishment. They found sanctuary and a flourishing life in the world's only Jewish state. These communities also include large numbers of Ethiopian Jews, along with a vast contingent of Jews from Ukraine, Russia, and Central Asia, who sought refuge in Israel following the dissolution of the Soviet Union, and later after the Russian invasion of Ukraine.

The kibbutzim along the border were founded as predominantly socialist communities, which still to this day support left and center political parties and advocate for a two-state solution. If Israeli election outcomes were based solely on the votes from some of these kibbutzim, Netanyahu's Likud party, whose coalition now includes some of the most extreme actors in Israeli political life, would most likely not have cleared the electoral threshold to enter the Knesset.

All in all, almost sixty kibbutzim, moshavim, and cities in an area known in Hebrew as the "Gaza Envelope" (*Otef Aza*) bear the brunt of the hostilities. Not many Israelis have understood the Israeli-Palestinian conflict better than these residents of the border, and not many Israelis have suffered more of its consequences. Take Kibbutz Be'eri, for example, whose members volunteered to transport Palestinian patients to Israeli hospitals and annually donated thousands of dollars to families in Gaza. On 10/7, one in ten residents of Be'eri was either murdered or kidnapped, many of them elderly and children. Most of their houses were destroyed and burned. Or take Kibbutz Kfar Aza, which held an annual peace-themed kite festival, flying messages of coexistence high enough in the sky to be received by the children of Gaza. There, too, one in ten residents is either dead or being held captive in Gaza.

The terrorists of Hamas murdered and destroyed the very communities that did more than any others to promote peace between the two peoples.

In the course of my research, I asked some of the bereaved families if and how their views had changed following the murder of their loved ones. It was a difficult question, but then those are the questions Israelis have been conditioned for—to ask and to answer, and to exist within.

While some progressive families have recommitted to their principles and insist on making an immediate peace with the

Palestinians, others I have spoken with have gone in the opposite direction, at least for now, saying they'd been naive or foolish to think that Israelis and Palestinians could ever live together on this land. They are enraged by Hamas, but also by their own government, which they feel abandoned them.

On the other side of the political divide, among the bereaved that identified with the right, those who supported Netanyahu also describe a deep crisis. They, too, have the sense that everything they'd trusted and invested in has failed. If even the most right-wing government in the country's history couldn't protect them, perhaps nothing could, and the only available solution, or protection, might lie in the individual: Israeli applications for gun licenses and gun purchases have skyrocketed since 10/7.

The shared political ground has never been narrower: what unites the poles of Israeli society is a sense of utter collapse. Beyond Israeli society, however, there is no shared political ground at all: Israeli-Palestinian relations are at a nadir. Israelis and Palestinians have become blind to each other, and deaf to each other's wailing, unwilling or unable to acknowledge the mutuality of pain, the common lot of loss; each tragedy only serves to reinforce and expand the walls between us, as each side denies the other side's facts, emotions, and even right to exist.

While I share the grief of Palestinians, and bear the weight of our entangled histories, I know that Palestinian stories, especially now, are not my stories to tell. I wait with all humility to read the books of my Palestinian colleagues, which will surely tell the stories of the innocents of Gaza, who suffered and died from my country's reaction to their leadership's violence.

Most Israelis and Palestinians were born into this violence. Half of Israelis are under the age of thirty, while half of Palestinians in Gaza are under eighteen. I myself am a child of this demographic—of this lost generation—born at the end of hope, at the end of the administration of Israeli prime minister Yitzhak Rabin, one year after he signed the first of the Oslo Accords and one year before he was assassinated.

It was the official end of the First Intifada (which wasn't then called "the First"), a series of terror attacks perpetrated on Israelis by a newly formed Islamist terror organization called Hamas. The Egypt-based Muslim Brotherhood had spawned a Palestinian branch that was almost as dedicated to destroying Yasser Arafat's secular Fatah party as it was to destroying Israel itself; its founding charter called expressly for the elimination of the Jewish state.

I was two months old when a Hamas suicide bomber blew himself up in a bus full of passengers a few meters away from where my mother stood, with me in her arms. At the moment of the explosion, she whisked me away.

But even as every bus ride, or casual stroll, became fraught, peace was on the horizon. It even had a date—and though the date kept changing, the prospect of a final accord between Rabin and Arafat, and so between Israelis and Palestinians, hovered in the humid air of the Mediterranean.

"We have come from an anguished and grieving land. . . . We have come to try and put an end to the hostilities," Rabin said at the ceremony presided over by US president Clinton on the south lawn of the White House, "so that our children, our children's children, will no longer experience the painful cost of war, violence and terror. We have come to secure their lives and to ease the sorrow and the painful memories of the past to hope and pray for peace," he said, in a rare and then-controversial acknowledgment of the pain of the Palestinian side. "We, the soldiers who have returned from battle . . . we say to you today in a loud and clear voice: Enough of blood and tears. Enough!"

Arafat responded: "Our two peoples are awaiting today this historic hope, and they want to give peace a real chance."

Some of my earliest memories are of being taken by my parents to peace rallies in Tel Aviv, pushed in a stroller, carried on their shoulders—and of being told that soon, soon, the days of sorrow and war would be over.

And yet this was precisely the thing my parents had been told by their own parents, who knew the sorrows and wars of an earlier generation.

In the 1920s, my father's family, the Katz family, were refugees many times over, initially fleeing the persecution of Russian Jewry that came with the establishment of the Soviet Union. They managed to make it to Romania, where they stayed for two tenuous generations, trying to rebuild their lives. During the Holocaust, they were interned in labor camps, a relatively lucky fate when compared to the millions murdered in the extermination camps and the hundreds of thousands killed in the territories the Germans handed over to the Romanians.

In the 1960s, after enduring renewed persecutions under the communist Romanian government, they became refugees again. My paternal grandfather, Dan, was a professor of philosophy; my paternal grandmother, Lili, a translator and interpreter for the theater, a woman who spoke seven languages. Arriving in Israel, they had to start over, finding only low-wage jobs as a municipal clerk and a secretary and struggling to adapt to a new climate, culture, and language in their fifth decade of life.

If my father's family is an exemplary Ashkenazi story, my mother's family represents the other half: Sephardim.

My ancestors on my mother's side were among the tens of

thousands of Jews deported from Portugal solely for the crime
of being Jews, an event that lived on in their surname, Adato.
The Hebrew language avails itself of a system called gematria, in
which each letter is assigned a numerical value: *aleph*, the first
letter, is 1; *bet*, the second letter, is 2, and so on. My mother's
surname is Adato, which in Hebrew is made up of four letters:
aleph, *daled*, *tet*, and *vav*, which together spell out the number
1496, the year of the expulsion of Jews from Portugal, making
their surname a constant reminder of their plight.

Many Jews from Portugal, who found themselves in Italy,
took on this surname because they enjoyed its double meaning: to Jews, Adato meant 1496, while to Italians, it sounded like
adatto, the Italian word for "suitable, qualified, adaptable," and
adaptability was certainly a quality they possessed in abundance.

From Italy, the family migrated to Turkey, where they settled in
Istanbul and Izmir, living in extreme poverty. My maternal grandmother, Malka, worked as a maid in a rich household and never
learned how to read or write in any language. My maternal grandfather, Avraham, worked in a candy factory from childhood. With
the establishment of the state of Israel, they decided to leave the
oppressive strictures of their official minority status and boarded
a ship for Jaffa. Their first years in Israel were spent in temporary
housing, little more than a shack, and then in a small apartment in
the impoverished city of Bat Yam, where they continued to speak
Ladino, the ancient dialect of Judeo-Spanish. They didn't teach this
language to their children, insisting once again on their "adaptability": the future, as far as they were concerned, belonged to Hebrew.

In flight from Jewish history, both sides of my family came
to Israel, and became Israeli, struggling to make a new life in a
state whose primary purpose for existing was to end thousands
of years of persecution and slaughter. This was their dream, as

it was the dream of every Jew in exile for millennia to found a
Jewish state.

This book comes early, and in a way it's a first line of defense—a
defense against distortion, a defense against forgetting. As I
wrote it, as I interviewed the bereaved, I thought often of those I
couldn't interview, among them the young women who sit keep-
ing watch at the border.

This job is given only to female soldiers—that's why the as-
signment is referred to by its feminine form, *tazpaniyot*: spotters.
There's a misogyny at work here—a military-grade misogyny—a
male upper-echelon belief that Israeli border technology was in-
fallible and that these women were merely backup, less capable
than sophisticated sensors and state-of-the-art computers.

But the truth of the matter has since come out: it was these
young women who first spotted that Hamas was conducting
exercises and testing Israeli defenses on the border. A number
of them spoke up, weeks and months before October 7, and reported suspicious activity to their superiors. But like Cassandra,
their reports were ignored. Their concerns were dismissed. No
action was ever taken.

Spotting is a thankless job—the spotters sit lonely for hours
and hours on end, staring out into the wastes. But these women
must remain vigilant, despite everything.

On 10/7, Israeli border defenses were overwhelmed and sixteen spotters were killed, seven were taken hostage. They were
among the first to be hurt that Sabbath.

Now all of Israel sits, if not in vigilance then in vigil. The end
of shiva is not in sight, and none can yet foresee the moment or
manner of our rising.

Sderot

Eleven people gathered in the three-by-three-square-meter room of two-month-old baby Yishai Azougi on Ehvat Israel Street in Sderot that Saturday. His father, Yanon, age twenty-three; his mother, Hillel, twenty-two; Yanon's parents, Eliyahu and Dalia; Aunt Moriah (who was three months pregnant); her husband, Haim; Uncle Yadida; Aunt Tahila; Aunt Amunah; and Aunt Shira.

Also present were three-year-old Lia Suissa and six-year-old Romi Suissa.

The members of the Azougi family knew almost nothing about the two young Suissa daughters. They did not know where the girls lived or who their parents were, or even how they came to be left next to the police station, covered in blood.

The girls were quiet—the family was afraid to ask.

At half past six that morning, Yanon had made the three-block walk to synagogue, as usual for him on a Sabbath morning. But he'd returned home shortly afterward, with two little girls in tow.

Home was a modest third-floor apartment of an older building, redolent with the smells of holiday cooking from the night before.

"Happy holidays to sweet Romi and Lia, who are celebrating Simchat Torah with us," Yanon called out as he opened the door, trying to explain the unusual situation through the intonation of his voice. The girls timidly entered the apartment's narrow white-walled vestibule, Lia's mouth hanging open. Romi was crying, her feet covered in broken glass.

Yanon couldn't even explain to his family who was the stranger driving a black car who stopped just next to him, shouted "I am a Jew," shoved the two girls into his hands, and gave a terse order: "Run!"

Run he did, holding the girls in his shaking arms, barely registering the absurdity of the situation: he still did not know how to comfort his own newborn, let alone the children of strangers. Almost by instinct, he brought them home: two girls with wavy dark hair and the family's signature bushy eyebrows and dark eyes.

Yanon's mother, Dalia, a nurse, immediately took the girls to the bathroom to check the source of the blood. Hillel, his wife, joined her, each of them bathing a child. Yanon could hear them singing to the girls from the shower. Romi and Lia were unharmed; the blood they'd been covered in wasn't theirs. Yanon's sisters braided the girls' hair and dressed them in clean clothes, much too big for them.

Yanon stepped outside again, heading toward the area near the police station where Lia and Romi had been handed to him, trying to piece together what had happened. He saw bodies on the sidewalk; he heard shooting in the distance. He wanted to get closer, to check if he could help, but a neighbor yelled at him to go home and take shelter.

Sderot, a city in southern Israel that like a lot of cities along the Gaza border has long grappled with systemic poverty and high unemployment, is located just over a kilometer from the border. Founded in 1951, a few miles from the ruined Arab farming village of Najd, Sderot began as a *maʼabara* (transit camp) of about seventy tents. The initial settlers were immigrants from Iran, Iraq, and Kurdistan, fleeing their homes due to antisemitic harassment and pogroms. The city expanded with new waves of immigrants: from Morocco and Romania in the 1960s, the USSR in the 1970s, and Ethiopia in the 1980s. By 1990, Sderot's population was about ten thousand. In 2000, the rockets from Gaza began.

Over the past two decades and counting, the city of Sderot has borne the brunt of Hamas's onslaught of rockets, an often nightly terror that despite Israel's Iron Dome has resulted in dozens of fatalities. Notable incidents include the death of three-year-old Afik Ohion Zahavi and fifty-year-old Mordechai Yosifov in June 2004, caused by a rocket that struck near a kindergarten. In September 2004, two-year-old Dorit Inso and four-year-old Yuval Abba were killed by a rocket while visiting their grandmother. In 2006, forty-three-year-old Yaakov Yakovov and fifty-seven-year-old Fatima Slotka were killed in two separate attacks; in 2007, thirty-two-year-old Shir-el Perdiman and thirty-six-year-old Oshri Oz were killed in two separate attacks; in 2008, a barrage of more than seventy Qassam rockets resulted in the death of Roni Yahya, a promising young student at Sapir College.

These events had led around 5,000 residents to leave Sderot since the start of the Second Intifada in 2000. The ones who stayed—35,000 in 2023—thought of themselves as survivors, even before October 7.

Just a few weeks before the two Suissa girls were shoved into his arms, Yanon had converted the house's only shelter—its only missile-proof space—into the baby's room. He and Hillel had painted the walls green and white, assembled a wooden crib for Yishai, their firstborn, and installed a small bamboo chest of drawers for diapers and wipes. They'd also placed in the room all the gifts they'd received at Yishai's *brit milah*, his circumcision celebration. Now, Hillel unwrapped the gifts and gave the toys to the Suissa sisters, hoping to distract them.

Around noon, Dalia, Yanon's mother, decided it was time. She took Romi to the bedroom and asked her, "Tell me, my girl, what happened to you?"

The six-year-old told her everything she could remember, or understand, from what happened to her that morning: a broken monologue, punctuated by shy pauses.

"I woke up early because there were alarms, and Mom and Dad said we were going to drive to the north so that missiles wouldn't hit us. They said I could bring my phone to take pictures, and my dog Simba could come too. I was happy and sang songs. Then there was a loud explosion in the car. Mom and Dad shouted that we had to get out quickly. Simba disappeared, and Mom told me not to worry about Simba but to run with her. We hid in a bush."

"What happened to your father?"

"Dad took Lia, and they ran in another direction. Lia went back to the car without Dad; she said he was dirty and that he told her to go back to Mom. Then a policeman told us to follow him. There was another explosion, and I tried to wake Mom up. I hid my baby sister and covered us with a sheet. When the 'boom boom' stopped, I shouted 'help' in my loudest voice, then one man took us out of the car and gave us to Yanon."

"What are your parents' names?"

"Dolev and Odia Suissa."

Meanwhile, Yanon had called the police to tell them that he'd found two girls; the parents were missing, perhaps injured or dead. The police said they were sorry, but they couldn't help at the moment; terrorists were still shooting in the streets. Yanon then called child welfare services, but they also apologized: they already had too many cases. Yanon contacted the medical rescue services—hoping they'd heard about Dolev or Odia Suissa—but it was too soon for them to check; they were still actively trying to rescue people.

Yanon located Dolev Suissa's Facebook page, which featured a picture of Dolev and Odia with Romi and Lia in a field of flowers. He wrote and deleted four messages before he sent Dolev this: "Dolev, your girls are at our house, everything is fine with them. Send me a number to get in touch." He checked his phone every few minutes, hoping for an answer.

"Romi, do you have any other family in Sderot?" he asked after an hour of waiting.

"My grandmother Eliana lives on Yitzhak Sade Street," the six-year-old remembered.

That was a five-minute drive away, but the municipality had issued a notice that terrorists were roaming the neighborhoods and shooting passersby. They advised residents to remain locked in their shelters and safe rooms. Yanon remembered that his wife's friend, Ronal, lived on the same street as Eliana. He called Ronal's husband, Elazar, asking if he knew the elderly woman. It turned out that Elazar knew Dolev, but not his mother. Yanon asked if Elazar could help locate the grandmother and send her a message, despite the municipal order to remain locked indoors, and Elazar agreed. After knocking on about thirty doors, he found the Herstein-Suissa house.

A woman with half-blond, half-gray hair and oversized

eyeglasses opened the door after he identified himself as Dolev's friend. "Eliana, your granddaughters Romi and Lia are perfectly fine. Call this guy, Yanon; he is watching them and needs to speak with you. I have to run home to hide. I'm sorry I can't stay."

Eliana Anna Herstein-Suissa has lived in Sderot for fifty-eight years, since she immigrated to Israel from Transylvania as a six-year-old girl alongside her parents, survivors of the Holocaust. Her father's entire family was murdered by the Nazis in the Dachau and Auschwitz concentration camps. Her mother never spoke about what happened to her family. Eliana raised her four children in Sderot: Carroll, Ophir, Ortal, and Dolev, the youngest. Just two months prior, they had celebrated Dolev and Odia's birthdays together, with only a year and a week separating their ages. He was thirty-four years old, and she was thirty-three. Dolev was reserved, while Odia was outgoing. He was passionate about nature; she was an avid and adventurous cook. Both were told that their daughters resembled them closely, sharing the same olive complexion. The couple met while still in their teens and lived with Dolev's mother, Eliana, for two years in Sderot until they had saved enough money to get married and rent an apartment a few blocks away.

Two years before this attack, a five-year-old boy named Idan Avigal was killed in their neighborhood by a rocket, despite hiding with his mother in a supposedly rocket-proof shelter.

Since that incident, the family had taken to leaving Sderot every time they heard the distinctive rising and falling siren indicating an incoming rocket attack. They had a pink suitcase prepared for such occasions, prepacked with winter and summer clothes for the girls, along with shoes and toys. Eliana guessed this day was no different: her son and daughter-in-law and grandchildren left, except this time the couple hadn't called or picked up her calls all morning.

Eliana called Yanon the moment Elazar left. He asked if she wanted to talk to Romi.

"Hello, Grandma."

"What happened, my sweet?"

"We wanted to go outside the city because there were sirens, and we drove near the square of the mall when the car stopped. There were many 'boom boom booms'—and a man came and took Dad away."

"And what about Mom?"

"She had a lot of blood. I talked to her, and she didn't answer me. I think Mom is dead."

"They murdered my child, they murdered my child," Eliana screamed, and Yanon took the phone off speaker and told Eliana that Romi didn't really know what happened.

"Let's wait, Eliana," he urged her. "Maybe they're just shocked. The girl doesn't understand."

He then put the phone back on speaker and Eliana told Romi to take care of Lia. "You're a hero. It will take some time, but we will come and pick you up as soon as it's allowed to leave the house."

Eliana told her daughter, Dolev's sister, Ortal, about the conversation and Ortal decided to venture out and search for the couple at the nearby Barzilai Medical Center. At thirty-nine years old, the mother of two daughters, she considered her brother Dolev as something like her first child. She was the one who took him to school, made his lunches, and comforted him during the rocket attacks that marked his youth.

Ortal lived in the nearby city of Ashkelon, which was also

attacked by a massive rocket barrage from Gaza. The siren went off sixty-two times that day, warning of incoming missiles. When she went down to the parking lot, she found that a missile had hit the house next to hers; the blast had broken her car's windows and mirrors, and the door had an enormous hole in it. But still, it started, and she drove to the hospital, praying all the way.

At Barzilai, the entrance floor was flooded with injured people. Ortal struggled to make her way through the chaos of running doctors and nurses and shrieking patients. Her friend, who worked at the hospital, assigned a social worker to her. She gave the social worker a picture of the couple, asking, "Can you find them for me?" The social worker promised to do everything she could. After forty minutes, she returned with news: Odia was not in the hospital, but Dolev was. He was in the operating room and alive. Ortal briefly felt light-headed as if she were about to collapse, but managed to make it to the operating room area to wait for him: "He'll be okay, he'll be okay," she kept telling herself.

While waiting, Ortal had the receptionist show her the files of female patients who matched the description of Odia—brown eyes, light brown skin, and black hair. They sat down in front of the computer and clicked through dozens of pictures of young women who'd been murdered or injured that morning. None of them was her.

Hours later, Ortal's name was called. The medical team informed her that Dolev was out of surgery and in the recovery room, and they would let her see him soon.

Twenty-five minutes from Sderot, in the Bedouin settlement of Abu Talul in the northern Negev, Amar Abu Sabila's wife, Rada, was searching for her husband. He hadn't returned home since the night before, when he'd gone to substitute for his eldest brother Salam, working the night shift as a security guard at a construction site in Sderot. She'd repeatedly tried calling and texting, but there was no response. Their sons, Salama and Faiz, were about the same age as Odia and Dolev's daughters—two and four years old. Amar and Rada had met five years earlier when Amar worked for Rada's father; she was nineteen years old, and he was twenty. Now, Rada was pregnant with their third child while Amar was working extra shifts as a security guard in Sderot, trying to earn enough money to support the newborn. Amar's mother, Naama, and father, Auda, were parents to eleven children, whose ages ranged from four to twenty-six. Amar was their second child. He lived with Rada and their children just one hut away from his parents in their Bedouin village. His ten siblings also resided within the same ramshackle compound. When the rockets began falling, Amar called Auda and said he was on his way home.

He was aware that missiles had also fallen on Abu Talul and that there was no missile protection available there. Yet, he preferred to be near his wife and kids without shelter rather than in a municipal shelter in Sderot. While he spoke with his father, a woman started screaming, "Help! Can someone help me?" Amar said he needed to go and hung up.

Every quarter of an hour after that, Auda tried to call his son again. He was hoping Amar had taken shelter or left his phone in the car. By one o'clock in the afternoon, Amar's phone wasn't even ringing: the calls went straight to voicemail. Muhammad and Omar, Amar's brothers, who'd also been working in Sderot, got in touch with their father and told him that they were hiding in a shelter, still waiting for Amar to pick them up. Amar's cousins were going from one hospital to another, showing pictures of Amar to the nurses. Naama was refusing to eat until her son was found.

In Barzilai Hospital, Ortal returned to the operating rooms, hoping to see Dolev. The medical staff directed her to room 12 on the surgical floor. Rushing there, she inadvertently knocked people over in her path and burst into room 12, where an injured stranger sat gaping at her in surprise.

Disappointed, she apologized: "Sorry, it's probably a mistake." Once again, she provided the hospital staff with Dolev's ID number and picture, saying, "You sent me to the wrong room."

A nurse dialed someone, and then the social worker from the morning arrived again. She escorted Ortal to an operating room, where the surgeon came out to speak with her.

"Dolev didn't survive," he said. "He was shot in the stomach and died after losing too much blood; we couldn't save him. I'm so sorry."

"That's not true! They said Dolev is alive!" she screamed at the surgeon. "This is a mistake! You're confusing things again! They told me Dolev is alive!" The surgeon showed her a picture: a body bag wrapped around a man, with only his head peeking out. There was no doubt; it was Dolev.

Ortal called her mother. She felt on the verge of collapse but knew she needed to find Odia. It was late in the evening when she obtained the cell phone number of Sderot's mayor, Alon Davidi, and pleaded with him to personally assist in locating her.

A short time later Yanon's phone rang; it was the mayor. They spoke briefly. Davidi inquired about any information regarding Dolev and Odia. Yanon could only provide the six-year-old's testimony of the events and direct him to search in the area of the police station. A few hours later, Auda's phone rang as well, displaying Amar's number on the screen.

"Hello? Amar, my love? Are you okay?"

"Who is this?" an unfamiliar voice answered.

"I'm Amar's father."

"This is the mayor of Sderot. Could you provide details about the phone's owner?"

"The owner of the phone? This is my son, Amar, an Israeli Bedouin."

"What was he doing in Sderot?"

"He has been working in the city with the rest of the family for years."

"When did you last speak with him?"

"Yesterday morning. He was on his way home when he stopped to help a woman. Since then, I haven't heard from him. Where is Amar? How did you find this phone?"

"We found it in a car that isn't his. Can you describe Amar?"

"He's young, strong, with beautiful brown eyes. He was wearing jeans, a black shirt, and black sports shoes. Is Amar okay?"

"Someone will call you soon, sir."

Shortly after, a policeman called Auda.

"Please tell me what happened. Tell me the truth. We're going crazy with worry."

"Your son was hit by a gunshot from a Hamas terrorist."

"Where is he? Which hospital? Where did you take him?"

"I'm so sorry, sir. Your son has passed away."

Auda was deeply offended. One should not announce such news over the phone without preparation. He wondered if the police had mistakenly identified another Arab man as his son. That same evening, Rada also received the news via a call from a stranger. A policeman answered her call to Amar's phone and said, "The owner of this phone was murdered but saved the lives of two girls," hanging up without giving any further details.

Naama kept calling Auda that evening, asking him for news, but he told her nothing: he didn't want to say anything until he saw the body himself.

Back in the Azougi home, Romi and Lia and the nine family members spent the night on mattresses in baby Yishai's room. The terrible noise of the sirens and the gunfire went on through the night, as did Lia and Romi's crying.

In the morning, Yanon decided that the girls should be with their family, even if the reunion would require some danger. It was nearly twenty-four hours since the invasion had begun, and terrorists were still roaming the region. Yanon phoned Odia's brother Ronan, who requested that the girls be brought to his house in the city of Rehovot, forty miles northeast. Ronan also told Yanon that Odia had been found dead that night in her car, from which the girls were rescued. She had been shot, wearing her pajamas. Beside her, an unknown Arab man in the driver's seat had also been shot. Yanon, along with Lia and Romi, immediately headed to Rehovot. On the tense drive, which was interrupted three times by police checkpoints, Yanon attempted to explain to Romi that they would soon part and she would be reunited with her family. "I will call you tomorrow if I have a phone," said the six-year-old, and added, "Thank you for helping with my baby sister."

Two weeks later, security camera footage provided answers to the three families: a document of the brief moments when the lives of Dolev, Odia, Romi, Lia, Amar, and Yanon intersected. The footage from Yitzhak Shamir Square shows a white van with ten armed Hamas militants entering the square just a second before Dolev and Odia's black car entered from the opposite direction. They were only three minutes from their home when the terrorists opened fire on their car.

Odia and Dolev stopped their car in the middle of the road and got out; Odia, in pajamas, was carrying Romi by the hand and running toward the bushes, while Dolev, dressed in red shorts, carried Lia and ran in the opposite direction, toward the square. Another van with another squad of terrorists appeared in the square. Dolev managed to run with Lia for about six seconds before they shot him. The terrorists continued driving, while Dolev lay on the pavement bleeding, Lia in his arms. Dolev yelled at Lia to leave him and go back to her mother. The three-year-old girl, barefoot in a white dress, stayed with her father for another twenty-five seconds until she followed his instructions. An ambulance and a private car passed the wounded man on the sidewalk without stopping. Lia took a few steps forward, then returned to her father. Dolev lifted himself up to Lia and begged her to find her mother. Lia slowly returned to the family car, repeatedly looking back. After a long minute, a police car entered the square and the officer noticed Dolev. Inside the vehicle was Golima Samzeo, a forty-eight-year-old policeman whose parents had immigrated to Israel from Ethiopia and who volunteered with Holocaust survivors in his time off. Samzeo assured Dolev that he was in good hands.

Two seconds later, Odia emerged from the bushes with Romi and returned to the car, where Lia was waiting. She stepped back to check on Dolev, who gestured for her to stay away, save the girls, and keep on driving. Just then, another vehicle pulled up near Dolev. It belonged to Ofek Shetrit, a twenty-six-year-old resident of the city. Shetrit serves as a sergeant in the army and studies mechanical engineering. Officer Samzeo asked him to take Dolev to the nearest first aid station. Dolev's gunshot wound did not appear to be fatal; he managed to stand and get into Ofek's car.

"Terrorists shot me. I have two daughters. There are terrorists in a white van. I have two daughters. I don't want to die. Take care of my girls," Dolev repeated over and over as Ofek drove him to get medical treatment.

"Are you sure? Maybe you were hit by shrapnel from a missile?" Ofek, certain that Dolev was disoriented from the pain of his injury, questioned him.

"There are terrorists, driving white vans," Dolev reiterated.

"We'll get you medical treatment soon and you'll return to your daughters. Everything will be okay," Ofek reassured the bleeding man in his car, whose name he never even managed to catch.

"Open up, I have an injured person here," he shouted upon arriving at the first aid station. The medics had begun to treat Dolev when Ofek heard gunshots coming toward them and realized that his passenger might not have been mistaken.

Ofek returned to his parents' home, where he lived with his mother, Naomi, father, Yuval, and two younger brothers, and exclaimed, "There are terrorists in the city. I've picked up a wounded man. Everyone's staying home."

His father answered him, "Mom went for a run. She isn't answering her phone."

Naomi Shetrit Azoulai, a fifty-two-year-old fitness trainer and gym manager, worked in a dental clinic for twenty years and only discovered her fondness for sports in her midforties. That morning, she went for a run with her friends Kobi and Ram. The three met early in the morning and had run four and a half kilometers when a barrage of rockets began. They took shelter behind a concrete wall by the roadside when they heard gunfire and shouts of "*Allah-hu Akbar.*" They found a large drainage pipe and hid under it while an armed terrorist approached and appeared to shoot Kobi, who hadn't managed to fully hide. For five hours, Ram and Naomi lay silently on the ground, covered with leaves and branches, as terrorists passed by on the road. When they heard a vehicle with Israeli soldiers, Naomi called for help. Suddenly, Kobi emerged. He explained that he'd only fallen—the terrorist had missed his shot. Naomi called her family saying, "We're fine; the terrorists passed by and didn't see us. We're safe now." But they weren't safe for long. The soldiers said they couldn't rescue them immediately, but would leave a force to secure the area and then return. A moment later terrorists arrived and started firing and throwing grenades at them. Kobi, bleeding, tried to run and escape but was shot dead. Another terrorist shot Naomi.

Yuval Shetrit went to look for his wife in Barzilai Hospital. This was at the same time Ortal was searching for Dolev and Odia. At the hospital, Yuval met Ram, who'd survived with two broken ribs and a partially collapsed lung. Ram knew that Naomi was dead but withheld the news from Yuval: he couldn't bear the thought of telling him. During Naomi's shiva, Yuval and Naomi's son, Ofek, came across a picture of Dolev in an article about his death. It was only then that he learned the name and fate of the man he had driven.

After Ofek had sped off with Dolev, Amar's car arrived at the square. Officer Samzeo hailed Amar's car, told him that Odia was unable to drive, and asked Amar to help her to safety. Amar agreed and decided to leave his car and drive Odia's, and she stepped out of the driver's seat and let Amar take the wheel. Lia and Romi were seated in the back of the car. Amar drove and Officer Samzeo drove ahead of them.

They approached the police station just as Hamas terrorists were laying siege to it. A group of terrorists turned and shot at them, hitting Officer Samzeo in his car and Odia and Amar in theirs. All three were killed. Romi and Lia, in the back seat of Odia and Amar's car, were left unharmed, though covered in blood. Romi unfastened Lia from the car seat, got down with her on the floor of the car, and covered them both with a white sheet. In a brief moment when the gunfire subsided, Romi shouted from the back seat, "Help us."

Meir Yair Avinoam, a corrections officer and a member of the Sderot emergency department, who was part of the combined force of police officers and civilians who'd arrived at the police station to retake it from the terrorists, heard the shouting and, dodging occasional crossfire, approached the car.

When he opened the door, Romi whispered, "No, please no."

"I'm not shooting, not shooting," Meir assured her gently.

"Are you the police?" Romi asked.

Gunshots echoed in the background.

"There are fatalities here," Meir said into his radio, looking at Odia and Amar in the front of the car.

"Are you from Israel?" asked Romi.

"Yes, sweetie, yes."

"Take us!"

"We will take you." He opened the door.

Roni was crouched in the back, clutching her sister.

"I'm here with a baby girl."

"Okay, I'm with you. Jump on me and we'll run."

"I don't want my sister to die."

The video stopped a moment before Meir gave the girls to Yanon.

The girls subsequently lived for a period with Odia's sister, while Eliana and Ortal visited them regularly. The bodies of Odia and Dolev were given to the families five days later.

For seventeen days, Auda traveled three hours every day to Camp Shura, a military camp where the bodies were kept, to search for the body of his son, Amar.

Every day, he watched trucks unload corpses as if they were new goods being delivered to a store. He saw boys and girls, Jews and Arabs, Thais, Eritreans, and the elderly—many of the more than fifty who'd been killed in Sderot that day—but none of them was Amar. Seventeen days felt like seventeen years for Auda. Sometimes, his sons accompanied him to the military camp, crying with him all the way there and back. Naama lost almost twenty kilos during these days of waiting. She was taken to the hospital four times during this period after losing consciousness, fainting from worry.

Sderot's police station had been besieged on October 7, and twenty police officers had been killed—that fact and his own fear as an Arab Bedouin had prevented Auda from more aggressively foisting his suspicions on the authorities. Finally, however, he ran out of patience and called the police, asking them whether it was possible that his son's body had been placed mistakenly with the bodies of the terrorists. He sent a picture of Amar's shoe, to aid in identification. Later that day, he was informed that Amar's body had been found—but where it was found was never specified.

Trip to the Dead Sea

Located between the Judean mountains to the west and the Moab mountains to the east, the Dead Sea is one of Israel's favorite vacation destinations. At restaurants such as the Mexican Dead Sea, the Taj Mahal, and the local McDonald's, Jews and Arabs in swimsuits order in Russian, Hebrew, and Arabic, and jostle one another in line. They leave sandy footprints on the wet faux-marble floors of the aggressively air-conditioned Dead Sea Mall and Hordus Shopping Center, where plastic packages of mud and salts are sold with the promise of rejuvenating the skin and reversing time.

The pseudo-modernist, palm tree–lined resorts along the water's edge rank among the country's most diverse—and most affordable—"beachside" spots, yet nobody stays in any of the tourist complexes for more than a few days.

The Sprebchikov-Tumiib sisters, Nadezhda (seventy-five) and Natalya (seventy-one), were planning to stay for just a few hours. The forecast for that Saturday in early October was 30 degrees Celsius, 86 degrees Fahrenheit, with low humidity. It was a perfect day for taking a dip.

The resorts' relentless Russian and Arabic advertisements

nearly always fail to mention that, due to the presence of heavy industry and mineral extraction facilities at the Dead Sea, the only beach still open for bathing is actually an industrial pool—a so-called dead pool. Artificial Industrial Pool Number 5 is a vast evaporation pond used by Dead Sea factories, constructed atop the remnants of the dried-up southern basin of the sea. Still, the sisters Sprebchikov-Tumiib delighted in the sensation of its dense and salty water enveloping and supporting their aging bodies, allowing them to imagine themselves young and agile again, free from joint and muscle pain.

Nadezhda and Natalya's trip, organized by Alexei Tours, offered rock-bottom prices of $25 per person per day with the purchase of three trips, guides and meals not included. The price dropped to $18 per person when seven trips were purchased in advance. The itinerary included a 6:15 A.M. pickup from the cities of Ofakim, Netivot, and Sderot; 8:00 A.M. arrival at Ein Bokek "beach"; and time for independent swimming and meals at the local restaurants, until the minibus departed at 12:00 P.M., returning them to their homes by 2:00 P.M.

The Soviet Union may have collapsed in the 1990s, but nearly every week Alexei Tours brought together the elderly Ukrainians, Belarusians, Russians, Moldovans, Georgians, Azerbaijanis, Kazakhs, Uzbeks, Kyrgyz, and Tajiks in something of a reunion in the Israeli desert. Almost every Saturday, a different Bedouin driver operated a small minibus, transporting the group of elderly retirees who spoke only limited Hebrew. The Bedouin drivers would complain to Alexei about their insistence on listening to Russian radio, to which they'd sing along.

Alexei Davidov, the owner of Alexei Tours, is a sixty-year-old Israeli, born in Dagestan, a resident of the city of Ofakim. He launched his small tourism company about a decade ago with a colorful Russian website and advertisements in Israel's thriving Russian-language media. Two years without tourism thanks to the COVID-19 pandemic nearly destroyed the business. Trying to recover, he started organizing small travel groups in 2023 via WhatsApp. It was a side job, a modest enterprise that remained tax-exempt because it earned less than $25,000 a year. In the mornings, he worked as a forklift operator at a food factory.

Two days before the October 7 trip, Alexei called Nadezhda Sprebchikov to ask if he could reschedule her and her sister for the following week. He explained that twenty-seven people had signed up for this week's trip, but there were only nineteen seats on the minibus.

Having paid in advance for three consecutive weekly trips to the Dead Sea, Nadezhda refused to change her plans. Alexei didn't argue, and instead canceled the bookings of two other women in order to accommodate Nadezhda and Natalya, who were, after all, regular customers. Following the death of their ninety-four-year-old mother, Lydia, Nadezhda had told Natalya that enough was enough: it was time for them to live. In the following seven months, the sisters had gone on three Dead Sea trips, one trip to Eilat, and one trip to the Sea of Galilee. They'd also booked trips to Eilat and the Upper Galilee for November, for which they'd already paid.

The sisters lived in the same old building in the center of Netivot: Nadezhda on the first floor and Natalya on the second. Every morning, they took their coffee together. If a child or grandchild called during that time, they'd each respond, "We'll talk later. I'm with my sister."

They'd grown up in Dushanbe, the capital city of Tajikistan, a mountainous, predominantly Muslim country in Central Asia, as part of a small Jewish community with Persian roots.

Nadezhda had had a respected career as a chemist, while Natalya had worked as a police officer. The two experienced considerable institutional and personal antisemitism. Most of Tajikistan's fifty thousand Jews had fled the country following the collapse of the Soviet Union and the advent of civil war in 1992. Natalya had left early, in the late 1980s, but Nadezhda had initially refused to leave, and it was only after her two sons and daughter joined a group of Jewish students moving to Israel in 1993 that she changed her mind. By the end of that year, the sisters were reunited in Netivot, a diverse but economically stunted city of newer immigrants, including a large contingent from the former Soviet sphere.

Moving to Israel at age forty-five, without any Hebrew, came at a price. Nadezhda was forced to abandon her scientific career. At first, she found a job as a supermarket cashier, which required her to be on her feet—her aching feet—for long hours. When she saw an opening for a caretaker for Russian-speaking senior citizens, she jumped at the opportunity. For two decades, she cooked, cleaned, and sang for the Russophone elderly population of Netivot—until she herself reached the retirement age of sixty-five. Natalya, for her part, was a stay-at-home mother and caregiver who'd had little opportunity to interact with Israelis outside her community.

On the morning of their Dead Sea trip, Nadezhda put on a long green dress with appliqué sunflowers, along with a pair of gold earrings set with small green stones. Natalya chose a simple pink T-shirt and black stretch pants for the occasion.

The minibus driver, Sharif Abu Taha, came from the Bedouin city of Tel Sheva, the first major permanent Bedouin town in Israel. He picked the women up just after 6:15 A.M. in Netivot. Seven other passengers had already boarded the bus in Ofakim:

Igor Kortzer, a jovial seventy-three-year-old from the city's Golden Years Citizen Club, was seated in his usual spot, dressed in his usual attire: a white T-shirt, round sunglasses secured with a string, and a gray hat; he had to do everything he could to protect his fair skin from the Israeli sun.

Igor was born in Mazir, Belarus, on the banks of the Pripyat River, five years after the end of the Second World War. His mother, Fira, was four years old when the first pogrom occurred in the city; thirty Jews were murdered. At age twenty-one, Fira witnessed the German occupation of her city; upon their arrival, the Nazis massacred more than two thousand Jews. Some were killed in their homes; others were forced to dig their own graves before being shot. Fira, along with her one-year-old daughter and five-year-old son, were among those ordered to dig. Just before the Nazis were to shoot, however, a soldier whispered to her in Russian, "Fall now!" And she complied—she fell, as everyone around her was shot. After hiding among the bodies for hours, Fira and her two children escaped. Later, Fira was rounded up in a separate "*aktion*" and marked for relocation to a ghetto, and she handed her son his baby sister and told him to run with her as far as he could. The five-year-old ran with the one-year-old barefoot in the snow until they reached a nearby village, where they were taken in by a Christian family. Two years later, Fira managed to escape the ghetto and find her children.

Fira's husband died during the war, and Igor was her first child with her second husband. The family's life was still hard after the war; they often went hungry, and long into adulthood, Igor recalled searching for potatoes under the snow. At age nineteen, he enlisted in the Red Army, and the following year he met Berta, a beautiful Jewish woman his age, and they soon married. In the early years of their marriage, Igor was often called away to the Red Army reserves, serving in Siberia and later in Chernobyl, where he was ordered to clean up after the infamous nuclear accident, unaware of the radiation's dangers. (Years later, he would be recognized as a so-called Chernobyl Disaster Neutralizer, a designation that made him eligible for a government grant of approximately $2,000 per year.) During his vacations from the army, he would take his three children mushroom and strawberry picking in the forests around Mazir. Like Nadezhda and Natalya, he emigrated with his children to Israel when he was already in his forties, struggled to learn Hebrew, and worked occasional jobs to support his family.

In the next seat of the minibus sat Michal Zarbailov, an apple-cheeked sixty-year-old grandmother of eight. Her husband, Avshalom, had tried to persuade her to spend the holiday morning at home. "You just woke up; how is it that you're already bored and want to leave the house?" he asked. Avshalom, who suffered from diabetes and struggled to keep up with Michal's pace, almost never joined her on her regular Sabbath trips.

They'd met at her grandfather's funeral, in the city of Quba in northern Azerbaijan, a city with a significant population of Caucasian or Mountain Jews. Avshalom was a distant relative from Derbent, Dagestan, just across the Azeri-Russian border. They married within a year and soon had three children: Daniel, Miriam, and Rami. Their fourth child, Iris, was born in Israel. The immigration office had initially placed the family in a coastal city, but they preferred the drier climate of Ofakim, where they joined a large community of Jews from the Caucuses. Avshalom worked as an apartment painter, while Michal worked in a produce-sorting factory, which had been located in Gush Katif, in the southern Gaza Strip, until Israel's withdrawal from Gaza, after which it was relocated to Sderot. She and her son, Daniel, worked there together, putting in sixteen-hour days at minimum wage. Four years ago she finally quit, and only last year did she find a new job, the first that she'd ever enjoyed: kindergarten assistant.

There were nine passengers aboard the small minibus; ten more were scheduled for pickup at two different stops in Sderot. At 6:30 A.M., they arrived at the first bus stop, Yitzhak Shamir / Public Library, located at the entrance of Sderot, near the municipal first aid station. Valerie Friedman, a father of three and grandfather of two, was waiting at the stop, wearing a black Nike hat and carrying a backpack.

It was just after they'd picked up Valerie that Abu Taha realized that the minibus had a flat. He stopped the bus to check and discovered that two tires had actually been punctured. He set up the jack and was trying to lift one of the problem tires when missiles began whistling overhead.

The elderly passengers, some with mobility issues, hurried to the so-called self-operating shelter at the bus station, which was intended to open instantly and automatically at the first alarm. The sign designating the safe area reads, "Dear citizen, this protected transportation station was established by the Home Front Command and the Ministry of Defense for the protection and well-being of residents and passers-by. Please take care of it." But would it take care of them? They soon realized that the electronic mechanism had malfunctioned, leaving them to wait, unprotected, on the street, among the dilapidated gray benches, for Abu Taha to finish changing the tires.

They had nowhere to hide. Behind them stood Beit Yad Lebanim Sderot, a memorial to Sderot residents who'd lost their lives to terrorist attacks. The memorial was erected five years previously, to replace another that had been criticized by the families of the bereaved for having been disrespectfully located adjacent to the municipal swimming pool.

At 6:45 A.M., Leonid, Natalya and Nadezhda's younger brother, called to check on them. Natalya told him their situation and mentioned that they'd unsuccessfully tried to contact the municipality to get them to open the locked shelter.

After the call ended, all they could do was wait. Igor stood against the shelter's exterior wall with Nadezhda and Natalya. Zinaida Beilin and Luda Furman were on their phones and chain-smoking cigarettes. Valerie Friedman just stood and gazed up at the missiles, deadly projectiles that seemed serene in the sky and made colorful clouds when they were intercepted by the Iron Dome.

Reuven, a volunteer police officer, happened to pass by at this moment; Igor and Michal waved him down and explained the situation with the shelter. Reuven attempted to kick in the door, but it was not designed to be so easily breached. Next came Danny, a Sderot resident out for a morning walk with his dog, who was surprised to find a group of scared elderly people crowded by the bus station opposite his house. He offered to lead them to his home shelter, but they declined; many of them said they had difficulty walking, and they were sure the missiles would be over soon and their driver would quickly replace the minibus's tires. However, Danny took one look at the jack the driver was using and realized it wasn't strong enough to lift the minibus, so he hurried back to his house to fetch a suitable one.

Just after he arrived at his house, Danny heard a series of gunshots. Then the sound of bullets striking one of his windows— one grazed the head of his high school–aged daughter. Looking out the other windows, he saw a white van filled with Hamas terrorists pull up next to the bus stop.

Reuven, who'd still been searching for a way to open the shelter, fired his gun at the attackers emerging from the van, and managed to escape. Abu Taha yelled to his group, "Run!" but it was almost a joke: most of his passengers could barely walk, let alone run. And even if they could run, where to?

Through his window, Danny helplessly watched the old people fall to the pavement one after the other, as they were shot repeatedly in the head, chest, and stomach.

Sofia Popov's body, clad in a pink dress with a black bathing suit underneath, lay in a pool of blood. Berta Shamayev, wearing a black-and-white floral shirt, fell atop Sofia. Michal Zarbailov's body lay next to her spilled beaded purse, along with one of Luda Furman's red flip-flops. On the other side of the minibus, the bodies of Nadezhda and Natalya sprawled out next to each other. Abu Taha managed to evade the bullets. He covered himself with the blood of his passengers and feigned death for an hour until he heard voices speaking Hebrew. Then he ran to the nearest gas station and called Alexei, his boss, crying out, "Everyone's dead . . . everyone's dead!"

Every person who traveled south from the center of Israel through Sderot passed the thirteen corpses of this elderly tour group lying at the edge of the road. Their bodies stayed out in the sun for hours, without cover, giving many the opportunity to take photos and videos of the grisly scene and share them on social media.

This was also how their families received the news of their deaths. Irit, Nadezhda's daughter and Natalya's niece, recognized the two from one of the posts—about an hour and a half after they were murdered.

Looking at the posted photos and videos, Michal's daughter,

Iris, recognized her mother's body from her clothing, but hoped she might only be injured.

On Monday morning, while on shift at her work as a nurse at Beilinson Hospital, Igor's daughter, Yelena, was called to the cemetery to identify his body; her husband would take the perilous trip with her. The road was lined with the husks of burned-out cars. Missiles fell, forcing them to take shelter in roadside culverts, covering their heads with their hands. At every intersection, soldiers stopped them and directed them to alternate routes for safety. Near Sapir College at the Sderot intersection, soldiers alerted them to the presence of escaped terrorists. They hurried to find refuge in a roadside pit, Yelena all the while imagining a social worker informing her children that their parents died as well, on the way to identify her father's body.

The burial process was brief: Igor's funeral was held at the cemetery in Ofakim. There were sixteen other funerals at the cemetery that morning—victims from throughout the area.

Each family was called upon to identify their murdered loved one. Following each positive identification, there was a short prayer and then the burial.

There were no further prayers or eulogies.

Igor's daughter, Yelena, and her husband, and Igor's ex-wife, Bertha, laid Igor to rest. None of his other children managed to attend.

Since October 8, the hotel complex near the Ein Bokek beach at the Dead Sea has served as temporary housing for approximately fifteen thousand residents of the city of Sderot and the kibbutzim around Gaza—people who were evacuated and whose homes were burned. Tourists have been replaced by mourners, people who have collectively lost hundreds of family members and friends, along with all their possessions.

Psychologists have taken the place of masseuses, and hostage retrieval consultants have replaced bartenders and waiters. Lobbies have become coordination centers, mustering points for those seeking transportation to hospitals and funerals. Teenagers who lost their parents get drunk on the boardwalk, late into the night.

The sixteen hotels that form the Ein Bokek complex have four thousand rooms but lack basic essential services required by people who stay for longer than a holiday weekend. To compensate for the lack of a supermarket, two large trucks arrive twice weekly in the hotel complex's parking lot, bearing diapers, food, and drink. To compensate for the lack of a school, the construction site of a future hotel was converted to hold fifteen classrooms.

No one knows when, if ever, they'll be able to return to their homes—if their homes are even still standing—near the Gaza border.

The passengers who had their Dead Sea trips canceled by Alexei have reached out to him to express their gratitude.

Odessa to Ashkelon

1

The orphanage was housed in a large stone building surrounded by a fence; its gate was guarded. Jews in Odessa rarely felt safe.

Its yard, gray and bare in winter, was home in spring to a garden tended by the orphans, who cultivated cucumbers and tomatoes.

Inside, the children, who ranged in age from newborns to seventeen-year-olds, were divided into separate areas: infant ward, girls' ward, boys' ward. Each room of the girls' and boys' wards accommodated six children, sleeping on three sets of rickety, thin-mattressed bunk beds.

The younger Kusenov brother was assigned to an upper bunk in an upstairs ward, while the older Kusenov brother slept in a lower bunk in a downstairs ward. Their mother, Marina, visited them every month and called almost daily. Most of the other children had alcoholic, abusive, neglectful parents—or simply no parents at all.

The Kusenov brothers were born in Kharkiv, northeastern

Ukraine—Eduard in 2006 and Radik in 2003. Marina was Jewish; their father, Yuri, was Christian, an alcoholic who abandoned the family when Eduard was three and Radik was six. Marina found work at a local casino, where she often had to defend herself from the advances of drunken men. Their neighborhood, Odrada, was poor and often dangerous. In Eduard's first year at the local school, when he was five years old, a fellow student slammed his head on the floor and kicked him. He was hospitalized for weeks.

Following Eduard's release, Marina decided to explicitly embrace her Jewish heritage—if not calling on the mercy of God then on the mercy of God's believers. She had her two sons circumcised and changed their names: Eduard became Eitan, a Hebrew name meaning "firm" or "stalwart," and Radik became Natan, meaning "he who gives."

She had been told of a Jewish orphanage in Odessa—a place called Tikvah (Hope) that offered Jewish children free room and board, education, and medical care.

Eitan was six and Natan was nine when Marina took them on the twelve-hour night train from Kharkiv to Odessa. There, she showed them the city's wide streets and dazzling beaches before dropping them at the orphanage and telling them that in Odessa they'd have a better life than any she could provide.

2

Odessa was founded by Catherine the Great in 1794 as Imperial Russia's gateway to the Mediterranean, the Moscow on the Black Sea, the Petersburg of the south. A charming amalgam of broad boulevards and twisting alleys, it was one of the most ethnically diverse, liberal, and dynamic cities in the empire. A Russian-speaking haven, it attracted Jews from throughout Ukraine who for centuries had faced restrictions, blood libels, and massacres. In 1815, there were 4,000 Jews in the city, but by 1897, there were about 140,000, approximately 37 percent of Odessa's population.

This population explosion helped to make Odessa the cradle of modern Zionism. Gaula, the first Zionist company dedicated to the purchase of land in Ottoman Palestine, was established in Odessa, and the foundations of modern Hebrew culture were laid by a circle of the so-called Sages of Odessa, a loose group that included one of the major modern Yiddish writers, Mendele Mocher Sforim; the essayist and Zionist intellectual Aḥad Ha'am; the historian Simon Dubnow; and the future patriarch of modern Hebrew poetry, Ḥayyim Naḥman Bialik.

Bialik had run away from his yeshiva in Volozhin, present-day Lithuania, and arrived in the city in 1891, at the age of eighteen. The following year, he published his first poem, "To the Bird," an imagined inquisition of a bird that had flown back to Odessa from Palestine:

> *Is there, dear bird, tell me,*
> *much evil there too, and pain*
> *in that land of warmth, of beauty?*
>
> *Do you sing greetings*
> *from fruited valley and hill?*
> *Has God pitied, comforted Zion,*
> *or is she a graveyard still?**

Despite Odessa's philosemitism, the city was often a site of Jewish persecution. These contrasting facets of Odessa's Jewish

---

* Translated by David Aberbach.

history are inseparable: the city's identity as a center of proto-Zionism was largely shaped in response to the pogroms, which returned with a vengeance following the outbreak of the first Russian Revolution. Between 1903 and 1906, about two thousand Jews were slaughtered in the area of present-day Ukraine, Romania, and Moldova. One notable incident was the April 1903 Kishinev pogrom, where forty-nine Jews suffered deaths by beating, stabbing, and being drowned in raw sewage. Numerous women and girls were raped. The Jewish quarter of Kishinev was devastated.

Bialik, who was thirty years old at the time and already recognized as the preeminent Hebrew-language poet, was appointed by Odessa's Jewish Historical Committee to lead a commission investigating these atrocities. From his research into Kishinev came one of his most famous poems, "On the Slaughter":

> *Skies—have mercy.*
> *If you hold a God*
> *(to whom there's a path*
> *that I haven't found), pray for me.*
> *My heart has died.*
> *There is no prayer on my lips.*
> *My hope and strength are gone.*
> *How long? How much longer?**

Two years later, in October 1905, there was another pogrom in Odessa. Policemen distributed bottles of vodka and pistols to the mob, who killed four hundred Jews and one hundred non-Jews.

---

* "On the Slaughter" by Ḥayyim Naḥman Bialik, translation by Peter Cole, *Yale Review*, online, November 2, 2023.

Each wave of pogroms brought a new wave of *aliyah*—
Jewish immigration to British-mandate Palestine. Between 1904
and 1914, nearly forty thousand Russian Jews made the trip—
immigrants who were instrumental in the foundation of the
Jewish state.

They left just in time.

Following the First World War and the Russian Revolution,
the Red Army's invasion of Ukraine in 1918 began a war that resulted in the massacres of more than one hundred thousand Jews
in more than one thousand pogroms, in what would become a
rehearsal for the Nazi slaughter. In the early days of the Second
World War, the Nazis occupied Odessa, the major city of the
territory they referred to as Transnistria, and in summer 1941
handed control over to Romania. The city's Jewish population
had already been halved: from 200,000 before the war, approximately 90,000 remained, of which the Romanians immediately
killed 8,000. Between October 22 and October 25, 1941, another
44,000 Jews were massacred, and the roughly 40,000 remaining
were moved to a ghetto in the suburb of Slobodka. From then
until January 1942, the vast majority of Odessa's Jews were murdered either on death marches or in concentration camps.

The post-Holocaust remnants of Soviet Jewry tended to collect in the cities, and Odessa was no exception. The 1959 census
recorded 106,700 Jews in Odessa, though the Soviet ban on religious activities led to the disappearance of institutional Jewish
life.

With the fall of the Soviet Union in 1991, Odessa witnessed
a genuine renaissance, fueled by Jews from Israel returning to
their ancestral city. One such individual was Shlomo Baksht,
born in Petah Tikva in 1960 to an Orthodox Jewish family with
Russian roots. His father, Rabbi Haim Menahem, served as the

deputy chief rabbi of the Israel Defense Forces. In 1993, Rabbi Baksht moved to Odessa, where he sought out the remaining Jews and reopened synagogues and schools. He didn't plan on opening an orphanage, yet upon encountering hundreds of local Jewish children suffering from abuse and neglect, he made that one of his life's central missions.

Ukraine's independence from the Soviet Union had led to widespread poverty due to the closure of Soviet-era factories and industries, causing rampant unemployment. Many people lost their homes, and with low wages and inadequate social safety nets, parents abandoned their children out of desperation. The Tikvah Jewish orphanage was faced with more children than it could accommodate.

3

The Kusenov brothers' lives in the orphanage were as good as one could hope for in Ukraine in the early 2000s. Hunger, crime, and homelessness were as common in Odessa as in Kharkiv, but Eitan and Natan now had three meals a day, warm clothing, and teachers who recognized and appreciated their intelligence and humor. They visited their mother twice a year, feeling happy for her when she met Anton (a man they sometimes even called "Dad"). Their mother and Anton had a baby together, a new brother named Yonatan. They weren't even jealous that Yonatan wasn't sent to the orphanage to be with them but kept at home. In 2019, Natan completed his studies at the orphanage and subsequently returned to Kharkiv to live with Marina, Anton, Yonatan, and his grandmother Ira, leaving Eitan, then thirteen years old, at the orphanage alone.

Eitan Kusenov had grown into a tall and handsome young

man. By his bar mitzvah, he was fluent in Hebrew, a promising student, and an excellent soccer player.

Odessa had become his playground. He knew every street and every bar that served alcohol to minors. At night, he and his friends would scale the orphanage's high walls and go out carousing. They'd smoke cigarettes, drink whiskey, and sometimes eat non-kosher shawarma at The Turk's in Odessa and kosher pizza at Hava Nagila near the Potemkin Steps. During the day, they'd sometimes feign illness, slip past the guard at the gate, and spend the day at Otrada beach near the city center. On Shabbat, the orphanage residents would gather with the greater Jewish community at the synagogue. Eitan liked the holidays, but especially Purim, when the older boys would receive small presents of money. His other source of income was his work at the kosher market, a portion of which he sent to his family.

His early memories of Kharkiv began to fade. Like many Jews before him, Eitan had come to call Odessa his one true home.

4

"Skies—have mercy": Bialik's first words in the poem about the Kishinev pogrom echo the ancient Jewish prayer "El Malei Rachamim" ("God full of mercy"). Traditionally, this prayer is recited to grant rest to the souls of the dead, although it's too often the living who are in the greatest need of mercy.

In May 2014, Russia invaded and occupied Crimea. With Ukraine losing about a third of its coastline, Odessa, the major Black Sea port, became increasingly vulnerable. The city was simmering with tension, marked by clashes between pro-unity and pro-European protestors and anti-Maidan factions eager to bring the city under Russian rule. On May 2, a United

Ukraine rally was attacked by Russia-backed separatists. Stones and Molotov cocktails were exchanged; shots were fired by both sides. Forty-nine people were killed in the unrest, which was the bloodiest civil conflict in the region since the Odessa Bolshevik uprising of 1918.

Rabbi Baksht knew that such times were never safe for Jews and decided to evacuate the orphanage. A convoy of buses brought the children to the city of Mykolaiv, to the east of Odessa. They spent a week there before the rabbi deemed it safe enough to return. The orphanage, however, remained on high alert and increased its stocks of canned goods, water, and medical supplies.

5

In early 2022, the Russian army again mustered at the Ukrainian border, with war threatening to break out at any moment. Rabbi Baksht had meanwhile contracted with a private security firm to hire twenty-five Israeli guards, to compensate for the impending conscription of the Ukrainian guards previously employed by the orphanage. He got ahold of two large trucks and loaded them with food, water, and medical supplies, along with emergency generators and blankets, not just for the hundreds of children under his charge but also for the thousands of Jews in the Odessan Jewish community.

Eitan, now sixteen, had little interest in politics. Putin? He only really knew the name from a soccer game he'd attended with his stepfather, Anton, where the crowd had chanted against Putin. Anton had explained that Putin would erase Ukraine if he could. Eitan hadn't realized Putin would actually try. Zelensky? Eitan mainly knew him as the TV comedian. During visits to Kharkiv, he enjoyed watching Zelensky's TV series *Rassmeshi komika*—it was funny, and it was fun to know that Zelensky was Jewish.

By the morning of February 24, 2022, when the Russian invasion of Ukraine began, Rabbi Baksht had already identified five potential evacuation destinations, and he now got on the phone to determine the safest option. That many of the orphans lacked passports further complicated the situation. He ordered the trucks to leave before the children, so that all could be organized before the children arrived.

The main thrusts of the invasion progressed from Belarus in the direction of Kyiv, and from Russia itself toward Kharkiv. In the south of the country, another front was launched from Crimea against Luhansk and Donetsk. The Kusenov family's apartment, just nineteen miles south of the Russia-Ukraine border, shook from missile strikes. Early that morning, Russian airstrikes targeted Odessa, and the orphanage's children were woken by the sound of exploding artillery rounds.

Eitan woke up with a sore throat and fever. There was shouting in the halls: "War has started! Russia's attacking! Gather your things; we're leaving soon."

The orphanage was in chaos; the children were crying and packing, reading the news, posting online, calling their families. The orphanage counselors reassured the youngest that they were just going on vacation; they told the older ones that they'd likely return to Odessa soon. Each age group got its own fiction. The tension was so palpable that one of the counselors began distributing cigarettes to all children over fifteen, telling them, "Smoke to relax." Eitan smoked one cigarette after another but didn't become any calmer. Marina informed him they were under attack in Kharkiv and urged him to flee along with the orphanage. Eitan approached Rabbi Baksht to ask if his family could join them, wherever the orphanage was planning to escape to, and the rabbi promised him that they'd do their best to help.

At 1:00 P.M., it was announced that all children with a passport should board the buses bound for Moldova, departing at 2:00 P.M. Eitan, along with 150 other undocumented children and babies, stayed back. Following explosions near the girls' ward at 8:30 P.M., plans were accelerated. By 10:30 the next morning, which was a Friday, the entire orphanage was emptied out and fifteen buses, including one carrying Eitan, were on their way to the Carpathian Mountains near the Romanian border.

On a typical day, the drive would take nine hours, but the roads were backed up for miles. Air-raid sirens sounded again and again. A few hours after leaving Odessa, the orphanage staff was informed that Russian missiles struck near the community buildings they'd just vacated.

Eitan sat at the back of the bus, watching Ukrainian tanks mobilizing in the opposite direction. He texted with his mother, Marina, who told him she was frantically looking for a way to flee Kharkiv and join the orphanage group with six-year-old Yonatan. Despite the Shabbat observance requiring phones to be turned off, Eitan was allowed to keep his on.

After twenty-seven hours, Eitan and the orphanage reached the Carpathians, where they found temporary shelter in a rented guesthouse that was bitterly cold and had spotty electricity. The trucks stocked with goods that'd been prepared for years had been lost on the roads, maybe stolen. All the males above the age of eighteen, who were eligible for conscription, had been separated from the rest, with the result that the orphanage was left with hardly any teachers. Eitan took up the role of a counselor, setting up a field kitchen and helping to cook three meals a day; he was constantly working, battling fatigue from lack of sleep, illness, and the cold.

During the week the orphans spent in the mountains, Rabbi Baksht coordinated the children's entrance into Romanian territory without passports.

The next week, they drove another twenty hours and crossed the border. Their destination was a seaside summer resort town called Neptun on the Black Sea.

In the depths of winter, Neptun was deserted.

An empty hotel, the Agora, became the new home for Jewish Odessa. In the first week, about eight hundred Jewish refugees from Odessa joined the orphanage in Neptun. In the first month, about fifteen hundred Odessan Jews arrived, filling three hotels. Eitan's sea-view room in Neptun did little to cheer him; the beaches here couldn't compare to those in Odessa. Eventually, Eitan received the news he'd been praying for: Marina, little brother Yonatan, and grandmother Ira had managed to escape and were on their way to Neptun. Eitan ran out barefoot into the snow to welcome them. Two months later, Anton and Natan managed to join the family.

The Kusenov family lived together in that small room overlooking the Black Sea. The room was cramped and cold but it was the first time Eitan had shared a roof with his family since he was placed in the orphanage at age six.

6

Like many Ukrainians, the Kusenov family faced a difficult decision. Returning to Ukraine was unsafe, but in Romania they lacked permanent status. The solution, it seemed, was Israel, where Ukrainian friends spoke of a higher standard of living and promising opportunities in education and employment. Natan chose to stay in Romania with the Odessan Jewish community, while Eitan, Marina, Anton, Yonatan, and grandmother Ira decided to make *aliyah*. The only question was, where to settle?

Masha, a friend of Marina's who lived in Ashkelon, suggested they join her in that southern city, known for its large community of Ukrainians and people from other regions of the former USSR. In Ashkelon they had the best chance of finding jobs in Russian. In February 2023, one year after fleeing Ukraine, the family arrived in Israel.

Eitan now found himself strolling another beach, in Ashkelon, searching the sands for a hint of Odessa. If he squinted slightly and overlooked the scattered plastic bags, he could almost convince himself he was still back home. The main difference, the hot winter days, exceeding 29 degrees Celsius, 84 degrees Fahrenheit in February, were warmer than most days of Ukrainian summer. From the balcony of their new apartment, they could enjoy the sunshine and gaze at the Mediterranean.

Life was gradually returning to a semblance of normalcy. Marina and Anton found jobs at a clothing factory, while Eitan and Yonatan made friends at their new schools.

Of course, there were the rocket attacks from Gaza. During one attack in May of their first year, they sat on their balcony, beers in hand, watching the Iron Dome intercept one missile after another. Marina said that after managing to escape Putin's bombardment of Kharkiv, she wasn't afraid of anything.

7

The family planned a trip to the Dead Sea for Saturday, October 7. They'd been invited by Marina's friend Karina to join her family there for a day of rest and relaxation.

At six in the morning, the Hamas missile barrage began. The constant roar of the rockets was unlike anything Eitan had heard in Odessa. The family's apartment lacked a safe room, but initially they assumed the Iron Dome would do its job. Then Karina phoned, advising them to "get out of Ashkelon as soon as possible and drive to the Dead Sea. It's usually calm in a few hours, and you can head back home." In haste, they grabbed their bathing suits and left, still hoping to enjoy a swim.

Jumping into their gray Kia Niro, they mistakenly took the more circuitous and dangerous route, heading south. As they passed towns near the Gaza border, the car was engulfed in the smell of smoke. While listening to Kan Reka, 100.3 FM, a Russian-language station, they heard reports of Hamas terrorists, disguised as IDF soldiers, attacking nearby kibbutzim and moshavim. As they sped along highway 34, they noticed bodies strewn about, corpses littering the shoulders, and abandoned cars, some with bullet holes in the windows. Anton put his foot to the floor, eventually reaching 125 miles per hour, passing armed figures whose affiliations they couldn't determine.

Eitan was sure he was going to die, he just didn't know whether by a missile strike or a terrorist's bullet. At least, he thought, he would die with his family, not as an orphan.

8

Two weeks later, Eitan returned to Ashkelon to collect the family's belongings, only to discover that their apartment building had been hit by a missile.

The blast had broken the windows and brought down walls, burying their living room and balcony under concrete rubble. Eitan quickly gathered a few items into suitcases and left. Just days later, another missile struck the rubble that had been their apartment building and rendered almost everything that remained unsalvageable.

Reluctant to move yet again, but with nowhere to stay, they made the decision not to return to Ashkelon.

The Kusenov family resettled in Migdal HaEmek, a cluster of dull housing projects far from Gaza, a hundred miles north of Ashkelon, a little more than twenty miles southeast of Haifa, and two and a half miles southwest of Nazareth. There was no beach in their new town, but the Sea of Galilee was close. Marina and Anton managed to find new jobs at a local electronics factory. Eitan enrolled in an engineering class.

About one thousand of the Ukrainian refugees who fled Ukraine after the Russian invasion and settled in Ashkelon and Ashdod were again forced to flee in October 2023. In total, around forty-five thousand Ukrainians have sought refuge in Israel since the outbreak of the Russia-Ukraine war, a quarter of them under the age of seventeen. Since October 7, dozens have been serving in the IDF, and to date nearly twenty-five hundred of these new arrivals have left Israel to wander—to search yet again for a new home.

Israel: The land of warmth, of beauty. She is a graveyard still.

Ofakim

Ofakim, located about twenty-five miles from the border with Gaza, is one of Israel's poorest cities. Established in 1955, it was intended to become an urban hub that would provide essential services to the surrounding region, which is largely a mix of agriculture and desert. The city's initial residents were Jewish immigrants from Morocco and Tunisia, followed by Jews from Iran, Egypt, Ethiopia, and the former USSR.

Unemployment and crime have continuously plagued the city. "The most consistent phenomenon in the history of Ofakim is how quickly people leave it," stated the sociologist Nathan Marom. Many families, upon achieving financial stability, depart Ofakim for neighboring cities such as Be'er Sheva, Ashdod, or Ashkelon.

On the eve of the current war, the average monthly salary in Ofakim was $2,500, 45 percent of its roughly thirty-six thousand residents had not completed high school, and 30 percent of its houses were government-owned. Even Mayor Itzik Danino, who comes from a founding family of Ofakim, used to claim as a child that he was from "near the city of Be'er Sheva" when asked about his origins.

On October 7, more than twenty heavily armed Hamas terrorists with hundreds of hand grenades and dozens of RPG
rockets entered the city. They invaded homes and opened fire
in the streets, particularly targeting Mishor Hagafen, a neighborhood whose homes lacked shelters and safe rooms, forcing
residents to flee into the streets, where they were easier targets.
On Tamar Street alone, dozens of citizens were murdered while
trying to find shelter or protect their families and neighbors. In
all, forty-nine residents of Ofakim were murdered.

October 7, 2023, corresponds to the Jewish date 22 Tishrei 5784.
It was a Saturday, the Sabbath, and not just any Sabbath, but Simchat Torah, the final holiday of the major sequence of holidays
in the Jewish year: Rosh Hashanah, the New Year, is followed by
the Ten Days of Repentance, which is in turn followed by Yom
Kippur, and Sukkot, and the days of Shemini Atzeret—a parade
of observances and fasts, prayer days and commemorations
(including the Fast of Gedaliah and Hoshana Raba) that finally
ends with Simchat Torah, which celebrates the annual comple-
tion of the cycle of Torah reading, when religious Jews gather in
the synagogue to dance with the Torah scrolls and observe the
commandment to begin reading them again.

Chaim Rumi, fifty-five years old, woke up early on Simchat
Torah and hurried to the synagogue of the Moroccan community in the Eli Cohen neighborhood of Ofakim.

A religious man, Chaim believed that a city as down on its
luck as Ofakim deserved an honest prayer. Unlike the mayor,
he'd never been ashamed of living in Ofakim. On the contrary—
he'd voluntarily moved to the city from Tel Aviv.

He was twenty years old at the time, a newly married young
man relocating due to a work opportunity in the south of the

country. In Ofakim, he became a father of four sons and found a steady livelihood: Chaim was the director of the municipal cemetery. Some might find this work emotionally and physically overwhelming, but he felt he'd found his calling. He enjoyed pruning the flowers and digging the graves. He appreciated the routine, the orderliness of the work. And that he was able to help bring comfort to families made the work all the more fulfilling.

All told, an area of fifty dunams, or 12.5 acres, encompassing 5,800 graves, was under his care. A few years ago, the local newspaper had noted that it was more pleasant to walk through the well-kept paths of the cemetery than on the streets of Ofakim.

Chaim was sometimes referred to as "the mayor of the dead," a moniker that originated from an innovation he'd introduced eight years prior: dividing the cemetery into streets. He installed fifteen street signs among the boulevards of graves to simplify navigation. Rather than sections and plots, people were now buried on streets named after notable individuals, such as Hasida Mor Yosef Street, Tami Afalo Street, and Masouda Zagori Street—all women who'd volunteered to assist him in ritually washing the deceased and preparing them for burial.

He even reached out to the Israel-based company Waze to incorporate his new streets into their navigation app. His goal for the following year was to enable people to enter the name of the deceased and have the app guide them to the grave. But until he could realize that goal, he relied on a photographic map he made himself with the help of a drone. Chaim's efforts in this regard earned his cemetery a rating of four and a half stars in customer reviews on Google.

It was also in Ofakim that Chaim found God. He often noted that "I used to make it difficult for the rabbis, asking a lot of questions, asking about the dinosaurs, asking for proofs. Little

by little I was convinced." His parents had immigrated to Israel
from Egypt and Turkey in the 1950s, but he found his community among the Moroccans, in their synagogue.

Typically, at least fifty men attend the Moroccan synagogue
for holiday prayers. The morning of October 7, only six of them
turned up, including Chaim.

"Where are the people, Gabbai Eliyahu?" (*Gabbai* is a term
for a helper in a synagogue, a man who facilitates the prayers.)

"Missiles are falling, Chaim, people are afraid."

"I understand, but this is an important day."

For Chaim, missiles are not a reason to cancel prayer. There were
years when more missiles fell from the sky than rain in Ofakim.

They decided to wait for more people to come. Eventually,
they had a minyan—the quorum of ten men required for public
prayer—and could begin:

> *Remember the twelve tribes, whom You brought out of*
>   *Egypt through the divided waters;*
> *for whom You sweetened the bitterness of the water.*
> *Their descendants, their blood was spilled for Your sake*
>   *like water.*
> *Turn to us, for our soul is engulfed with sorrow like*
>   *water.*
> *In the merit of their righteousness grant us abundant*
>   *water.*
> *For You Lord, our God, cause the wind to blow and the*
>   *rain to fall*
> *For blessing and not for curse. Amen.*

Half an hour into the prayer, Osher, the gabbai's son, burst
into the synagogue.

"There are terrorists; there are terrorists in Ofakim."

"What did you say, boy?"

"Terrorists in the city center, they are shooting people in [the neighborhood of] Mishor Hagafen."

"We didn't hear a thing; we are close enough that we would've heard if there was shooting."

Chaim was unsure what to make of it. Osher was known to be mischievous, and it was always hard to tell what was true and what wasn't with him. Yet, something seemed amiss on this Sabbath.

"Okay, sit down, boy. We'll finish the prayer and go home."

They quickly sang the holiday hymns and then read "The Bridegroom of Genesis" as fast as they could. There were no traditional three or even seven circumambulations, carrying the Torah around the reading desk; on this day, there wasn't even one.

Chaim walked slowly back home. He debated whether to turn on his phone to check if something was happening but ultimately decided against it. "Shabbat is Shabbat," he reasoned to himself. He thought he heard airplanes but wondered if it might just be the noise from his air conditioner. He decided to take a nap, as was his weekend habit.

His nap was cut short when his wife shook him awake. "Chaim, Chaim, the head of the religious council and three soldiers are at the door. Wake up." He jumped out of bed, in shorts and a tank top. Soldiers at his door? He has no soldier sons. Why had they come?

"We're sorry to wake you up, Chaim, but there's been a massacre in our city and all over southern Israel by Hamas terrorists. You need to open the cemetery now and start receiving bodies."

Osher had not lied.

Chaim quickly changed into his work clothes, telling his wife that he had no idea when he would return.

"Be careful, and look after yourself," she cautioned.

"Okay, okay, I will," he replied.

Five soldiers accompanied Chaim to his cemetery that morning. The commanding officer, either a major or lieutenant colonel—Chaim couldn't determine his rank—requested his drone; they needed to check for any ongoing active shooting. Chaim looked calm to the soldiers, but one thought kept recurring to him: What did *massacre* mean in terms of the number of dead?

Upon reaching the cemetery, Chaim opened the gate and then showed the soldiers into the low-slung plaster-walled offices. He turned on all the air conditioners, preparing the space for the expected influx of bodies. In matters of life and death, Jews have rabbinic dispensation to break the Sabbath, whether that involves driving an ambulance or using a phone. Chaim made sure his phone was on in case the police or medics got in contact.

He launched the drone, a Chinese model with an iffy battery, and invited the soldiers to view the images it transmitted through the application on his phone. At first the city streets appeared peaceful, with no one walking outside. It was on Tamar Street where they saw bodies upon bodies strewn along the sidewalks, uncovered. After forty-five minutes, the first ambulance arrived.

Chaim recognized the first body brought in. It was Rabbi Binyamin Rahami, a member of the synagogue he used to attend. Rabbi Rahami had often sat in the row in front of him. Such a kind person. The father of young kids. Chaim sighed as he carefully enclosed the body in a plastic bag.

After several ambulances had come and gone, a bus arrived.

Bodies and body parts were piled atop one another. A bus had collected every human remnant it had passed from the Nova music festival in Re'im all the way to Ofakim, a journey made considerably more challenging by the terrorists still firing along the thirteen-mile route. In all, about fifty bodies were crammed into the bus's luggage compartment. Chaim had never before seen people with bullets in their eyes, their brains spilling out of their heads. For half an hour, he tried to match one severed hand to its corresponding body. He recognized too many faces from his neighborhood, though he couldn't recall all their names. There was the man he always nodded to during his morning walks, some women he often saw at the grocery store. Then there was Moshe Ohayon, a local political and philanthropic figure. Everyone knew Moshe.

Next to Moshe's body was that of his son, Eliad, a young man in his twenties. Had the father seen his son die, or the son his father? Chaim tried not to dwell on these thoughts.

A truck arrived.

God forbid, Chaim knew this boy well. It was Aaron Chaimov, the son of the rabbi of the Bukharian community, a leader of the local Jews from Uzbekistan and Tajikistan. Rabbi Yosef Chaimov, a frequent visitor at the cemetery, always accompanied members of his community in their final journey. He had been so proud of Aaron, his eldest, twenty-five years old, a medic and ambulance driver and a father of two toddlers himself. Aaron was on the way to treat the injured when he was shot. A bullet entered his chest and he lost control of the ambulance.

Nahorai Said. Chaim felt that it was just a moment ago that Nahorai had been a baby in his wife's kindergarten class. Now he was already nineteen years old and dead.

Chaim worked for fifty hours without sleep. Cleaning, covering, cataloging. The Jewish ritual of preparing the bodies was a comfort: it dictated to him his actions, and the actions postponed his thoughts.

That week he conducted twenty-five funerals for the victims whose families wished to bury them in Ofakim—interring half of the forty-nine residents that were murdered in the city that day. Even in death, some still seek to leave Ofakim, and an out-of-town grave is cheaper than an out-of-town apartment.

Each family, each sect, has its funeral customs, and Chaim knew them all. Russians prefer not to carry the stretcher with the deceased by hand, opting instead for a cart. People from the Caucasus usually attend funerals in large numbers. Ethiopians, similarly, come in droves, but they do not approach the deceased, gathering at the grave only after interment. Moroccans carry the deceased to the grave with the feet forward, while Tunisians do the opposite.

It was only after the funerals that Chaim began to feel the pressure in his head: a mounting tension behind his eyes. His family suggested he talk about what he had seen. Initially, he resisted. Why should he burden others? What could he possibly share? Could he mention the wife who came screaming in the middle of the night, desperate to find her husband, although Chaim was legally prohibited from assisting her in identifying the body? The more pain he felt in his head, the more he felt trapped, in his own memories, and in others' pain.

Sarit Ohayon, who did not yet know of her husband and son's passing, waited quietly for news at her home in Ofakin, still caring for the twenty children with disabilities who her family had invited over for the holiday.

In the late 1990s, Sarit and Moshe Ohayon, a young couple

living in Jerusalem, moved to Ofakim in search of a challenge, or a purpose. They heard about a group of families affiliated with a national religious movement moving to the impoverished city to promote economic and social change. They decided to give it a try, for a year.

At the end of the year, Eliad, the second of their five sons, was born. They never left the Mishor Hagafen neighborhood.

Moshe, who became a prominent city figure, established a student village and a center for children with disabilities in their first years in the city. In 2013, he nearly won the mayoral race with the slogan "Doing, Changing, Leading." Some believed he lost because he acted more than he spoke, but there was no doubting his commitment to bettering the city. In recent years, Moshe led a national organization aiming to bridge the secular-religious divide through scripture study. A devout believer, he taught his secular students that commandments governing how people relate to other people are more important than commandments governing how people relate to God. He also chaired the executive committee of the Shaharit think tank, which was concerned with the escalating conflict between different groups in Israeli society: right versus left, Jews versus Arabs, religious versus secular, and Mizrahi versus Ashkenazi. He implemented the Sukkat Shalom (Shelter of Peace) initiative across the country, aimed at further breaking down these polarizing divisions. All in all, a busy man whose aim was to bring people together.

On October 5, coinciding with the minor holiday of Hoshana Rabbah, during which many traditionally engage in all-night Torah study, Moshe and his family hosted fifty guests at their home for one of these Sukkat Shalom events. For the occasion, Moshe invited two influential figures known for their divergent views. The first guest was Nimrod Shafer, a general in the reserves and a leader of the protests against Netanyahu's so-called Judicial Reform. He was known for supporting the reservists who refused to serve as a form of protest against the government's efforts to undermine democracy. The second guest, Sara Eliash, played a significant role in the establishment of settlements in the West Bank and was a prominent leader of the Religious Zionist community. Until the early hours of the morning, the two sat in Moshe's sukkah and discussed the Talmudic parable of the sailor on the ship:

> Rabbi Shimon bar Yochai taught a parable: Men were
>   on a ship.
> One of them took a drill and started drilling.
> The others said to him: What are you doing?
> He replied: What do you care? Isn't this my area of the
>   ship that I'm drilling?
> They said to him, Yes, but the water will rise and drown
>   us all.

The following evening, Eliad hosted an event at his family's home. It was the third year in a row he had invited children with disabilities such as cerebral palsy, muscular dystrophy, and brain trauma to celebrate the Sukkot holiday with his family. In the first year, he invited thirty children. The following year, he hosted fifty. And on what turned out to be the last evening of his life, he welcomed eighty children into the family's yard.

Eliad organized sleeping accommodations for all eighty guests around the neighborhood, with the family themselves hosting twenty children overnight.

At the first siren on Saturday, the whole Ohayon family started rushing among the five rooms of the house, helping to get the disabled children into the missile-proof room. Their house was one of the few in the neighborhood with such a shelter.

Aware that public shelters were locked and municipal help would probably be delayed as always, Moshe ran to the neighborhood's shelter, smashed open the locks, and ushered local residents inside.

"Stay with us, don't go outside," some of the neighbors begged him, but with reports of shooting coming in, he wanted to go investigate.

Eliad, arriving in Moshe's car, drove his father toward the gunfire on Tamar Street—with Moshe holding his gun out the window.

Five terrorists had seized Tamar Street 1, the residence of the Adri family. They were shooting at the street from inside, holding an elderly couple, Rachel and David, hostage. Rachel, who was raised in a family of fourteen children with parents from Iran and Morocco, was able to somewhat endear herself to the terrorists by conversing with them in Arabic and offering them pineapples and cookies.

At Tamar Street 16, Moshe and Eliad came across a group of terrorists firing at the Biliya house and attempting to break in. Looking up, Moshe saw eleven people trying to escape through a roof window. Among them were Ariel Biliya, his wife, Shoshana, their children, and other family members. Moshe and Eliad parked at Tamar Street 20, in a yard clear of terrorists, aiming to distract the attackers from the fleeing Biliya family.

Standing at the window, Ariel Biliya was helping his wife and children onto the roof one by one. He was shot while using his body to block the window.

Meanwhile, Amitai, Eliad's brother, Moshe's eldest son, was on the other side of Tamar Street, treating thirteen injured people, applying tourniquets. With no ambulances in the immediate vicinity, he loaded the injured into his car and transported them to a police checkpoint thirty minutes away. Amitai made three trips back and forth from Tamar Street. Ambulances wouldn't arrive on the street until evening.

Sarit remained at home, focused on feeding the twenty disabled children and reassuring their anxious parents. She was so occupied that she barely had time to worry about her husband and two sons. One of the volunteers who stayed with her and the children received a distressing video showing a family member of theirs, Doron Asher, being kidnapped along with her two young daughters from Kibbutz Nir Oz and brought to Gaza. It was difficult to understand what was happening amid the chaos.

At noon, Amitai returned home and broke the news to Sarit that Ariel Biliya had been murdered. The rest of the Biliya family had managed to hide under a solar panel on the roof. Sarit was concerned about how Moshe would react to his friend's death upon his return home.

In the evening, with Moshe and Eliad still not in touch, an increasingly anxious Sarit made a call to the police hotline to report them as missing. She'd been receiving a range of accounts from different people; some claimed they saw the father and son assisting people at the Nova festival at Re'im, while others speculated that they might be among the unidentified injured in one of the hospitals.

The next morning, Amitai decided to take matters into his own hands and search for them himself. He intended to drive to the area of the party but was prevented from doing so due to active shooting. While waiting, he chose to check their neighborhood just to be sure. As soon as he entered Tamar Street, he spotted his father's car, doors ajar and pocked with bullets, but with no signs of blood. While Amitai was inspecting the area around and under the vehicle, a member of the Biliya family happened to walk by.

"I'm so sorry about Ariel," Amitai said.

"We can't believe we lost him, we can't believe we survived. How's everyone in your family? What about your father, what's he up to?"

"I don't know, we haven't heard from him or from Eliad since yesterday. I actually just found their car here," he replied, pointing to the vehicle.

Amitai was searching around the car for any indication of what might have happened when another neighbor, a man he hadn't met before, began yelling from his yard across the fence.

"Are you looking for the owner of this vehicle?" he asked.

Amitai nodded.

"I saw everything from my window! It was insane, just insane! They fought against the terrorists, a father and son!" he exclaimed, gesturing with his hands to mimic shooting weapons and bodies falling.

"How do you know they were father and son?" Amitai asked, perplexed.

"Because the older man was shot first and the younger man was shouting for someone to help his father. The poor boy was shouting for help and then he was shot himself."

Attracted by the loud conversation, yet another neighbor approached and joined in. He, too, had witnessed the battle. "Their bodies were lying right here on the sidewalk until just a few hours ago," he said. He then took out his phone and showed Amitai a photo. Amitai saw his father and brother, pierced by bullets, in an embrace.

The bodies of Moshe and Eliad Ohayon had lain on the

pavement outside Tamar Street 20 for nearly a day before being evacuated to Chaim's cemetery on Sunday morning.

Amitai ripped his shirt in the traditional expression of mourning, and waited in tatters and tears for the city's social workers to accompany him home, in order to inform his mother and siblings. They arrived at the front door just as the last of the child guests was being evacuated from their house.

The Negev Bedouins

The Negev is a vast triangular expanse of desert in southern Israel, an eerie, arid stretch of sand and occasional mountains, dotted with stunted acacia trees. This harsh but often holy-feeling landscape is home to the Bedouins, an indigenous minority group of Arab Muslims who maintain characteristics of their traditional tribal way of life, living in extended family clans. Many engage in sheep and goat herding; others work as doctors, lawyers, and engineers. Polygamy is practiced among approximately one-third to one-fifth of Bedouin families in Israel. Although officially illegal, the ban is not widely enforced by the Israeli authorities.

Though the Negev Bedouins are full Israeli citizens and serve with distinction in the Israel Defense Forces, they have faced discrimination and suffered from poverty and lack of access to basic governmental services since the very founding of Israel.

Historically, the Bedouins were nomadic or seminomadic, originating from the Hejaz region of the Arabian Peninsula, and arriving in the Negev between the fourteenth and eighteenth centuries. On the eve of Israel's founding in 1948, there were about seventy thousand Bedouins in the Negev. During and after the war, most Bedouins left or were expelled from their traditional lands, relocating to the Sinai, Trans-Jordan, and Mount Hebron. Only about eleven thousand remained in the Negev, and they were subject to a military government for the first two decades of the state's existence. The 1965 Planning and Construction Law marked a significant change in land categorization throughout the country, one that still affects the Bedouin today; many villages, especially those in agricultural zones, were officially classified as "unrecognized" and deemed unsuitable for settlement. As a result, existing homes in these areas were suddenly considered illegal.

Today's Bedouin population in the Negev is approximately three hundred thousand, living in three distinct types of communities: government-planned towns, newly recognized villages, and those older, officially illegal, "unrecognized" villages. There are thirty-five of the latter in the Negev, and they are home to about 30 percent of the Bedouin population.

Conditions in these villages are dire: they lack basic infrastructure, including water, electricity, and roads. Access to education and medical care also remains limited. In addition, they face legal challenges regarding construction permitting, meaning that any attempt to repair or renovate their dwellings can result in fines, even demolitions.

During times of war between Israel and Gaza, no Israelis are more vulnerable than the Bedouins of the Negev. Most unrecognized villages lack warning sirens or access to municipal shelters. Even the Iron Dome rocket interception system, which offers substantial protection to most Israeli cities, does not extend to certain villages. This absence of protection is a direct result of the Israeli government's classification of the Bedouin areas as "open areas," meaning not officially populated—the same designation that denies these villages connectivity to the national water supply and electricity grid.

In 2014, the Civil Rights Association petitioned the High Court of Justice to provide protection against rocket fire for residents of Bedouin villages. In 2017, a relatively quiet year for rocket attacks, the court decided not to interfere, and refused to mandate the installation of shelters in these villages. The court ruling expressed trust in the authorities to "provide protection when necessary." While many Israelis were concerned about potential judicial reforms weakening democracy, the Bedouins laughed.

When Hamas launched the October 7 attack, numerous rockets struck Bedouin areas. Nineteen Bedouins, including six children, were killed on this day alone. The regional council for the unrecognized villages in the Negev calculated that the residents of these villages have a 2,200 times higher risk of dying from rocket attacks compared to the rest of the Israeli population.

Three days had passed since her October 3 due date, yet Sujood Abu Karinat patiently anticipated her baby's birth. She was already well acquainted with waiting.

The mother-to-be was a daughter of the Abu Karinat family, a family so large and well-established in the Negev that it had its own village, called Abu Karinat, a formerly unrecognized village that was granted official status by the Israeli authorities in 1999, a year before Sujood was born. Her childhood was spent waiting for the government to come and set up links to the water and electricity supply. When she was eighteen, an access road was finally paved, and the first permanent buildings, including a children's club and a public health clinic, were constructed. When she was nineteen, the district committee approved the development of new neighborhoods with concrete buildings, and the water and electricity soon followed. Not for her, though—like many others in Abu Karinat, she still lived in a dilapidated tin shack. At twenty, she married thirty-year-old Triffy Abu Rashid, a member of the second-largest family in the village, becoming his second wife. Triffy was already the father of six children, and was himself one of thirty-five siblings born to his father, Muhammad, by three different women.

Sujood was expecting her first child, a baby girl. Months before the birth, she'd prepared a crib, chosen the girl's name, and bought pink clothes and diapers. Triffy, the less patient of the two, suggested they visit a doctor to ensure that everything was normal with their now-overdue baby. After completing the exam, which showed that the baby was healthy, they decided not to return home to sleep in Abu Karinat.

Instead, they headed to their family field near Kibbutz Re'im, where their flock of nearly 350 sheep were grazing. They struggled to sleep that night, kept awake by the sounds of a giant nearby party—the Nova music festival.

A little after five-thirty in the morning, Sujood woke up screaming, "I'm in labor! Get up, Triffy, get up. I need to go to the hospital immediately, like the doctor said."

Leaving Triffy's younger brother, Bilal, to care for the sheep, Triffy, Sujood, and their soon-to-be baby girl set off.

It was early on a holiday Saturday; the roads were empty, and the day seemed promising, until the sirens started. Despite the warnings, they continued toward Soroka Hospital, Sujood praying all the while: What did her baby have to do with military conflicts? They hoped to be at the hospital within forty minutes, and to become parents within a few hours.

Several kilometers away, sixty members of the Al-Kran family were woken by explosions. They live in a dense hive of tiny huts in East Maluda, an unrecognized Bedouin village. When a son marries in East Maluda, families slightly reduce the size of the other rooms to add a new one for the young couple. Despite the open stretches of desert beyond the walls, the rooms of their huts are so closely situated that every movement can be heard, and it can be hard to sleep if someone in the next room is awake.

These tight quarters are not even a consequence of poverty: the Al-Kran fear that new construction might trigger demolition orders from the authorities. In a neighboring village, residents daub their houses with mud to give them an aged appearance, hoping to avoid Israeli inspectors.

The village of East Maluda lacks a formal entrance and its location cannot be found on online maps. Dirt roads lead through the desert to a plot with about thirty olive trees, frequented by camel herds for grazing.

In 1880, during the Ottoman reign, Saleh Al-Kran migrated from Saudi Arabia to the Negev and settled in this village. His grandson, Muhammad Al-Kran, was born there in 1940, eight years before Israel's founding. He became a respected mediator, a resolver of conflicts in Bedouin society. Muhammad fathered seven sons; the eldest, Said, age fifty-seven, and the youngest, Jasser, age twenty-eight. His other sons, Ebrahim, Akal, Dib, Taleb, and Sajr, also resided in the village, raising their children there as part of a large, close-knit family.

Dozens of the Al-Kran men, women, and children awoke to find that a missile had landed just a few meters from their compound. Vehicle windows were shattered, a fire ignited, and a plume of smoke rose into the sky. The men of the family congregated to pray and express gratitude to Allah for what they considered a miracle: only property was damaged.

A few minutes later, another missile struck the nearby village of Alabat, landing in the middle of Faiza Abu Sabeih's shack. Her fourteen-year-old granddaughter, May Abu Sabeih, was at that moment administering Faiza's high blood pressure and choles-terol medication. Adal, Faiza's son and May's uncle, was sitting on a bench by the kitchen waiting for breakfast.

May, the second child of Faiza's eldest, Zuhir, chose to live with her grandmother even though her parents resided in a nearby shack. Every day at seven in the morning and seven in the evening, she diligently administered her grandmother's medication, bathed her, and tucked her into bed. Faiza's ten chil-dren acknowledged that May took care of their mother alone more effectively than they could collectively.

At times, when Adal, a respected architect and former teacher, came to dine with his mother, May would stay seated, refusing to serve him. She didn't care about traditional cus-toms; men could serve themselves. When called, May didn't al-ways respond, and she often danced around the house with her headphones on, listening to songs in English. "You call yourself educated and only speak Arabic and bad Hebrew?" she would tease her uncles and cousins, teaching them English words.

The Abu Sabeih family is among the most educated in the region. Faiza's cousin, Ibrahim Abu Sabeih, a Labor Party Knes-set candidate, was among the founders of the Regional Council for Unrecognized Villages, the first autonomous Bedouin entity to protest against the injustices of the Israeli government. Faiza herself was only allowed to complete her education up to the eighth grade, and yet she became the main breadwinner after her husband, Muhammad, became disabled. She crafted traditional Bedouin *thobe* dresses, produced high-quality cheeses from their herd of six hundred sheep and goats, and traded in gold, buying low and selling high.

Just before the missile struck her home, Faiza was teaching six of her young grandchildren, aged five to nine, how to make pita bread on the *saj*, a metal griddle. One of them, eight-year-old Zuhir, became distracted by a white puppy outside the hut and, despite Faiza's remonstrations, chased after the dog, leading all his cousins except May and Adal in pursuit.

They'd just left—they were only a dozen or so meters away—when the missile destroyed their shack.

Zuhir was wounded by shrapnel in his leg and back, while Adal lost consciousness when the shack's tin walls collapsed on him. "Mom! May! Where are you? Mom! May!" he called out before passing out. Regaining consciousness a few minutes later, he found the shack on fire and navigated through the destruction searching for them, unaware of his own injuries from shrapnel that had penetrated his head, back, and hand. He found Faiza and May lying motionless, with their arms outstretched.

The ambulance, upon arriving at the village entrance, failed to reach the Abu Sabeih shack due to the absence of a proper road. Neighbors transported Faiza, May, Adal, and Zuhir in their private vehicle to the ambulance, which then took them to Soroka Hospital.

As the rockets began falling on Road 232, Triffy apologized to Sujood, who was experiencing labor pains: they'd have to take a detour. He was concerned for the safety of his little brother, Bilal, left alone in the family's pastureland, and decided to turn back and pick him up.

As they neared the Re'im intersection, close to the site of the Nova music festival whose noise had disturbed them throughout the night, two white vans boxed them in: one in front, the other behind. Triffy squinted to confirm what he was seeing: a man armed with a submachine gun was standing on one of the vans. The man opened fire on them. Triffy swerved sharply to the right, narrowly escaping the ambush. As he glanced over, he saw Sujood bleeding from her abdomen—a bullet had penetrated the car and struck her pregnant belly. Another bullet hit one of the car's tires.

Triffy's attempts to get emergency help were met with no response from the national emergency medical services or the police. He called his father, Muhammad, pleading for medical assistance at the Urim junction, which he was trying to reach despite the flat tire. After the car stalled out, just shy of the intersection, Triffy and Bilal stepped out onto the road, waving for help. Three cars, all driven by Bedouin residents from the area, pulled over. Triffy was explaining the situation to them and begging for assistance to transport Sujood to the hospital when another white van appeared. Six or seven Hamas militants began firing indiscriminately at the group of Bedouins, who pleaded in Arabic for them to stop. Among the Bedouin were women wearing black hijabs, similar to the one Sujood was wearing in the passenger seat of the car. A bullet grazed Bilal's neck, and Triffy urged him to take cover behind the car as he turned to check on Sujood. Just then, another bullet flew by and hit Sujood in the stomach once again.

"Two bullets in the stomach? Have the Bedouin fights gotten that bad?" The ambulance driver callously mocked Triffy when he finally arrived.

"There are terrorists shooting at civilians," Triffy yelled. "Come on, take them and drive quickly to Soroka."

Dr. Eyal Sheiner, head of the obstetrics and gynecology division at Soroka Hospital, was in the process of moving expectant mothers to rocket-proof buildings with his team when they received a message about the day's first injury:

"Advanced pregnancy, abdomen penetrated by shrapnel, hurrying to the trauma center . . ."

Sujood was semiconscious when Dr. Sheiner and his team, consisting of two senior surgeons, two obstetrician-gynecologists, an intern, and a pediatrician, began their initial examination.

The ultrasound revealed a viable fetus with a normal heartbeat and amniotic fluid level. Forgoing further imaging, they rushed to the operating room. The team opted for a cesarean section with a longitudinal incision to avoid intestinal damage. The surgeons were astounded to find that a bullet had passed through the uterus and struck the fetus. The pediatrician noted entry and exit wounds on the lower abdomen and leg of the fetus, who was now a newborn and moved immediately into intensive care. Sujood's internal organs were unharmed; her unborn child had acted as a shield. The medical team stitched up her intact uterus. In the room, with hundreds of years of combined medical experience, nobody had ever encountered such a case.

As Triffy waited for Sujood's operation to be over, he encountered Said Al-Kran, the eldest son of the Al-Kran family. They embraced; Triffy had already heard about the disaster that had befallen the Al-Kran children. After the missile had landed near their home, the family members had gathered in the *shige*, the traditional Bedouin guest room reserved for male gatherings, to pray and express gratitude for their survival. After their prayers, they dispersed. Ibrahim went to inspect the missile fragments, while Said prepared tea. The children, opting to rest, stayed behind with Uncle Taleb. A second rocket then fell in the center of the *shige*, amid the red carpets and orange-yellow pillows. Said pulled the children from the debris himself. Ebrahim's two boys, sixteen-year-old Malak and eleven-year-old Jawad, had been killed instantly. Said Al-Kran carried sixteen-year-old Muhammad and ten-year-old Amin in his arms. He rushed them into a car and drove them to Soroka, where they were declared dead on arrival. Their uncle Taleb, seriously injured, was the only survivor of this second missile.

A few floors away, in Soroka's internal medicine ward, Adal Abu Sabeih had just arrived at the hospital when his grandfather Ali—Faiza's eighty-two-year-old father—passed his bed by chance. Ali had been in the hospital since the day before for a routine dialysis treatment. He was accompanied by his grandson, Hitam, Adal's cousin.

"Hitam, do you know what happened back home? Did May and Faiza survive?"

"We have to wait, Adal, we don't know yet."

"Are they alive?"

"It'll be all right, it'll be all right, Adal."

They couldn't finish the conversation. The surgeons rushed Adal to the operating room. As he regained consciousness post-surgery, he found himself surrounded by family members. He was told that the doctors had managed to remove most of the shrapnel from his body—he would recover, but Faiza and May would not.

Paramedics had declared them dead at the scene; they hadn't even made it to the hospital. Adal was released for several hours, in order to attend the funeral. He wore his hospital gown, having no other clothing.

On October 7, Soroka Hospital treated a total of 676 wounded. At noon that day, about two hours after beginning the procedure on Sujood, Dr. Sheiner left the operating room and called Triffy in to see his daughter for the first time. He informed Triffy that Sujood was no longer in danger; the baby had absorbed the bullets and saved her life. He assured him that Sujood's uterus was intact, allowing future pregnancies.

Triffy gazed at his small, stitched-up daughter, who bore a striking resemblance to his wife. He wasn't allowed to hold her. When Sujood woke up from surgery in the afternoon, he informed her that their baby was alive and in intensive care, after which she soon fell back asleep. At 10:24 P.M., the fourteen-hour-old baby passed away. Sujood never got the chance to see her. The next morning, she asked Triffy to bury their daughter in the village without her presence; she couldn't bear to see the face of her dead firstborn.

Adal Abu Sabeih paid a visit to the mourning tent of the Al-Kran family. Ebrahim, the father of two of the deceased children and a colleague of Adal's, taught mathematics at the elementary school in one of the Bedouin villages. Jawad, his youngest, an eleven-year-old boy, was known for styling his hair with gel, wearing branded shirts, and reciting the Quran loudly every Friday to the adults. Amin, the son of Akal and almost the same age as Jawad, was known for his humor; he had the reputation of being the funniest among the nearly thirty Al-Kran cousins. Malak, Ebrahim's sixteen-year-old middle son, stood out for his maturity and excellence in mathematics. He also participated as a young nature guide in a Ministry of Education program. Muhammad, Dib's only son and Malak's classmate, joined him as well.

Following their deaths, the ministry issued a statement: "Muhammad and Malak were outstanding students. They possessed excellent social skills and their potential for leadership was widely noted. They completed the Nature Guide youth training program with honors. Malak aspired to study medicine, and Muhammad aspired to be a teacher."

At the Al-Kran mourning tent, the three grieving mothers of dead children watched with disdain as a procession of men with bowed heads arrived at their home, bearing makeshift rocket shelters as gifts. The first group, members of the Israeli Islamic Movement, brought large concrete cylinders: these would be placed a four-minute walk from their houses. The mothers questioned the feasibility of reaching these shelters in time, especially given the village's lack of an alarm system. Days later, officers from the Israeli Home Front Command visited, offering condolences and installing Hesco barriers. These structures, made of large sandbags covered with steel mesh and jute cloth, lacked an effective roof to protect against rockets. Lastly, representatives from ICL—Israel Chemicals, a company routinely identified by the Ministry of Environmental Protection as one of the country's major polluters— donated a concrete safe room to be placed adjacent to the houses. While the mothers appreciated the gesture, they were left wondering how to choose which of their remaining children to save. There were fifty-six people left in the family, and the safe room could only accommodate six.

Fathers and Sons

1

It was a time of weddings.

Nahal Oz, in 1956, was a young kibbutz, just five years old, the first outpost of the Nahal program, a government initiative that combined service in the newly formed Israel Defense Forces with the founding of agricultural cooperatives. The kibbutz population was mostly Ottoman and Mandatory Palestine-born Jews, alongside new immigrants, including refugees and Holocaust survivors. Weddings were a way of starting over.

Four couples were to be married. A fifth wedding, which had been planned, had to be postponed because the groom had been wounded by shelling from Gaza.

Moshe Dayan, the chief of staff of the Israeli Defense Forces, a relative of one of the four grooms, had been invited to the festivities.

The preparations for the celebration were almost complete; a large sign bearing the phrase "I am my beloved's and my beloved is mine" from the Song of Songs stood at the center of the kibbutz farm. Four rows of tables flanked by bales of hay were arranged to serve as benches; the choir and accordion players were in the midst of rehearsals and the brides were ironing their dresses.

But seven hours before the event, at half past six in the morning, two shots were heard. The early-rising wedding organizers observed a group of Arabs from the Egypt-controlled Gaza Strip crossing the open border, only a few miles from the kibbutz.

Roi Rotberg, a twenty-one-year-old thin, bespectacled security coordinator who always carried a small comb for his blond hair in his pocket, rode toward the infiltrators, unarmed, in an attempt to chase them off, as was his normal practice. But he rode into an ambush. A group consisting of Jamil Wadiyah, a thirty-year-old corporal from the Gaza police, and Mahmoud Zaira, a fifty-year-old Gazan farmer, along with an Egyptian army officer and two soldiers, murdered Rotberg and took his body to Gaza, where they gouged out his eyes—an echo of the same fate the Philistines visited upon Samson.

The party was canceled, but the wedding ceremonies themselves were held that day as planned, brides donning white with tears, following Dayan's advice: "Never cancel a wedding."

At noon that day, UN observers from the Israel Egypt Mixed Armistice Commission brought Rotberg's desecrated body back to Israel. As Nahal Oz didn't yet have a cemetery, two kibbutz members quickly identified a hill for the burial, one kilometer away from their farm, overlooking the houses of Gaza on one side and on the other, the fields of the kibbutz.

Zvi Gershuni, the forty-four-year-old secretary of neighboring Kibbutz Nir Am, arrived at the funeral straight from tending chickens, still wearing his everyday khaki shirt and pants. He stood next to Moshe Dayan near the freshly dug grave. Dayan's military uniform was similar to what Gershuni was wearing—the

same khaki—but Dayan's was adorned with the badges and insig-
nia of the highest ranks of the IDF, and, as always, he wore a Vertia
eye patch for the eye he lost in Lebanon fifteen years earlier.

All told, about a thousand people gathered atop the hill that
afternoon, all clad in nearly identical khaki outfits and bucket
hats, as if they could camouflage themselves amid the arid
wastes. It was Dayan who delivered the eulogy. Standing above
the open grave, with Gershuni at his side, Dayan read a speech
he'd handwritten:

Early yesterday morning Roi was murdered. The quiet of the
spring morning dazzled him and he did not see those waiting
in ambush for him, at the edge of the furrow. Let us not cast the
blame on the murderers today. Why should we declare their
burning hatred for us? For eight years they have been sitting in
the refugee camps in Gaza, and before their eyes we have been
transforming the lands and the villages, where they and their
fathers dwelt, into our estate. It is not among the Arabs in Gaza,
but in our own midst that we must seek Roi's blood. How did we
shut our eyes and refuse to look squarely at our fate, and see, in
all its brutality, the destiny of our generation? Have we forgotten
that this group of young people dwelling at Nahal Oz is bearing
the heavy gates of Gaza on its shoulders? Beyond the furrow of the
border, a sea of hatred and desire for revenge is swelling, awaiting
the day when serenity will dull our path, for the day when we will
heed the ambassadors of malevolent hypocrisy who call upon us
to lay down our arms. Roi's blood is crying out to us and only to
us from his torn body. Although we have sworn a thousandfold
that our blood shall not flow in vain, yesterday again we were
tempted, we listened, we believed. We will make our reckoning
with ourselves today; we are a generation that settles the land

and without the steel helmet and the cannon's maw, we will not
be able to plant a tree and build a home. Let us not be deterred
from seeing the loathing that is inflaming and filling the lives of
the hundreds of thousands of Arabs who live around us. Let us
not avert our eyes lest our arms weaken. This is the fate of our
generation. This is our life's choice—to be prepared and armed,
strong and determined, lest the sword be stricken from our fist
and our lives cut down. The young Roi who left Tel Aviv to build
his home at the gates of Gaza to be a wall for us was blinded by
the light in his heart and he did not see the flash of the sword.
The yearning for peace deafened his ears and he did not hear the
voice of murder waiting in ambush. The gates of Gaza weighed
too heavily on his shoulders and overcame him.

On the day following the funeral, Dayan reread the eulogy
on the radio to the general public but with three lines omitted
from the original text—the words expressing sympathy for the
pain of the killers from Gaza. In 1956, this would've been a difficult statement for Israelis to hear. Over the course of the first
decade of statehood, about one thousand Israelis were murdered
in hundreds of terror attacks committed by Palestinian *fedayeen*
based in Egyptian-controlled Gaza and Jordan.

The public Dayan was addressing on the radio still well remembered when Amin al-Husseini, the Muslim leader of British
Mandatory Palestine, paid a visit to Adolf Hitler at the Reich
Chancellory in Berlin and, according to the official Nazi record
of the meeting, seized the opportunity to stress that "the Arabs
were Germany's natural friends because they had the same enemies as had Germany, namely the English, the Jews, and the
Communists." Hitler declared that among the Nazi goals was the
struggle against a Jewish homeland in Palestine. Four years later,

one-third of the world's Jewish population was exterminated, and Palestine was all but closed to the surviving remnant.

Dayan's radio audience also vividly remembered their Arab neighbors' refusal to countenance the United Nations Partition Plan for two independent states, one Jewish and one Arab, which was approved by the UN General Assembly and the Jewish Agency in November 1947. A people who had barely escaped the Nazis had found broad international support for their right to an autonomous Jewish state, though the country's neighbors rejected the legitimacy of the UN's decision. The Arab Higher Committee of the Grand Mufti of Jerusalem denounced the plan, arguing that it was unjust to assign 52 percent of the land to the Jewish state and 45 percent to an Arab state, a particularly disproportionate distribution given the larger Arab population. Meanwhile, Jamal al-Husayni, head of the Arab delegation to the UN, declared, "The dividing line will be nothing but a line of fire and blood." Azzam Pasha, Arab League secretary-general, remarked, "This will be a war of extermination and momentous massacre."

The Jewish state was born into war.

Two-thirds of the sixty-seven thousand Israelis who fought the combined five Arab armies that attacked them were recent immigrants, many survivors of the Nazis' camps.

After more than a year and a half of fighting, Israel won the war it called its War of Independence, albeit at the cost of about six thousand lives, approximately 1 percent of the young nation's population. About half of the dead were Holocaust survivors, some of them the last surviving members of their families.

The Arabs also lost thousands of people in the war they called the Nakba (the Catastrophe), some killed in battle and some killed in massacres committed by Jews: Deir Yassin, al-Dawayima, Lydda and Ramle and Safsaf. About half of the region's

Arab population, between 700,000 and 750,000 people, were either expelled from their lands or fled, and were forbidden from returning. Israel destroyed about four hundred abandoned or evacuated Palestinian villages, along with vast swaths of Palestinian neighborhoods in cities occupied by Jews. The names of these villages and neighborhoods were erased from maps and replaced with Hebraicized versions.

Many of the Palestinians fled to the Gaza Strip. After the war's conclusion, the territory was occupied by Egypt, which refused to extend citizenship to Palestinians, who because they weren't able to return to their homes were left stateless.

It was this legacy of Palestinian suffering that Dayan was trying to communicate in the original version of his eulogy for Roi Rotberg—a legacy that contained a warning that the Israeli public was not ready to hear.

2

Moshe Dayan was the second child born in the first-ever kibbutz, Kibbutz Degania, in northern Israel, in May 1915. Zvi Gershuni was born in Balti, then part of Bessarabia (present-day Moldova and Romania), four months earlier in January 1915. His most formative memories involved witnessing his Zionist father's official political persecution at the hands of the Soviets. From earliest childhood, he longed to become a part of the kibbutz movement that Dayan had in his blood.

As a high school student, Gershuni joined Gordonia, a youth-socialist-Zionist organization named after Aaron David Gordon, one of the forefathers of Labor Zionism (Gordon, a native of Troyanov, Russia, later became a resident of Kibbutz Degania, and died there in 1922).

Gordonia and Labor Zionism emphasized the importance of rural manual labor and the revival of the Hebrew language in the creation of a new state, and Gershuni went on, as a high school student, to become one of the group's leaders in Bessarabia. At the age of twenty-one, he, along with fifteen young men and women from the movement, immigrated to Israel on one of the Ma'apilim ships, or illegal chartered immigration ships, overcrowded and beset by illnesses. On board, he met Hana Roitkov, a girl born in Orgeye, Bessarabia, and asked her to join the group. Not long afterward, he asked her to marry him. The growing group first settled in Rehovot, working in orchards, and then spent several years doing hard physical labor at the port of Haifa. Soon enough, the group was looking to establish a more permanent agricultural settlement for itself and began to search out likely locations in the Upper Galilee. However, Avraham Herzfeld, a member of the Knesset and the founder of many kibbutzim, advised the group to instead focus on the barren, forbidding Negev: "If you search for too long," he quipped, "you'll remain an old bachelor like me. Take what is needed. These days, the Negev is needed—go there."

In 1943, the young group followed his advice, establishing Kibbutz Nir Haim, the southernmost kibbutz in Israel at that time, later renamed Nir Am (the government names committee ruled that there were "too many places named Haim").

For the next two years, the fledgling population of Nir Am struggled to build homes, grow food, and find water, relying on water barrels purchased from the Arabs in Beit Hanun.

The kibbutz maintained warm relations with the nearby Arab villages, especially with the Mahuj Abul Eish family. This family assisted the kibbutz with supplies and equipment, facilitated connections with local Arabs, and educated the residents about Arab customs to avoid misunderstandings.

Everything changed after the approval of the United Nations Partition Plan. According to the plan, the kibbutz was now located at what was supposed to be the southern border between the independent Arab and Jewish states, which Israel recognized but the Arabs did not. In January 1948, two months after the unveiling of the plan, two sons of the Mahuj Abul Eish family were killed in Gaza by Arabs due to their cooperation with the Jews of Nir Am. This was just the beginning of the cycle of bloodshed.

Four months later, the armies of Syria, Jordan, Iraq, and Egypt attacked Israel, and Kibbutz Nir Am found itself under siege. During this period, Gershuni served as the head of the Negev Council. At the inaugural meeting of the Workers' Party of Israel in June 1948, in the presence of David Ben-Gurion, Gershuni testified about the war's impact on the Negev: "I come from places that were attacked, even severely, yet the Negev did not lose its sense of morale. We understood the necessity of continuing life. Thus, we constructed an underground dining room and kitchens, not just shelters. There is underground life, a determination to persist despite the circumstances."

By 1952, Gershuni had become the interior secretary for the Union of Kibbutzim, earning respect as one of the most determined and talented young men in the young ruling party. In 1969, he was elected to the Knesset as part of a revived party called Alignment—created from the joining of the Israeli Labor Party and the United Workers' Party—which won a majority of fifty-six seats. Of those fifty-six seats, Prime Minister Golda Meir was first, Moshe Dayan was fourth, while Gershuni was thirty-seventh.

"My belief is to engage in an unceasing pursuit of peace, and a society characterized by greater justice and equality," Gershuni said upon being sworn into the Knesset, adding, "I want to remember that my home is the chicken coop, and it will stay such, when the time comes to retire."

3

In the same year of 1969, at a government-sponsored Hebrew language course known as Ulpan in Migdal HaEmek, an extravagantly bearded twenty-eight-year-old new immigrant from Rosario, Argentina, named Alfredo Wax met a lively blond nineteen-year-old new immigrant from Queens, New York, named Suzy Galnik. Born in Germany, Suzy had fled the Nazis and came to the United States with her parents. Soon overwhelmed by New York, she decided to leave everything behind once again and start anew by herself.

Alfredo and Suzy both made *aliyah* in the wake of the Six-Day War—the third of the Arab-Israeli wars, when Egypt, Syria, and Jordan attacked Israel. On May 13, 1967, Soviet officials informed Syria and Egypt that Israel had amassed troops near the Syrian border. Despite the inaccuracy of the report, which might have been purposeful disinformation, Egyptian president Gamal Abdel Nasser responded by deploying a substantial number of troops to the Sinai Peninsula. Israel declared that any Egyptian blockade of Israeli shipping in the Straits of Tiran would be considered a declaration of war. Nasser announced the closure of the Straits of Tiran to Israeli vessels and ordered a mobilization of the Egyptian military along the Israeli border, also demanding the withdrawal of the UN Emergency Force from the area.

On June 5, 1967, Israel initiated a series of airstrikes against Egyptian airfields and military installations. Over the course of five days, Israel defeated the combined forces of Egypt, Jordan, and Syria, in the process occupying territory in the Sinai and the

Gaza Strip from Egypt, the West Bank and East Jerusalem from Jordan, and the Golan Heights from Syria.

It was in the newly Israelized Sinai that newlyweds Suzy and Alfredo decided to settle. They'd tried living in Tel Aviv, Herzliya, and even New York, but never felt at home in a city. A white Peugeot 203 carried the young couple, their baby, Yigal, and their Danish dog, Shiba, to the white sands of the Sinai—the biblical landscape par excellence. Adapting to the heat was challenging, as was learning to drive a tractor, especially while pregnant. Their second boy was named Amit, but everyone called the two boys "Vex" and "Vexy," based on the pronunciation of Alfredo's last name.

Alfredo and Suzy cultivated cucumbers and flowers and felt for the first time that they had found a real community. Together with fifty-eight families, they worked to build a small town in the desert—a town they called Moshav Netiv HaAsara, the Path of the Ten in Hebrew, in memory of ten soldiers who died there in a helicopter crash.

Another one of the founding families was the Taasas—two parents and three sons around the ages of the Wax boys. Shoshana and Abraham Taasa were Yemeni Jews who had lived in Moshav Mishan near Ashkelon but had long wanted to have a farm of their own. In 1972, a friend suggested they check out the Sinai. "When I saw the sea, we decided to move," Shoshana recalled years later, in a documentary on the community. On the day they arrived, they were greeted by a house full of sand—it was everywhere, in the kitchen, in the drawers, even in the shower. Their fourth son, Gil, was born atop those endless sands soon after.

What none of the new residents of Moshav Netiv HaAsara knew in advance of their arrival was that about fifteen hundred Bedouin families had been secretly expelled from the area under orders from Defense Minister Moshe Dayan and Southern Command head Ariel Sharon, without government authorization.

It was once this expulsion was revealed in spring 1972 that the local residents of the kibbutzim demanded justice for the Bedouin. The chief of staff of the IDF, David Elazar, formed an inquiry commission, and Ariel Sharon was reprimanded for exceeding his authority. Eventually, the Israeli Supreme Court legitimated the expropriation, officially citing "security reasons." The Bedouins received compensation, some in the form of money, others in the form of land in the territory of Gaza.

4

MK (member of the Knesset) Gershuni never retired as promised.

He rose through the ranks of the Knesset and found himself appointed, in succession, head of the Agricultural Lobby; member of the Finance Committee; member of the Economy Committee; and member of the Constitution, Law, and Justice Committee. His days consisted of pursuing various ministers with problems for them to solve. Once, he managed to pass legislation ensuring better regulation of water prices; another time, he fought a decision to grant better medical insurance to Knesset members, calling the decision part of "a feudal regime of special privilege for those with privileged status"; he worked tirelessly to promote a law to change the Knesset election system from a national to a regional system, aiming to strengthen the obligations of elected representatives toward their constituencies. In early 1974, under Meir's new government in the aftermath of the Yom Kippur War, Gershuni was among the first to propose Yitzhak Rabin for the prime ministership. He speculated that Meir's tenure would be brief due to a combination of public outrage and internal party pressure following her handling of the war, and concluded that Rabin, who was then Israel's ambassador to the United States, was the only viable candidate to replace her. After Meir's resignation, Gershuni supported Rabin's candidacy with a zeal that made it easy to understand why, over the course of his years in politics, he suffered three serious heart attacks.

On Wednesday, September 1, 1976, Gershuni was scheduled to present a proposal to the Finance Committee—an idea for the establishment of a new government housing bank. Gershuni prepared a speech advocating for an end to government funding of privately capitalized banks, which he believed enriched private citizens at the public's expense. He was to argue in favor of a state bank that would provide loans and mortgages to those eligible for public housing, catering to the needs of hundreds of thousands of new immigrants.

That morning, MK Adi Amorai, a member of his party and of the Finance Committee, left the bus to the Knesset and saw Hana, Gershuni's wife, waiting at the bus stop. He wondered why Hana would accompany Zvi to a regular meeting of the Finance Committee. Upon entering the Knesset, Amorai found Gershuni in the corridor, sitting on a chair, taking off one pair of shoes and changing into another. He was pale and agitated. "Gershuni, relax," he pleaded.

During the committee discussion, Gershuni took meticulous notes. Just before his turn to speak, he excused himself to go to the restroom. When the topic of his proposal was reached, the committee chairman requested the staff to call MK Gershuni to the podium. At that moment, MK Gideon Patt burst into the room, exclaiming, "A man is lying unconscious by the toilets."

Everyone rushed to the bathroom, where they found Zvi Gershuni on the floor, having suffered another heart attack and sustained a head injury from hitting the enamel sink during his fall. MK Amorai accompanied Gershuni in the ambulance that rushed to Shaare Zedek Hospital.

Gershuni passed away half an hour later, at the age of sixty-one. Before his death, Gershuni expressed that his greatest satisfaction in life was not his public achievements but the fact that all his children and grandchildren remained in Kibbutz Nir Am, the home he founded.

He didn't live to see the peace agreement with Egypt three years later. He never retired back to his chicken coop.

5

Israel's withdrawal from Sinai in 1982, in compliance with the newly signed peace agreement, meant that sixty-nine families of Netiv HaAsara had to leave—including the Waxes and Taasas. They decided to relocate together, aiming to preserve their agricultural community within Israel's newly revised borders.

On their last day in Netiv HaAsara, Suzy Wax let her young sons paint on the walls of what would soon no longer be their house. They left behind their tomatoes and the children's wall paintings for the Egyptians.

The families transplanted their Sinai palms to their new moshav (agricultural village), close to the Zikim beach, just north of the Gaza border, and retained the name Netiv HaAsara. They found the same soft quartz sand there, originating from the mountains of Ethiopia and Sudan, carried by the Nile, washed from Egypt's delta into the Mediterranean, and transported north to Israel. Each family was allotted a 2.5 dunam estate and an additional 40 dunams for agriculture. Shoshana replanted her loquat tree, which continued to bear fruit.

As the Netiv HaAsara families rebuilt their homes, most of the construction was carried out by Arab workers.

Many of these workers, like Hamis and Halil from the city of Beit Lahiya, formed friendships with the Israeli families. They invited each other to celebrate birthdays and weddings, shared home-cooked meals, and offered financial support when needed. When one of Hamis's children needed medical treatment, Alfredo and Suzy took them to an Israeli hospital. This uncommon kindness was a common occurrence and would continue to be, even after the establishment of the new Israel-Gaza border.

6

Fifteen years after Zvi Gershuni's death, his son, Yakovi Inon, left the kibbutz his parents established and moved to the relocated Moshav Netiv HaAsara, seven kilometers away from Nir Am along the Gaza border.

At that time, many kibbutzim were facing economic challenges, and the Inon family sought private family life without the collective intervention of the kibbutz in their work and financial decision-making. Yakovi, his wife, Bilha, and their five children chose the democratic route and held a family vote: they elected to leave the kibbutz (where all resources were evenly split among members) and move to a moshav (which allowed for more individual decision-making).

Yakovi, who resembled a young Gershuni, also inherited his father's deep connection to farming and agriculture. He became a well-known agronomist, specializing in field crops. He planted and plowed wheat, barley, chickpeas, corn, peas, and potatoes across the fields along the Israel-Gaza border. Bilha, born in the neighboring Kibbutz Ruhama, was a pixieish woman with a high forehead, light hair, and deep blue eyes. She initially worked as a school art teacher, then branched out to create her own mandalas and art made from recycled materials and conducted art workshops for women, often voicing her disdain for the rising influence in Israel of what she called "consumer culture."

They settled in family farm number 11, in the same block as the Wax family at number 7; the Taasa family resided at number 6.

They bought a 160-square-meter (1,700 square feet), ecologically friendly model kit home made of wood, the only wooden home in the moshav, whose buildings were otherwise built of concrete and plaster. They transformed the entrance into a showcase of Bilha's recycled art, surrounding it with old mill wheels overgrown with plants, a disused sewing machine adorned with a lion statuette, ceramic roosters, and metal fish arranged at the sides. Inside the house, the dark wooden kitchen cabinets were decorated with Bilha's mandalas and the living room was overlaid with colorful Afghan carpets. Suzy Wax enrolled as a student in Bilha's art classes, while Hadar Taasa, the son of Shoshana and Abraham, built horse stables. The Inon family grew tangerines, avocados, guavas, and sabras in their orchard.

In late July 1997, during the first week of watermelon season, Yakovi was working in the Judean mountains with Palestinian workers from the West Bank and Gaza. Two Hamas terrorists, disguised as ultra-Orthodox Jews, carried out a bombing at the Mahane Yehuda market in Jerusalem, causing 16 deaths and 178 injuries. Following the attack, all Palestinian workers left the area, leaving behind the Jewish farmers and thousands of watermelons in the open field. A month later, suicide bombers from Hamas struck the Ben Yehuda pedestrian mall in Jerusalem, killing five

Israelis. The Palestinian workers did not return for the rest of the summer. Frustrated by the accelerating conflict and the loss of life, Yakovi focused on what he could control: ensuring the success of the watermelon harvest. He received a grant for the development of mechanized equipment, and within two years he'd developed a machine capable of efficiently extracting seeds from watermelons, a device that has since harvested eight thousand tons of seeds every year, regardless of the status of the conflict.

At the time they made the move to the moshav, the family also reconsidered their surname. In Bessarabia, Zvi Gershuni was originally Zvi Pinkonzon. Upon immigrating to Israel, he, like many immigrants at the time, adopted a Hebrew name, as part of the same Israelization process that turned David Green into David Ben-Gurion and Golda Meirson into Golda Meir. Wishing to reconnect with their original heritage, Gershuni's children changed their surname yet again, five decades after its initial change, this time choosing Inon, a Hebrew name contained within Pinkonzon.

7

On Monday, June 19, 2023, the Finance Committee of the twenty-fifth Knesset convened for one of its rare discussions about the Gaza border that year. A mother of four boys from Moshav Netiv HaAsara, a community that now numbered about one thousand residents, requested to provide her testimony.

Sabine Taasa: "Hello. My name is Sabine Taasa. I've lived in Netiv HaAsara for twenty-three years and I am a beautician."

Chairman Moshe Gafni: "Netiv HaAsara?"

Sabine Taasa: "Netiv HaAsara, a moshav directly adjoining the fence of Gaza. My home is less than half a kilometer from the city of Beit Lahia in Gaza."

Chairman Moshe Gafni: "I was under the assumption only farmers resided there. Now I learn there are also beauticians."

Sabine Taasa: "I'm here to present to you a clearer picture of the situation. I came here today to speak to you of my pain."

Chairman Moshe Gafni: "Keep it short."

Sabine Taasa: "Your Honor, I am a simple, hardworking person. I've been self-employed for over fifteen years. I've been through every military operation and every war with Gaza. I'm also an EU citizen—I can start my life over anywhere else in the world, but I choose to live here. Unfortunately, I've reached a point where the state of Israel is pushing me to my limits. My community hasn't even recovered from the COVID pandemic, and now we need to recover from these recent military operations. A Korent rocket landed near my home. I left Netiv HaAsara at 4 A.M. and spent six days on the move with my four children. The horrors and fear stay with you even when the shooting is over. All the children of Netiv HaAsara are suffering, even the livestock are suffering. Every child growing up in Netiv HaAsara experiences bed-wetting, stuttering, anxiety, and requires medication in one form or another. I'm personally taking Cipralex and seeing a psychologist, I'm not ashamed to say it. We invest heavily in therapy for our kids' mental health. My business is collapsing. I'm exhausted. We know there'll be more wars, whether with Hamas or Islamic Jihad. All the time there are sirens due to rockets being fired at us, and we can't deal with it anymore without help."

Chairman Moshe Gafni: "Okay. I will arrange a discussion about Netiv HaAsara."

Sabine Taasa: "Let me finish, please."

Chairman Moshe Gafni: "Go ahead."

Sabine Taasa: "Please help me and my children stay here—"

Chairman Moshe Gafni: "Okay—"

Sabine Taasa: "My mother came from France. She experienced serious antisemitism in Paris. She gave up everything in her life in order to fulfill the Zionist dream. Let me continue this dream. Don't let it collapse. Help me and all the residents of Netiv HaAsara and the Gaza border."

Chairman Moshe Gafni: "Thank you. We'll have this discussion. You haven't spoken in vain. I don't think there's anyone in this country who disagrees with you—you should be helped—and the state of Israel is committed to helping you. We'll have a discussion about it."

Despite her pleas for help, Sabine Taasa was probably one of the most sympathetic—politically sympathetic—Israelis that Chairman Gafni could have invited to his committee in the summer of 2023. Prime Minister Benjamin Netanyahu's far-right government, of which Gafni was part, was then in the midst of passing the so-called Judicial Reform package designed to weaken Israel's judiciary, giving the Knesset the power to override Supreme Court decisions. Hundreds of thousands of Israelis across the country had been protesting, in a nationwide and even international movement that regarded itself as fighting for the future of democracy in the country. Just two days before Sabine's testimony, demonstrations had occurred in dozens of cities, marking the twenty-fourth week of protests.

Sabine wasn't one of these protestors; she supported "judicial reform," as she supported most of the actions and proposals of Netanyahu's government. She'd voted for Netanyahu in every election he'd participated in over the past two decades, believing that his leadership and only his leadership could bring safety to her family. It was precisely this safety that she was also seeking when she testified in front of MK Gafni, whose promised discussion of her concerns never materialized. Sabine spent Friday, October 6, reading Netanyahu's recently published autobiography, *Bibi: My Story*.

At 6:29 A.M. on October 7, Sabine was asleep when three Hamas terrorists parachuted into Netiv HaAsara. Her fifteen-year-old son, Zohar, was also asleep in his room. Her husband, Gil Taasa, from whom she was separated but not divorced, was sleeping in a small housing unit on the other side of the road with their twelve-year-old son, Koren, and their youngest, eight-year-old Shai.

The bespectacled, wavy-haired Sabine always maintained something of the refined, attractive air of a Frenchwoman. She was born in Paris—raised in the affluent suburb of Neuilly-sur-Seine, and immigrated to Israel at the age of fourteen with her parents and siblings following antisemitic harassment. The Israeli authorities relocated the family to a slum in the southern city of Ashkelon. Unfamiliar with Hebrew and the local culture of the impoverished immigrant city, the family struggled to adapt.

Three months later, her father left them and returned to Paris. Sabine stayed with her mother, learning to survive in the violent and impoverished city. This was where she developed her politics, having come to believe that the Israeli left was too naive about the chances for achieving peace with those who kept firing missiles at her home.

The city girl was in her early twenties when she met her future husband, the nearly six-foot-tall dark-skinned Gil Taasa. A mutual friend from Netiv HaAsara made the introduction. They married in 2004 and built their home in Netiv HaAsara next to his parents and three siblings.

In 2005, a year after their wedding, Israel withdrew from Gaza, giving the land over to Palestinian control and evacuating all twenty-two Jewish towns in the territory. Following the Disengagement—as the withdrawal is known in Hebrew—Netiv HaAsara became the closest Israeli moshav to the Gaza border, with some of its houses located only one hundred meters away.

Then–prime minister Ariel Sharon addressed the nation on the occasion of the Disengagement, saying, "I am deeply convinced, with all my heart and understanding, that this disengagement will reinforce Israel's hold on vital territories essential for our existence. It will garner blessings and respect from near and far, diminish hostility, break the boycott and blockade, and propel us toward peace with the Palestinians and our neighboring countries." Once again, as with the Sinai deal, "land for peace" was the presumption.

US president George W. Bush, in the midst of promoting his "road map for peace" plan to resolve the Israeli-Palestinian conflict, praised Sharon for the withdrawal decision: "These are historic and courageous actions. If all parties choose to embrace this moment they can open the door to progress and put an end to one of the world's longest-running conflicts."

President Bush's plan required the Palestinians to combat terrorism, recognize Israel as a Jewish state, and implement reforms toward establishing democracy. Israel's obligations included halting the construction of settlements and dismantling illegal outposts in the West Bank, withdrawing from occupied territories, and avoiding attacks on Palestinian civilians. None of that ever happened.

In July 2005, twenty-two-year-old student Dana Galkovich was sitting on the balcony of her home in Netiv HaAsara with a friend when a Qassam rocket struck, killing her. She was the first Hamas victim in Netiv HaAsara.

In response to the escalating intensity and frequency of shootings and missile attacks, Israel constructed an 8.5-meter-high security wall around the moshav for resident protection. The gray wall was decorated with colored stones and painted with blessings and prayers contributed by thousands of people. This collaborative artwork, named *Path to Peace*, features its title in large letters in Hebrew, Arabic, and English. The resulting creation can be seen from both sides of the wall.

In May 2008, a Palestinian suicide bomber detonated a truck booby-trapped with approximately four tons of explosives near the Israeli border. The explosion damaged about a hundred houses in Netiv HaAsara, with the blast's force throwing people out of bed and dislodging water tanks from roofs. Gil Taasa, the moshav's security coordinator at the time, described the scene to reporters: "When the explosion occurred, I initially thought a mortar had hit the house. I immediately grabbed my two-year-old son Or and ran to the safe room."

In 2010, the same year their third son, Koren, was born, a Thai guest worker in the moshav was killed by a rocket from Gaza. In May 2019, Or's bar mitzvah was interrupted by a Hamas missile attack. That week saw 690 rockets launched toward Israel, leading to the deaths of four Israeli civilians and four soldiers, along with approximately twenty-five Palestinians in the subsequent IDF response. The Taasa family celebrated Or's bar mitzvah with a cake in the shelter, and a ceasefire was declared the following morning.

Following her separation from Gil, Sabine had found herself grateful that Or, their eldest, now seventeen years old and in his final year of high school, stepped up to help support her. Or ensured that his mother didn't work too late; he routinely checked to make sure she was supplied with adequate nuts to snack on in the car, so she didn't fall asleep while driving; he made sure she didn't drink alcohol before she got into the car, and he even helped out with landscaping and house cleaning. Or also started working in a factory near their home, contributing money to the household. Sabine appreciated the effort but was slightly worried that he was maturing too quickly. She sometimes teased him, calling him an "old woman," saying that she could imagine him knitting in a nursing home.

That Saturday, October 7, morning, Or left the house around 6:10 A.M. to go surfing with his high school friends at Zikim beach, in the waters that brought his grandmother to build the adjacent moshav. A short time after he left the house, the familiar sound of sirens, alerting to a rocket attack, woke his mother, Sabine, and fifteen-year-old brother, Zohar. They closed the heavy iron front door, which Gil had insisted on installing and Sabine had often criticized for its lack of aesthetic, and ran as fast as they could into the safe room, and called Or.

"Or, where are you? There are missiles, are you okay?"

"Maman, Hamas is firing like crazy at the beach. Don't worry, I'm in a shelter and won't move."

"Swear to me that you won't go out."

"Maman, I promise you, you know me, I'm careful."

She messaged Gil: "Go to Zikim beach, bring back our son."

Gil and sons Koren and Shai, now twelve and eight, just awakened and wearing their underwear, evacuated the small cottage he'd been living in and headed for the portable shelter.

Gil's cottage didn't have a proper safe room; installing one had been too expensive. He'd managed to purchase one of the cheap temporary structures made of aluminum and whitewashed concrete and had it delivered and set up just across from his cottage's front door. It wasn't too far to run—and he trusted himself to run fast enough when needed. When a siren goes off, residents of Netiv HaAsara have approximately fifteen seconds to take shelter—not enough time for Gil to bring the boys to the safe room in their mother's house.

It was from their portable shelter that the three Taasas heard Arabic being spoken, and gunfire. Gil instructed Koren and Shai, "Be quiet, don't say a word. I'm going to get a gun. I'll be right back." He dashed off, retrieved his personal firearm, and was returning to his boys when he encountered three terrorists. Gil fired his gun three times and ran back into the shelter.

Sabine heard the gunshots from her safe room in the main house. "It's Dad. I'm sure it's Dad fighting and saving us," she assured Zohar. A few minutes later, she heard a loud knock at her front door. Then another one.

Two people with green bandanas on their foreheads stood in front of Sabine. One had a weapon directed toward her, and the other held a grenade, declaring, "*Allah-hu Akbar*, death to all Jews." Sabine slammed the door in the two men's faces—the iron door she'd always hated deflected their bullets.

Just after Gil Taasa had made it back to the portable shelter with his boys, a grenade was hurled at them. Gil Taasa yelled, "Stay away" and threw himself onto the grenade, dying instantly to save his children. The boys were covered in his blood and theirs, and shrapnel was embedded in Koren's leg and Shai's eye.

The terrorists entered the shelter and shot Gil Taasa's corpse a few more times before leading the boys inside to their cottage's kitchen. As the boys cried out for their mother, one of the attackers casually drank a Coca-Cola from their fridge. Shai was quiet; he didn't cry. Koren attempted to use Google Translate to negotiate with the terrorists in Arabic, pleading with them to release him and his younger brother to their mother.

"Translate," Koren told the terrorist in English.

"Speak Arabic, speak Arabic."

"Translate."

"Speak Arabic."

"But I don't know! Can we go home, please? Please?"

"Wipe the blood off. No, no."

"Please, can we go home?"

"Do it like this, do it like this."

"What about my dad? What about my dad?"

Koren's translation efforts were met with a slap and the confiscation of his phone, which the attackers then used to upload a video of Gil's body to Facebook. Eventually, the terrorists handed the boys a blanket and left to target civilians in another house, unwittingly providing them with a brief moment to escape.

They ran to Sabine's door and knocked.

"Don't you dare open up," Zohar begged her.

"I have to. Maybe it's your brothers and your dad," she said, leaving him in the safe room and opening the front door.

Her two young children were standing in front of her, wearing only their underwear, covered in blood. Before she could hug them, Koren blurted out, "Dad was shot. He's dead."

Sabine carried the injured Koren and Shai to the safe room. She recorded a video of her children, lying in bed, as she desperately pleaded for medical attention: "Please, it's urgent. My children are injured and need help immediately. My sons have been shot, they're traumatized. Our house is covered in blood."

Sabine didn't know that about fifteen minutes earlier, her oldest son had been murdered while hiding in the toilets at Zikim beach. Terrorists shot Or and his two high school friends in the head at point-blank range. She would learn about her son's murder the following day when Hamas posted a video of Or's killing.

She was at a local hospital with Koren and Shai when she received the video. The boys were hospitalized for ten days, during which time Shai underwent three surgeries on his right eye. He ultimately lost his sight. Koren recovered quickly. It took seven days to identify Or's body. They buried him alongside his father, Gil.

After their funeral, Sabine wrote a message on Facebook to the chairman of the committee that had, just four months earlier, promised to look into the safety of her community: "Dear Mr. Gafni, I lost my dearest, my son Or and my husband Gil. I would be grateful for your response regarding the special discussion promised to us, the residents of Netiv HaAsara."

8

Since October 7, about two hundred thousand Israelis have been evacuated from their homes to hotels and private apartments, including those whose homes were destroyed or located in areas of heavy shelling. The Taasas were one such family.

Fifteen-year-old Zohar, now the eldest Taasa son, was in his new temporary apartment in Netanya when he discovered that the family's old next-door neighbor, Yigal Wax, whom he had always regarded as something of an uncle, had also been murdered that terrible morning.

Yigal, a fifty-three-year-old graphic artist, amateur carpenter, and painter, had returned to the moshav just two years prior, following his divorce.

His close friends Sabine and Gil Taasa had allowed him to live rent-free in the cottage they had built for rental purposes—the same one that Gil used later, after his separation from Sabine. A few months after his arrival, Yigal moved to his father, Alfredo's, cottage. His mother, Suzy, had died from cancer a few years before, yet three of the four Wax brothers were still living in the moshav near the eighty-three-year-old Alfredo.

On the morning of October 7, Yigal Wax didn't hear the Hamas terrorists attempting to break into his father's house. The first indication of danger came when Yigal heard the grenade the terrorists threw into the Taasa cottage explode.

Aware that his brother, Yigal, was unarmed but impulsive, forty-eight-year-old Amit Wax urged him to stay at home. Nevertheless, Yigal was concerned for Gil and his children, so he armed himself with only a machete. As he opened his door, intending to retrieve a proper weapon from Ziv, the moshav's current security coordinator, he was shot in the back. Despite his wound, he managed to run another 150 meters to Ziv's home. "Open, open please," he begged.

Ziv hesitated. "Who is this?"

"It's Yigal, please."

Ziv let him in, and Yigal briefly explained what had happened, muttering, "There are so many of them" before dying in Ziv's arms.

As an armed member of the Yishuv's emergency squad, Amit Wax had been one of the first to confront the terrorists. They struck him near the playground. Before rushing out, Amit had briefly called his father, Alfredo, urging him to take shelter. He knew his father as well as he knew his brother—stubborn Alfredo never hid during missile attacks. He was right. At the time of the call, Alfredo was standing in front of the window, stirring his black Turkish coffee, unaffected by the sound of falling missiles. The dog was still sleeping on the couch.

While terrorists killed his two sons, an unknowing Alfredo had already left the shelter despite Amit's warnings and was watching an action movie at high volume on the television in his living room.

9

Down the road from the Wax and Taasa families, seventy-five-year-old Yakovi and seventy-one-year-old Bilha Inon still resided in farm number 11.

The decision to exchange kibbutz life for the moshav had worked out for them. Over the past thirty-two years, they'd prospered. Bilha had cut her long hair, which had turned white over the years, while Yakovi still had a full head of hair, only partly grayed. She was still a dedicated painter, while he worked in the orchard daily. Their house had become an eclectically decorated museum of their many and varied interests: crafts, woodworking, mosaic. Exemplary leftists, they joined protests against the Netanyahu government's Judicial Reform at the Sha'ar HaNegev Regional Council almost every Saturday. As the moshav's community committee chairman, Yakovi was leading a new initiative to establish a hospital for both Palestinian residents of Gaza and Israelis near the moshav.

Despite their children's pleas to move them to central Israel due to escalating wars and terror attacks at the moshav, they refused. They believed they were safe. They believed peace would someday come.

Their only concession was to add a safe room to their wooden house, where Bilha created large mandalas and inscribed what she called "words that give strength and encouragement" on the wall. "I transformed it from a place of missiles and war into a haven of art," she explained.

Every Friday afternoon since 1992, Yakovi has attended informal "parliament" meetings at a restaurant in Ashkelon. The group—more informal men's club than political entity—consists of about ten members from various kibbutzim and moshavim along the Israel-Gaza border. On Friday, October 6, Yigal Flash from Kfar Azza rejoined the "parliament" after a lengthy absence. He had been busy with renovations at his home in the kibbutz and proudly shared new pictures of the completed work.

After the "parliament" meeting, Yakovi and Bilha traveled to Tel Aviv for a holiday dinner with their five children and eleven grandchildren, all of whom had left the moshav. Maoz Inon, once an equestrian, had become an entrepreneur promoting social change and Jewish-Arab coexistence. He'd opened the Fauzi Azar Inn in Nazareth, reconstructing an old Ottoman-era mansion in partnership with a Palestinian family—a rare Jewish-Arab business. The Abraham Hostel group, his flagship project, is a hospitality company aimed at strengthening tolerance and building bridges through sustainable tourism and employing and hosting many asylum seekers from Eritrea and Sudan. More recently, he'd launched Abraham Tours, offering excursions to popular sites that feature both Palestinian and Israeli historical narratives.

Proud of their son, Yakovi and Bilha sometimes stayed at his hostels during military operations and wars, the rare occasions when they agreed to leave the moshav for a few days. The dinner in Tel Aviv ended late, and although their children suggested they stay overnight, they preferred, as usual, to return to their own bed in the Negev.

Around 7:30 the next morning, an RPG struck Yakovi and

Bilha's home. The moshav's lone wooden house was soon engulfed in fire, a conflagration that reached a height of twenty
meters. The eco-house was the only house in Netiv HaAsara
completely destroyed in the attack. Yakovi and Bilha Inon were
unable to escape the flames.

Years earlier, they'd expressed the wish not to be buried according to Jewish tradition but to be cremated, believing that the
land should be used for crops rather than for graves.

Upon finding two charred skeletons lying near each other
in the ruins of their parents' home, their children began sitting
shiva the following morning, without waiting for official confir-
mation.

During the shiva, Maoz Inon learned that many members of
his father's "parliament" had also suffered losses: Yigal Flash and
his wife, Cindy, were killed in their newly renovated home; Yonatan, Dodo Elazari's grandson from Kibbutz Beit Nir, was murdered in Ofakim during a break from his military training; Eshel
Gat from Kibbutz Be'eri survived an attack, having been in the
bathroom at the time, but his family, who'd gathered in Be'eri for
the holiday, were not as fortunate. His wife Kinneret, daughter
Carmel, son Alon, daughter-in-law Yardenne, and granddaughter Gefen were kidnapped during the attack. Kinneret was murdered, Alon and Gefen managed to escape, and Yardenne and
Carmel were taken hostage and abducted to Gaza.

Twelve days after the murder of his parents, Maoz Inon was at
his home in Binyamina when an IDF casualty officer arrived to
officially inform him of his father's death, confirmed through the
identification of burned remains. At that time, Bilha's remains
were still unaccounted for.

"Okay, okay," Maoz acknowledged the officer's message, but
had a response of his own: "I am giving the prime minister

twenty-four hours to resign, due to the government's failure to achieve peace or security." The officer listened in silence, then departed.

A month later, Maoz Inon started demonstrating in front of the Knesset. His protest turned into a protest camp, comprising bereaved families and families of hostages, calling for an end to the war and the resignation of Netanyahu. He believes his parents would have wanted him to forgive, not to seek revenge.

"I don't seek revenge; there's no benefit in it. I mourn every drop of blood spilled, every expansion of the circle of hatred. It's time for Israelis and Palestinians to understand each other's narratives and pain, to unite in opposition to their politicians, and advocate for peace."

10

On October 8, Isaac Herzog, the president of Israel and a veteran member of the Labor Party, addressed the nation:

"My Israeli sisters and brothers, I speak to you today in the midst of a fierce war.... We have all witnessed the inhuman cruelty of our enemies—attacking the elderly, women, children, whole families; people from all backgrounds and faiths in kibbutzim, moshavim, cities, and towns. These monstrous human animals show no distinction in their choice of victims, targeting innocent young people at a party whose only 'sin' was to be Israeli and seek happiness and joy."

Later in his address, Herzog quoted Moshe Dayan's 1956 eulogy for Roi Rotberg: "This is our life's choice—to be prepared and armed, strong and determined, lest the sword be stricken from our fist and our lives cut down."

However, Herzog—like the Israeli radio before him—saw fit

to omit some of Dayan's original, most controversial lines: "Let us not cast the blame on the murderers today. Why should we declare their burning hatred for us? For eight years they have been sitting in the refugee camps in Gaza, and before their eyes we have been transforming the lands and the villages, where they and their fathers dwelt, into our estate."

The empathy that came naturally to Dayan in 1956 was impossible for Herzog, or for almost any Israeli, to express in 2023, the day after the greatest massacre in the country's history.

In the seven decades of war that separate Dayan's and Herzog's statements, the complex legacy of Israel's founding split into two conflicting and eventually contradictory narratives, with broad swaths of each side of the Israeli-Palestinian divide refusing to recognize the other: in their claims, in their grief, and in their inalienable humanity.

Warring

A HISTORY, 1948–2024

The battles of 1948 never ended: in a sense, Israel is still fighting them in 2024, against Palestinians, against insurgent militias based in neighboring states, and even internally, with the result that existential conflict has become a constant Israeli condition.

The Six-Day War in 1967, the Yom Kippur War in 1973, the various skirmishes with Lebanon in the 1980s and after—all were extensions of Israel's foundational violence, which my generation took as its birthright, and regarded as a reality that could not be changed.

Hopes that were frustrated by the assassination of Yitzhak Rabin were disappointed again during the government of Ehud Barak, who offered the Palestinians most of Gaza and the West Bank in return for peace and was refused. Further disappointments followed—in 2005, when Prime Minister Ariel Sharon unilaterally withdrew from Gaza, evacuating all Israeli civilians from the land without any preconditions, only for the Palestinians to elect a globally recognized terror group, Hamas, to lead and administer its territory; and in 2008, when Prime Minister Ehud Olmert offered a full Israeli withdrawal to its borders before the

1967 war, along with an exchange of territories and the division of Jerusalem, and was again rejected.

The Palestinian side contended that none of these offers fully addressed their demands, chief among which was the right of return for Palestinian refugees to a future Palestinian state with Jerusalem as its capital. With each passing year, the Israeli-occupied territory of that putative state became increasingly fragmented through the government-sanctioned construction of Israeli settlements—Jewish impediments to the liberal goal of "two states for two peoples."

Following the failure of five Israeli prime ministers and two Palestinian presidents to broker a deal amid an atmosphere of escalating violence, many simply gave up on the ideal of coexistence and clung instead to the belief that no peace was possible.

Under Benjamin Netanyahu's leadership—a reign that has lasted more than sixteen years, longer than that of David Ben-Gurion—the peace camp dispersed to the margins; its members going underground, or online, or abroad. The voices calling for an "end to the conflict" were replaced by those calling for "managing the conflict"—"peace" had become "security."

Every few years, or few months, when a major attack on Israeli civilians occurred, the army would go out and "mow the lawn," which became the standard phrase for military reprisal despite the fact that few Israelis have a lawn, let alone mow it. The consensus in the government and in the press seemed to be that technology such as the Iron Dome defense system would protect Israel, as would the large sums of money—cash, passed in suitcases—that were being paid to Hamas, essentially bribes to ensure their acquiescence.

Year after year, those who believed in resolving the conflict on a national level were pushed to the political sidelines; they were exiled from the cabinet, and barely passed, then failed to pass, the minimum threshold for election to the Knesset. The very word *peace* gradually disappeared from election campaigns and the media: it became a word, almost a shibboleth, of the few, the new extremists, who refused to let go of the past.

Year after year we Israelis talked less and less about Palestinians, let alone Palestinian statehood, and more and more about ourselves. We became immersed in internal struggles, disputes between secular and religious, between Ashkenazim and Mizrahim, and above all, between left and right. In truth, we came to believe that despite the occasional terror attack and the increasingly frequent rocket attacks—despite the high cost of living and the frequent military "operations" (never "wars")—Israel had come into its own; it had become a world-class capital of the tech sector, a Western progressive country, dedicated to democracy and liberalism, and to the propagation of equality, civil liberties, and human rights. If you were a gay Jew—if you were a gay Arab—you wanted to live in Tel Aviv; Haifa became one of the most prominent and successful mixed cities, with a high proportion of Israeli Arab college graduates. Jerusalem was still Jerusalem, but tourism was up; the hotels, restaurants, and bars were full, as were the synagogues, mosques, and churches.

The appalling reality of the lives of the Palestinians in the occupied West Bank—from the everyday humiliations of long waits at border checkpoints and walls bisecting their neighborhoods to abusive arrests, killings, and the forced displacement of villages—were absent from the public discussion, much like the Palestinians in Gaza.

My newspaper, *Haaretz*, was the only newspaper to report

on Palestinians' issues with any regularity and sensitivity, and my involvement with the paper brought me a certain infamy: to work for *Haaretz* was to be regularly yelled at, spit at, and accused of betrayal—of treason. My colleagues and I found ourselves threatened online and in person, our work and motives impugned, our characters smeared. Following an exposé I wrote with a journalist named Gidi Weitz that aired allegations of criminality against David Bitan, the former chairman of the Likud coalition, Bitan was captured on police surveillance planning his revenge: "*Haaretz* is a hit squad . . . and they need to be crushed," he said. "They'll never leave us alone." His close associates in the Netanyahu government were also recorded bragging that they had ordered people to follow me and report on my meetings and communications.

Scary as that was, it was little when compared to what's been suffered by journalists reporting directly on the Occupation. Colleagues such as Gideon Levy, Amira Hass, and Hagar Shezaf, who publish reportage about the violence wrought by Israeli settlers in the Occupied West Bank, receive death threats on a regular basis. The bulk of Israelis are content to ignore the plight of the other side, and in that ignorance of Palestinian life lies Palestinian dehumanization.

This marginalization of the left in the media further licensed the marginalization of the left in society at large, and a denigration of its values. Media bias and civic bias interact in extremely direct ways, especially in small countries like Israel, with small media markets: few papers and few channels. Year after year, as the right came to dominate print, the airwaves, and finally social media, the window shifted: the right became the center, the center became the left, and the left became illegitimate. This was a new era in which idealism became aid and comfort to the enemy; the goal of coexistence became the grind of "containment" and "conflict suppression."

The peak of this process came with the Abraham Accords, a series of agreements between Israel and assorted Arab (or Muslim) countries, including the United Arab Emirates, Bahrain, Morocco, and Sudan. A common fear of Shia Iran led these Sunni Gulf countries to establish new ties with the Jewish state, to the profound dismay of Palestinians. Under American pressure, these countries opened themselves to Israel, without making any demands to support their co-religionists in the West Bank and Gaza.

In the wake of this success, Netanyahu sought an even greater prize—a normalization agreement with Saudi Arabia, the richest and most influential Sunni Arab nation. Approaches that had begun under the Trump administration, and had continued with Biden's prodding, seemed promising, and toward the end of September 2023, Netanyahu addressed the UN General Assembly, saying that he believed that "we are at the cusp of an even more dramatic breakthrough—an historic peace between Israel and Saudi Arabia. Such a peace will go a long way to ending the Arab-Israeli conflict." He was gesturing at a long-gestating plan not to negotiate a peace settlement, but to impose one. In his words, "I believe that we must not give the Palestinians a veto over new peace treaties with Arab states."

It was expected that a Saudi normalization agreement would emerge sometime around October, just after the Jewish New Year—the inauguration of a new Middle East.

In spite of this new era, all had not gone smoothly for the Netanyahu government. In fact, Saturday, October 7, was the first

Saturday without antigovernment protests in Israel since the early days of 2023.

For thirty-nine consecutive Saturdays, tens of thousands and often hundreds of thousands of Israelis went out into the streets after the end of Shabbat to demonstrate against the so-called Judicial Reform promoted by the Netanyahu government. This "reform" was actually a comprehensive overhaul, a legislative program that would allow the government to weaken and control the judicial system by preventing it from overruling certain decisions made by the Knesset.

Netanyahu, who was and still is facing several criminal trials for corruption, had his own interests in supporting the legislation, as did his coalition partners—Jewish extremists steeped in anti-Arab rhetoric who promote the Jewish settlement of the West Bank in contravention of international law.

These protests were attended by Israelis from every walk of life: young and old, right-wing and left-wing, religious and secular, many of them military personnel who declared their unwillingness to report for duty if the government didn't commit to preserving its democratic nature and system of checks and balances. Pilots threatened to skip training, reservists threatened to skip service; business leaders and entrepreneurs issued warnings of dire economic consequences should the legislation go through; while ordinary citizens marched, chanted, and waved Israeli flags; some blocked major intersections and lit bonfires.

Netanyahu's most die-hard supporters did their best to brand these protestors as traitors—people compelled not by civic duty but by their hatred of Netanyahu himself, along with an elitist desire to perpetuate the hegemony of bureaucratic rule, a court system that, in their interpretation, routinely tied the country's hands by protecting the rights of minorities, including Israeli Arabs.

The rift between the protestors and the so-called Bibi-ists was so deep, so hateful, that comedians and later more-or-less serious news personalities began speaking of a civil war—either that or a "three-state solution."

This Judicial Reform was led by the most right-wing government in Israel's history, a reverse mirror image of Rabin's last government. Its figures, who never before held such high office, were simply the people Netanyahu required in order to retain his hold on power, and they were frequently exposed as painfully underqualified for their positions—professionally, morally, ethically. One of the coalition's key members, the minister of national security, responsible for administering the police, was Itamar Ben-Gvir, head of the far-right party Otzma Yehudit (Jewish Power), who was convicted of a score of criminal charges and is a proud admirer of Baruch Goldstein, the terrorist who massacred twenty-nine Arabs in Hebron in 1994 and whose portrait used to hang in Ben-Gvir's house. Another prominent coalition member, Finance Minister Bezalel Smotrich, was one of the leaders of the movement opposed to Israel's 2005 disengagement from Gaza and was arrested for the civil actions—essentially antidisengagement riots—he helped organize.

After 10/7, the very Israelis who protested for democracy and declared their unwillingness to serve if the Judicial Reform went through showed up to fight in Gaza. They understood that the fate of the country was at stake and that it was up to them to prevent the further indiscriminate murder of Israeli citizens, and to attempt to return the hundreds of hostages whose chances of survival dwindled by the day. Among these reservists was Gal Eisenkot, a twenty-five-year-old student of computer science and bioinformatics. He'd worked as a medic treating Syrians wounded in the Syrian civil war and planned to dedicate his life to medical innovation. He had a room in a small apartment in south Tel Aviv and had just restarted a relationship with a love of his young adolescence. He was a dear friend of mine and my brother's since childhood, and he had grown up into a generous, humble, sensitive man, shy but quick to laugh, that rare type of perfectionist who forgave all flaws in others. He was the son of former chief of staff Gadi Eisenkot, who today is a minister in the emergency government and a member of the war cabinet, but Gal was not a military man himself. He did not want war, he did not want to hurt anyone, and he certainly did not want to die. He was drafted into the army reserves alongside hundreds of thousands of his peers who put their lives on hold to protect their country. He was sent out to fight a war he believed was justified: he thought that if Israel didn't respond, it would cease to exist. He was out on a hostage-rescue mission in the heart of Gaza when an explosive device in a tunnel shaft went off—a booby trap—and everything ended: he would be twenty-five forever. This book is dedicated to his memory.

Rave

"How long does it take for a corpse to rot?"

"I'm not sure I heard you correctly—can you repeat that?"

"How much time, how many hours, does it take for a dead body to rot?"

It was around seven-thirty in the evening on October 7 when Haim Utmazgin's phone rang. The Orthodox father of six was hosting twenty guests—his in-laws included—at his home in Petah Tikva for the holiday. The person on the other end of the line was a young rabbi whom Haim Utmazgin barely knew; they'd met only once or twice.

"And why are you asking me this?"

"I'm currently guarding about one hundred and twenty-five bodies . . . maybe more . . . I can't exactly count right now . . . They were murdered a few hours ago at the music festival . . . and I was put in charge of their bodies and I'm not sure what to do. Maybe you have some advice?"

"You're at the music festival near Kibbutz Re'im? On the news, they say the casualties there might only be thirty or fifty. Are you sure about the numbers?"

"I haven't seen the news. I'm here, in person, and let me tell you: it's a massacre."

"Can you switch over to video?" He needed to see for himself.

It was dark, but the video was clear: he saw bodies of young ravers stacked up near a bar; bodies piled by a DJ booth and wedged between the speakers; bodies strewn awkwardly around a yoga complex as if in some grotesque group pose; bodies of half-naked and naked women near the camping area; bodies heaped near a giant Buddha statue like sacrilegious sacrificial offerings. Some bodies had been burned so badly that they'd melted into one another.

"Do you have a team with you?"

"I'm alone. Hamas terrorists are still in the area, shooting. Everyone's busy fighting, so they put the rabbi in charge of the bodies. I need help."

"I'm on my way."

Haim Utmazgin is the founder and head of the special units of ZAKA, the National Identification and Burial Organization, which is a non-governmental aid organization responsible for collecting human remains to ensure their proper burial. The organization was founded in response to the spate of Palestinian suicide bombings of Israeli buses during the First Intifada, which often left grisly scenes of maimed bodies and severed limbs.

Haim Utmazgin's "special units," staffed like much of ZAKA mostly by Orthodox Jewish men, were experts in body identification and collection. Whenever his regular volunteers encountered a difficult case, such as retrieving bodies from the sea or mountains, the woods or desert, Haim would create a new special unit: a diving unit, a canine unit, and so on. For this task, he called in all units, coordinating the emergency response effort en route.

Despite the fact that the border was still an active terror scene, the ZAKA ambulances were required as soon as possible—a measure taken primarily to prevent the corpses from being taken hostage to Gaza.

Seeking to better understand the exact scale of the event, Haim called the young rabbi again:

"How many ambulances do you think we'll need?"

"How many? I can't even walk here without stepping on bodies. That's how many ambulances we need."

Haim continued making calls, trying to enlist refrigerated trucks, which had more capacity than standard ambulances. One volunteer offered his bread distribution truck, capacity: at least fifty bodies.

On Road 232, near the city of Netivot, fourteen kilometers from the Gaza border, two ultra-Orthodox men flagged down the ambulance, pleading for help. Haim slowly opened his window, asking what was so urgent for them to stop an ambulance.

"Help us, please; we have two bodies in the trunk."

"You have what?"

"We were at the party and just started helping to pick up all of the bodies lying on the road."

Haim asked them to open the trunk. Two young girls, each shot in the head, lay one atop the other.

Haim contacted the police, who told him to meet them at what they believed to be safe GPS coordinates in the nearby orchards, which became the general meeting point for later volunteers who arrived. From that bivouac, the police escorted Haim to the party area, as the main roads were still too dangerous to traverse. Driving through furrowed fields and rows of citrus trees, they came across a police car that had been hit by a missile. The vehicle was burned, and inside, a charred body was fused to the seat. Haim provided the policemen with bags and gave them instructions on how to handle and transport the remains.

It was around nine o'clock when Haim finally arrived at the site of the Nova music festival. Above, the stars shone in the darkness without competition from the dance floor's lasers or lights. The police escorting Haim explained to him that because any light source could attract Hamas fire, the work had to be done in complete darkness: "You have until sunrise to evacuate all bodies before we expect the shooting to resume."

About forty volunteers filtered into the festival area, answering Haim's call. They arranged all the bodies under one large tent, making a macabre dance floor of corpses. The missiles continued to fall near them all night; at times, they had to lie down among the bodies as a shelter. They needed to work quickly. The volunteers were divided into teams, each assigned two columns consisting of ten to fifteen bodies, treating one after the other: photographing it, cleaning it, wrapping it. Haim gave the teams only six minutes to spend with each body. After previous terrorist attacks, they'd typically had at least an hour.

After appointing the teams, Haim himself now searched the camping area—a resting spot between one trance set and another—a ramshackle clearing of dozens of pitched tents and smoldering bonfires topped with grills and *finjans* for making Turkish coffee.

Near one of these tents, he found a young half-naked woman in her twenties, her purple skirt pulled up to her stomach. Her underwear had been removed. She had been shot at least once in her vagina and again in the center of her head. Haim adjusted the girl's skirt before carefully tending to her body: photographing it, cleaning it, wrapping it, putting it into a bag. Nearby, he found another young woman, also shot, once in the head, once in the ear; her neck had been slit and she was topless. Yet another girl was lying on her back. She had been gutted, and her intestines had been ripped out of her and hung down in thick tubes between her legs. Haim covered her.

Further on, he found a woman half-naked, ripped out of her white dress. Another woman, shot in the head, wearing bold green hiking socks. There were so many, executed in so similar a fashion, that they became distinguishable by their clothing alone: this one wearing a tracksuit, that one wearing white jeans, another in a purple halter top, all of the clothing soaked through with blood.

Three women were tangled together; they'd all been shot in their vaginas, revealing to Haim what came to be a pattern: an almost ritual slaughter in which women, stripped of their party attire, were shot at close range in their breasts and genitals, or had their breasts and genitals sliced and mutilated with knives. In a few instances, their genitals had been specifically burned: the rest of their corpses were intact, but their vaginas had been set ablaze.

As more and more bodies were found, Haim adjusted the protocol: they couldn't spend more than a minute and a half per body.

By 4 A.M., they'd removed 257 bodies—only the ones that were easily identifiable.

Celine

It was the last weekend of Celine Ben-David Nagar's extended six-month maternity leave. The thirty-two-year-old, who'd emigrated to the city of Ashdod from the city of Lyon, France, at the age of sixteen, wanted to do something special to mark the occasion before returning to her stressful routine of managing the Tel Aviv office of Kasuto & Co., a boutique law firm.

Her husband, Ido Nagar, a lawyer at Kasuto & Co., was not keen on the idea from the moment Celine shared the invitation, which had read:

"We're excited to announce a new installment of the 'Nova' festival—two days of trance raving . . . The central conceit [behind the festival] is a set of fundamental human values: free love and spirit and environmental preservation."

It was more than just an opportunity to listen to trance and dance; it was an international gathering of a like-minded community, young people drawn together by a common desire for spiritual transcendence and a brief release from daily reality in a neo-hippie atmosphere free of judgment.

Ido had decidedly more local concerns. "What about the milk you're pumping? Won't it go to waste?"

The couple had been intent on freezing as much breast milk as possible before Celine returned to work and their baby, Ellie, started daycare.

She was their first baby—every drop of milk mattered. "Perhaps we could celebrate some other way?" he suggested. A skilled litigator, Ido nonetheless found his wife harder to persuade than most judges.

"It's not a debate. I—am—going—to—this—party," Celine insisted.

Having thought about it, Ido wasn't even sure why he was so bothered by the prospect of spending a few hours alone with their baby. Why wasn't he being supportive? What made him resist the will of the woman with the black curls and French accent who'd brought so much joy into his life from that moment one morning when they'd worked at the office together and he'd confessed his attraction to her.

There was only one appropriate response. "I'm happy when you're happy."

The first batch of tickets to the festival sold out within just eleven hours. Celine managed to snag tickets for herself and two friends, Shiraz Tamam, the secretary at Kasuto's Tel Aviv office, and her husband, Adir Tamam, the instructor of Ellie's baby swim class.

Celine arose early on Saturday morning to breastfeed Ellie. They departed at 4:40 A.M. to make the hour and fifteen minute journey from their hometown of Holon, just ten kilometers southeast of Tel Aviv, due south to the rave, located near Kibbutz Re'im.

Raz

At the same early morning hour, from the same city of Holon, twenty-three-year-old Raz Perry set off for the same party. "Nova is a healing party," he'd told his sister when explaining why he was going. He was in the midst of treatment for Hodgkin's lymphoma, and his doctors had recommended music as a distraction.

Shani and Orión

Ricarda Louk had her own plans for that weekend.

She'd just learned that not only was her twenty-two-year-old daughter, Shani, back together with her Mexican-French boy-friend but that the boyfriend was visiting Israel.

She decided to use that Friday's holiday dinner as an opportunity to meet Orión for the first time.

"Will you come to dinner today?" she asked Shani. "And bring Orión."

Ricarda wasn't the type of mother to meddle in her daughter's life or pass judgment, and even if she had been, Shani would not have listened. From childhood, Shani Louk was stubbornly independent and opinionated. She switched schools frequently and refused to do her mandatory service in the Israeli army. Skipping university, she taught herself whatever she found interesting—sometimes Buddhism, sometimes music, usually art. Ricarda respected her daughter's independence and had only one firm rule for her: no tattoos. So of course, Shani became a tattoo artist. She herself had only one tattoo, though, a design of her own inked by one of her favorite tattoo artists, which had been given to her as a gift from Orión for her twenty-second birthday. Its abstract shapes stretched across her lower legs, like the shin-guards of ancient warriors or superheroes.

Shani Louk and Orión Hernández Radoux had been together, off and on, for about eight months, helping to throw techno parties across Europe and South America with a group of friends, sleeping in hostels and camping out in tents. She was sensitive, daring, a caregiver but sometimes flighty, with a thick long mane of dark hair. He was funny, driven, a ponytailed adventurer with a penchant for organizing events and people. They'd met at a music festival in Croatia and since then had been in Switzerland, Italy, France, Hungary, Czech Republic, Guatemala, and Mexico—visiting Orión's family in Tulum. She'd also met his ex-girlfriend and his baby girl, Iyana. Orión had a tattoo with his daughter's name, ايانا, in Arabic on his chest.

In the last two weeks of September, Orión organized a three-day trance music festival in Greece—Shani designed the venue and invitations. By the end of the festival, however, they'd broken up, and Shani returned to Israel by herself, saying it was over. She was thinking about moving out of the increasingly expensive, hipster-ish Florentin neighborhood of Tel Aviv and finding some quiet village, where she'd start a business specializing in party design.

In the wake of Shani's absence, Orión realized he missed her. "She makes me happy," he confessed to his friends in early October, before boarding a plane to Israel to surprise Shani and try to reconcile. The couple picked up where they'd left off, and soon bought some of the last remaining Nova tickets, joining approximately 4,400 other young attendees for the two-day peace-and-love rave.

In response to her mother's dinner invitation, Shani said, "Can we do it next week? This weekend there's a party where our friends are DJing."

Matan and Alexndra

The featured performer on the opening of the main stage at the festival on Friday night was DJ Kido, Matan Elmalem to his friends.

Kido was his way of transliterating or spelling *kiddo*—a nickname he'd received as a ten-year-old boy who transformed his neighborhood air-raid shelter into a children's club. At age twenty, he flew to Japan to record with much older and well-known DJs, and now, by forty-two, Matan had spun at most of the major festivals across Europe, South America, and India and had become an influential figure in the local Mediterranean trance scene and helped to mentor the next generation of young DJs in the burgeoning genre of repetitive beats, which are supposed to inculcate a hypnotic, ecstatic state.

In fact, Matan was so in demand that he was scheduled to perform at two different trance parties happening consecutively in the same desert region, just a few kilometers from the Gaza border. The first party, UNITY, was set for Thursday night, and Friday and Saturday was Nova, where he was slated to play two sets: the opening set and the sunrise set, which was billed as the festival's highlight.

"Play well, my love," Alex, his girlfriend, texted him on Friday night.

"I love you," he replied as he prepared his set list.

Alex had told Matan that she couldn't make it to either event—saying that it was too far for her to drive, and she had work—but she was actually planning on surprising him at the Nova festival on Saturday morning. They hadn't seen each other for weeks.

Two and a half years earlier, Matan had met Alex Korobka at a party. She had a big laugh and long blond hair and wore a red pantsuit. Matan, by contrast, always wore black, along with a ring set with a purple stone and a skull bracelet, his black hair and beard were speckled with silver, setting off his soulful brown eyes. They'd lived together for two years and discussed marriage before deciding to live apart for a while—the issue wasn't so much the DJ lifestyle as it was personal drift, as they found themselves heading in separate directions. Matan had moved back to his parents' house in Dimona, spending time with his aging parents, Sherry and Shimon, and his younger sister Lin.

At forty-two years old, DJ Kido was a kid again.

Maya, Karina, Maayan, and Raz

They'd spent hours trying on different outfits and eventually decided to bring a second look to change into at sunrise. Maya Haim, a brunette, donned a tight white bikini top and wide-legged white pants. Karina Prithika, a blonde, chose a black crop top with black joggers. Maayan Tzubri, their gay male friend and the group's makeup artist, sported jean shorts and a tank top.

Both women were twenty-two and still living with their parents. Maya was the only child of a Polish mother and a Yemeni father, while Karina was the daughter of Russian immigrants. They and Maayan worked together as servers at a small beachside restaurant in Tel Aviv. They were saving their money for an upcoming trip to South America, which they planned to take in November.

Maya had been dating twenty-four-year-old Raz Cohen for two months, and invited him to join them at the party. In the week leading up to the event, the two spent many hours together; he'd just returned from a work trip in Africa, while she was preparing for her South American journey. Realizing they would soon be on different continents, they decided not to pursue a serious relationship and agreed the Nova party would be their "farewell."

By 2 A.M. Saturday, Maya, Karina, and Maayan were already dancing in front of the main stage. Raz arrived around 4 A.M.

Locating each other in the vast desert venue took time: the venue featured two large plazas, a camping area, expansive bars, dining areas, and spaces for yoga and meditation, plus an amply staffed "safe zone" for those having a bad trip (MDMA and acid were the drugs of choice).

When Raz found the girls, they were dancing, kissing, at one with one another and the music.

Shani, Orión, Jose, Dani, Sasha,
and Keshet

Shani and Orión were out on the main dance floor. They were very high—they were flying.

"This is the best party I've ever been to!" Jose Soto Grotewold yelled to them. Jose was one of their closest friends, a party producer in South America. "Everyone is beautiful, everything is beautiful. I love you guys!"

Jose was from Guatemala. He and Sasha, from France, and Danny, from Argentina, had been traveling together for months.

They'd flown to Israel to join Shani and Orión—the Nova party was just another stop on their seemingly never-ending global rave tour.

Orión and Jose first crossed paths four years earlier at a party in Guatemala. Two years later, at a festival in Croatia, Jose and Shani connected on the dance floor. Then, a year after that, Orión introduced Jose to his new girlfriend—Shani. In July, during a music festival in Switzerland, they met Keshet Casarotti from Kibbutz Samar, a ladies' man and a star attraction of every party he attended. The group had spent the previous September together in Greece. After the Nova festival, they planned to spend a few days at the desert kibbutz where Keshet grew up. His mother, Natalia, had prepared beds for everyone. From there, the group had a reservation at a Bedouin beach camp in Sinai, Egypt. Jose wanted to see some camels.

Keshet's arrival at the festival had been delayed. He'd been at his synagogue in Tel Aviv, celebrating the Simchat Torah holiday, and only got to Nova as the sun began to rise at half past five.

"Friends, we're all together now. Let's have a toast," Jose said.

"I have a bottle of tequila in the car," and he led everyone toward the parking lot, singing and hugging.

They toasted against the reddening sky of morning, calling out "*L'chaim*"—"To life."

Matan and Alexndra

Alex arrived at the party's parking lot at around the same time—sunrise. She was just in time to surprise her DJ boyfriend before he started his next set.

"Matan, my friend Shani Hadar is at the party entrance, she has a surprise for you, meet her in the parking lot," she texted him, still not saying that she herself was the surprise.

"I'm on my way," he replied.

The first rockets were fired before Matan reached her.

At 6:22, the sky lit up with what many of the non-Israelis at first thought were some new kind of Israeli fireworks. The production staff, under no such illusions, stopped the music immediately and the crowd responded with boos. Even some of the locals were momentarily confused. As far as they knew, the Gaza border area had been quiet for months, the army had approved the party location, and dozens of police officers were guarding the party area.

"Everybody spread out . . . protect yourself . . . code red!" the organizers announced, instructing everyone to "lie on the ground, put your hands on your head."

Three minutes later, by 6:25, the police made the call to end the party: "Everyone start making your way to the exits."

Alex didn't care about any sirens or Home Front Command instructions; she just wanted to find Matan. She left the car and began looking for a bearded man dressed in black.

He found her first. They hugged, but Matan told her to leave immediately—to leave alone.

"The party's over; there's nothing to do here. Get back in the car and get out of here. I don't want to be worrying about you."

"I can't believe I just drove three hours and the moment I showed up the party's over."

Nearby, a few young women were having panic attacks. Matan gave them water and helped calm them down. "Missiles are no joke. Get going before the traffic gets horrible."

"Come with us," Alex begged him.

He refused.

He said he felt responsible for helping to evacuate everyone first.

Maya, Karina, Maayan, and Raz

Raz Cohen searched frantically for his date. He looked for Maya in the parking lot, near the stage. They'd parted just before the air-raid sirens started, each going off to find their separate friend-groups. After about fifteen minutes, he finally found her and Maayan. He gave her a kiss and asked if they planned to leave by car or if they intended to stay and hide out at the party. Maya wanted to leave quickly; Karina was already in the camping area packing up their gear, but Raz thought the rocket barrages would soon be over. He wanted to ask Maya to stay with him, but didn't say anything. He wasn't sure which was the safest option.

Celine, Shiraz, Adir, and Raz

After insisting to her husband, Ido, that nothing would stop her from going, Celine, along with friends Shiraz and Adir, never made it to the party.

They were twelve miles from the rave site when the rocket attacks started. They decided to hole up in a bomb shelter at the entrance to Kibbutz Mefalsim, less than two miles from the Gaza border.

Shortly after they arrived, cancer patient Raz Perry entered the shelter. He too had been on the way to the party and had decided to stop and take cover. After a few moments of talk, the four realized they were neighbors.

Ido, at home with his baby, had been woken up by the sirens and immediately wrote to Celine.

"We're in a shelter, I'm in shock . . . there are missiles . . ." she responded.

"I knew you shouldn't have gone."

"Shiraz is having an anxiety attack."

"Should I wake up Ellie?"

"No, don't even think about it. I'll get back in the car as soon as the missiles stop and come home."

"You don't want to try going to the party?"

"We're already at a party—a rocket party!"

"Do you want me to come and pick you up?"

"Don't even think about it! We'll wait a bit longer in the shelter and then leave."

Shani, Orión, Jose, Danny, Sasha, and Keshet

Shani Louk, crying, yelled at her friends to hurry up as the sirens continued to wail. Orión tried to comfort her, telling her they'd be home soon, but Keshet was holding them up; he was back inside the party area and they couldn't find him.

The group decided to split up; Jose, Danny, and Sasha would

try to find Keshet, while Shani and Orión would drive back to Tel Aviv, hoping to get ahead of the massive traffic jam.

On their way out, however, Shani and Orión bumped into Keshet, who was stumbling around the parking lot. He'd been hit in the leg by a car scrambling for the exit. They helped Keshet limp to their car and managed to leave—or at least to join the line to leave. Keshet called Jose: "Drive without me; I'm with Shani. Meet in Tel Aviv." It was 6:37 A.M.

Celine and Raz

Celine was still on the phone with Ido, discussing when it would be best to feed Ellie, when she heard the first gunshots. She ended the call and the group huddled, shivering, afraid.

"What's going on?" Ido texted a minute later.

"Everything's good, we're safe."

"Still shooting?"

"Yes."

"Whoa."

"Sounds like soldiers have arrived," Celine wrote, when the shooting seemed to get closer. "I'm dying to get out of here."

Alexndra and Shani

Matan's advice appeared to have been good. Alex and her friend Shani Hadar were among the first to leave the music festival area, driving about twenty kilometers north on Route 232.

Just as they passed a roadside bomb shelter, a heavy rocket barrage struck the area.

Alex suggested stopping, but Shani refused, saying, "I have a thirteen-year-old daughter—I need to get home as quickly as possible." She didn't think it likely that a rocket would score a direct hit on their moving car.

Just a few minutes later, around 6:55 A.M., they saw a car break apart in front of them, its metal flying.

"Stop!" Alex shouted. "Stop driving! The next rocket's going to hit us!"

They took cover on the side of the road, as per protocol, lying face down, hands over their heads.

From her position on the ground, Shani Hadar noticed two legs approaching—two legs and a gun. She dashed back to her car's driver's seat, urging Alex to follow, and though she managed to close the door, she was shot twice in her arm.

A large group of armed men was positioning themselves along the route, firing at passing vehicles. "I'm bleeding! They hit me!" Shani yelled, driving at top speed, one hand on the wheel.

"Don't stop driving, no matter what. . . . If we stop, we die!" Alex was shrieking. Shani Hadar made a sharp left turn off the road into a field, then drove up a hill of scrub and through the desert sand.

Once out on the sand, they stopped and examined Shani's wounds. She'd been hit by at least two bullets and was losing blood fast.

Alex took off Shani's wrap and used it as a tourniquet.

After calling the emergency services, which told her they couldn't send help anytime soon, Alex called Matan. "Shani was shot. It's not just rockets. Can you give our location to the police at the party and maybe they'll come rescue us?"

Matan rushed between security personnel at the party, giving them Alex's GPS coordinates and begging them to do something. He kept calling Alex back, but reception was spotty and the calls kept getting dropped. "Alex, I'm begging you, answer me."

Shani Hadar lay on a mat next to the car, clutching a small doll that once belonged to her daughter, trying to ignore the pain and focus on her breathing.

Shani, Orión, Jose, Danny, Sasha, and Keshet

They headed north, with Shani Louk at the wheel, Orión beside her, and Keshet, still in pain from getting hit by the car, in the back.

They were only a few minutes behind Alex and Shani Hadar when, about twenty kilometers from the party, they reached the area of Kibbutz Mefalsim.

That's where a car, an Israeli's car, hit them from behind: part of a twelve-car pileup of motorists attempting to escape the rockets, many of them driving while impaired.

"I'm at the Gaza border, we need an ambulance, my friend was hurt, her leg is hurt."

Shani was injured from the pileup and unable to walk. Keshet managed to get through to the national emergency medical service and send them their coordinates at 6:59 A.M. "You have to send an ambulance . . . you don't understand what's happened to her leg . . . we need an ambulance here now. We're in a car, but she can't get out of the car, there are crashed cars everywhere, please, someone come."

He called them again at 7:06 A.M., asking where the ambulance was. They told him it was just a few minutes away.

But it wasn't.

About thirty heavily armed terrorists were standing along Route 232, shooting at the crashed cars and the other cars trying to escape. A Mefalsim resident looked out his window and saw militants cheering and congratulating one another for each kill.

"Hi, Dad. I'm calling you from Mefalsim." Mahmoud, one of the terrorists, called his father from a victim's phone. "Open WhatsApp and see how many I killed. Look how many I killed with my own hands! Your son killed Jews!"

"May God protect you," his father responded.

"Dad, I killed ten people with my own hands! Dad, ten with my own hands! Open WhatsApp and see how many I killed!"

Keshet managed to make one more call, to Jose, and warned him, "Don't come this way, don't keep driving, they're shooting up the cars . . . just leave your car and run for it . . ."

Jose then heard shots through the phone and Shani shrieking. Then the call was disconnected.

Keshet noticed an elderly man, the seventy-four-year-old Moti Zuarman, a grandfatherly hippie fixture at these parties, passing them by in his vehicle, and he asked the man for a ride to the hospital. It was decided that it would be better for Orión and the injured Shani to wait for the ambulance in her car, while Keshet—who could still walk—would seek out his own medical treatment.

A moment after Moti drove away with Keshet, a group of men seized Shani and Orión and headed with them toward Gaza.

Moti drove Keshet another four minutes and arrived at the Sha'ar HaNegev intersection, near Sderot, where a group of terrorists shot them at close range.

Maya, Karina, Maayan, and Roy

Maya, Karina, Maayan, and another friend, Roy, were driving in the opposite direction, southwest on Route 232.

Karina, seated in the front passenger seat, alternately feeling too hot and too cold, was taking off and putting back on layers of clothing. Maya, sitting behind her, called out to the group about rumors of a potential terrorist threat. "People are saying there are terrorists—what do you think?" Maayan, sitting next to Maya in the back, reassured her. "Sounds like nonsense to me."

He patted her on the back comfortingly just as gunshots hit their car. The shots came from several directions; the windshield shattered; Karina was shot in the head. Maayan, ducking low in the back seat, felt Maya collapse onto him and bite hard into his shoulder, perhaps trying to stifle her scream. She'd been shot in the chest. Maayan himself was hit in the pelvis, and Roy was hit in the legs, by bullets that had passed through the metal body of the vehicle. He swerved to the right, toward a gully with a stream at the bottom. The "girls' side" of the car was riddled with dozens of bullets, while the "boys' side" had much less.

Maayan and Roy dragged themselves bleeding from the car, into some nearby shrubbery. They hid there and tried to call for help while watching over the bodies of Karina and Maya.

Raz

Raz Cohen was still taking shelter under a tree in the party area, listening to falling missiles and sharing jokes with his friend Shoham, when his mother called. There was a terrorist attack underway. He laughed it off: "You're insane."

Two minutes later, he recognized the sound of a Kalashnikov being loaded coming from the direction of the road.

"Attack! Terrorist attack!" Two nearby police officers were suddenly repeating his mother's warning. "Hide! Everyone hide!"

They scattered; some hid in refrigerators and coolers in the bar area; some locked themselves in the porta potties; others ran into the open fields. Raz and his friend Shoham hid under the stage, along with many others. They lay still, trying to catch their breath.

About twenty minutes later, they heard shouting: "The terrorists are coming, they're here! Run!" Raz and Shoham dashed onto the stage floor and ran as fast as they could as the gunfire came closer. The area was teeming with heavily armed gunmen who were firing thousands of rounds at the still-intoxicated party-goers attempting to escape. Bullets whizzed past from several directions; no one knew where to turn.

A shot.

A shout.

A fall.

A rising laugh.

The terrorists were laughing as they were shooting.

Celine, Shiraz, Adir, and Raz

At the shelter, Raz Perry, Celine, Shiraz, and Adir heard voices in Arabic and realized that the shooting they were hearing wasn't coming from IDF soldiers.

Raz Perry urged everyone to stick close to the walls and remain silent.

Shelters, especially in that part of Israel, are essentially three-walled doorless structures of reinforced concrete, which provide more-or-less effective protection against rockets but on that day became traps—shooting galleries—for anyone hiding from terrorists.

When a Kalashnikov slowly appeared in the open doorway, Shiraz couldn't contain her fear.

She screamed, and the terrorist fired one bullet, which missed Shiraz and hit Adir in the leg.

Raz Perry, unarmed, jumped up and seized the terrorist by

his testicles, causing the terrorist to double over in pain. Raz then struck the terrorist, who fell to his knees and in falling began firing his weapon. Raz tried to wrestle the gun away but ended up being dragged outside and found himself surrounded by dozens of terrorists.

"A Jew, a Jew," the terrorist shouted as Raz tried to fight him off. The other terrorists opened fire, but the bullets hit the terrorist who'd dragged Raz outside, and Raz managed to crawl back to the shelter.

"Play dead—they're coming!" he yelled, and everyone in the shelter proceeded to lay in a pile, body stacked atop body, with the injured Adir on top. At least three terrorists now approached the shelter and hurled four grenades inside.

As the grenades flew in, Adir ran out and was shot in the head. Shiraz, witnessing her husband's murder, let out another scream, attracting the attention of other terrorists, who threw additional grenades from the doorway of the shelter. One struck Shiraz directly.

Celine watched her close friend explode.

Though the explosion was still ringing in his ears, Raz Perry tried to speak: "Celine, Celine, calm down, you're still alive," he told her, but he couldn't get through to her. Covered in her friend's blood, she was gripping her knees and rocking back and forth, not acknowledging his voice. He covered them both with Shiraz's ravaged body, hoping it would shield them from further grenades. "I'm sorry, Celine, but we don't have a choice."

Raz

Raz Cohen managed to dodge the bullets.

He spotted a dried-up streambed and a bush along the road

and took refuge between them, hiding behind the bush with his friend Shoham.

Three other young men soon joined them; one was shouting into his phone about a friend's murder. Raz asked him and the others to be quiet; if they kept shouting, they were going to get all of them killed.

Through the bush, they saw a white Savana van approaching. Five men, dressed in civilian clothing, got out of the van forty yards away. They all carried daggers, and one had a hammer. A light-haired young woman was with them; they were holding her tight. Raz Cohen watched as they tore her clothes off and gathered around her in a semicircle.

Raz Cohen wanted to intervene but knew he would die trying. The terrorists had weapons; he only had branches.

One terrorist grabbed the woman by the neck and another placed her hands on the van, then bent her over and started raping her. The others watched. Raz Cohen saw the terrorist stab her repeatedly while raping her. The woman stopped moving and screaming, but the terrorist continued moving inside her dead body.

Jose, Sasha, and Danny

"We have to make a run for it!" Jose shouted to Sasha and Danny upon hearing the shooting and Shani Louk's screaming through the phone.

They got out of the car and started running through the parking lot, not knowing where to go. They were still high, though full of adrenaline, and they couldn't understand the warnings being yelled at them in Hebrew. An Israeli, noting their confusion, told them to follow him to a shelter. They did, but as more and more people began crowding into the shelter, Jose started to feel unsafe. He thought it would be better to leave for an open area. A few minutes after they left, terrorists murdered all the partygoers hiding in the shelter.

Sasha suggested they split up to avoid drawing attention as a group. He decided to hide in a tree. Jose and Danny fled into a field, dashing from one hiding place to another, dodging bullets. They reached a grove of olive trees, filled with people, sheltering in the tree cover. They were huddled between the trunks, among the branches, listening to the steps and shooting as they seemed to grow closer, listening to their own breath and beating hearts.

Matan and Alexndra

Matan's battery was nearly drained when he dialed Alex to find out whether help had arrived. No answer. He called her another twenty-six times from a phone borrowed from a member of the party's production team. He refused to leave the party area until he got her help. At the same time, he was also trying to provide aid and comfort to partygoers under the influence of acid and MDMA and experiencing psychotic episodes. Matan soothed them, washed their faces, spoke gently to them, and guided them toward a safe escape route, urging them to run. For more than two hours, he dashed around an active terror site, trying to calm and help people under fire. Only when the gunshots were getting closer and closer did he seek refuge for himself. "Luna, they're shooting at us," he told his younger sister. He found shelter under a nearby abandoned ambulance and called Alex again, from the borrowed phone: "It's getting too close, I'm hiding now too, can't talk anymore, love you."

Shani

Ricarda Louk texted her daughter again and again:

"Have you reached a protected area?"

No response.

"Update us."

No response.

"Shani, update us. We're worried."

No response.

Amit Louk, Shani's twenty-year-old brother, was sitting on a couch in the living room when he received a text with a video clip from Shani's ex. He opened it and screamed. His parents and sister rushed over to see what had prompted the reaction. On the phone, they saw Shani, in the back of a jeep in what appeared to be Gaza, half-naked, bleeding from the head, surrounded by armed terrorists. Crowds of Palestinians cheered and spat on her.

Raz and Celine

Shiraz's body protected Celine but not Raz Perry. He'd been shot in the stomach. As he sat there bleeding, he heard the terrorists leaving and decided to flee the shelter. But Celine wouldn't move. "Come with me!" he yelled. "Please, we need to run!" He tried pulling at her arms and legs, shaking her, even slapping her, but Celine remained unresponsive. She just rocked back and forth and her eyes refused to focus.

Giving up, Raz Perry left the shelter alone, hobbling barefoot with grenade fragments in his leg and two bullets in his stomach. He made his way through a burning field, heading toward the houses of Kibbutz Mefalsim, praying he wouldn't be shot in the back.

Reaching the houses, he knocked on door after door, but no one answered. Everyone in the kibbutz had retreated to their safe rooms. Finally, he broke into a house and collapsed atop a sofa. He called a friend for help, but the call was dropped. There was no phone service, but he kept trying to make calls as he burst into tears and held his bloody stomach. The owner of the house timidly stuck his head out of his safe room and asked in Arabic, "What's your name?"

"Raz Perry," he answered in Hebrew. "I'm Israeli, I'm Jewish."

The owner of the house helped him into the safe room and gave him a towel to stanch the bleeding.

Alexndra and Shani

For nine hours, Alex and Shani Hadar lay on a mat in an open field near Kibbutz Mefalsim, surrounded by gunfire. Shani had already lost a significant amount of blood, and Alex had been unable to reach Matan for hours. No help was on the way.

In an effort to keep Shani conscious, Alex counted aloud with her to one hundred. She then phoned the emergency medical service and pleaded again for help, asking the operator, "How many terrorists are there? Be honest with me!"

"There are reportedly two thousand to twenty-five hundred terrorists. I'm sorry, but we don't have an ambulance for you now. I can stay on the line with you, though."

"No, thanks," Alex said. "I need to save my battery."

When they spotted a drone overhead, they signaled to it for help, but the moment they did, heavy gunfire came in their direction. Alex hid under the car while Shani feigned death, closing her eyes as the bullets whizzed by.

Then it was silent again.

Alex again called for help. The operator on the line was blunt: "No one is coming. You have to take care of yourselves. Get in the car and drive as fast as you can." While they were speaking, Alex noticed that a figure was approaching them—a man coming across the field. She strained to pick up her pale and weakened friend and put her into the car, and they sped away.

Turning left toward a hill, Alex saw people. Their dress and sense of disorientation revealed them as partygoers, not Hamas. She pulled up near an Israeli ambulance and army vehicles.

Raz

Raz Cohen waited in the bush for about ten hours, until twelve Israeli soldiers emerged, shouting, "Any Israelis here?" He was taken to a police officer's private house in Ofakim, which was also under siege.

"Do you need anything?" the police officer asked.

"Just a glass of water. And a paper and pen if possible." Raz Cohen wrote down everything that had happened since the morning. He didn't want to forget.

Maayan and Roy

Maayan and Roy were hiding under a tree for about eight hours, bleeding, until a civilian from a nearby moshav responded to a request for volunteers to aid partygoers, given the breakdown of the emergency response system. He took Maayan and Roy in his own car to the hospital.

Jose, Danny, and Sasha

Military forces rescued Jose and Danny around the same time; they arrived in their Tel Aviv Airbnb later that evening, reuniting with Sasha, who had been rescued as well. They had all seen the video of Shani Louk in Gaza. Calls and texts to Orión and Keshet went unanswered. Jose, Sasha, and Danny flew to Greece two days later, their families having begged them to leave the country. They were half the group that they were before, waiting for their flight at Ben Gurion Airport.

Shani

At 4:37 P.M., Ricarda Louk received an alert on her phone:

"Hello, a transaction attempted with your credit card at the store—MY PHONE—was not approved. Always at your service, Isracard."

Someone had attempted to make purchases in Gaza using Shani Louk's credit card, which was still linked to her mother's account.

Ricarda immediately called the credit card company, requesting the location of the attempted purchase. They confirmed it was made in Jabalia, Gaza.

Recognizing that Israeli authorities might not be able to rescue her daughter in time, Ricarda recorded a twenty-nine-second video in German, displaying a photo of Shani on her phone, and asking for any help:

"This morning my daughter, Shani Nicole Louk, a German citizen, was kidnapped with a group of tourists in southern Israel by Palestinian Hamas. We were sent a video in which I could clearly see our daughter unconscious in the car being driven around the Gaza Strip. I ask you to send us any help or news. Thank you very much."

Later, at 11:23 P.M., another message came:

"Hello, a transaction attempted with your credit card at the business—UBER—was not approved. To verify your identity and continue using this card, please contact 03–6364677 extension 2. Always at your service, Isracard."

Someone had tried to use Shani Louk's credit card to book an Uber in Gaza.

Celine

The next morning, the unofficial assessment was that Celine Ben-David Nagar had been kidnapped, a conclusion based on the absence of a corpse.

At home, Ido was consumed by worry; days passed with no sign of his wife.

He reached out to anyone he thought could help, managing even to get through to French president Emmanuel Macron before any Israeli official was in touch with him (Celine was a dual French national). He made daily calls to the French embassy and the French and Israeli media and reached out to survivors of the party. Desperate for any clue, he drove to the last known location of her phone—the rocket shelter of Kibbutz Mefalsim. There, he found the vehicle Celine, Shiraz, and Adir had driven to the party. The only human trace was some blood smeared near the vehicle. Bodies had been removed from the site—whether by ZAKA or by the terrorists—before he arrived.

All work at the law firm of Kasuto & Co. was paused.

In Celine's absence, hundreds of Israeli women donated breast milk for baby Ellie.

Matan

After visiting every hospital and finding no trace of Matan, his family set up an impromptu information center at their home in Dimona. They combed through every video posted from the party, searching for any clue that might reveal Matan's fate.

As time passed, they received more and more phone calls and messages from people claiming they'd seen him at the party late into the morning. Many recounted how he'd helped them escape. None could provide information on what happened to him.

Alex received a call from the phone Matan had tried calling her from twenty-six times. The voice was a woman's; she sounded confused: "What's your connection to my husband?"

"What?" Alex said. "I don't know your husband."

"Really? So how come his last calls are to you?"

"No, no, it's my boyfriend who used this phone—my boyfriend, the DJ Matan Elmalem. He borrowed a phone and called me from this number after his own phone died."

The woman on the other end had also been looking for her missing husband for days.

Orión

Sergio, Orión's father, was in Mexico when he got a call from friends in Sweden: they'd gotten a call from Orión's phone from a man speaking Arabic. The friends and Sergio arranged for the services of an Arabic translator and called the phone back. "Orión's been kidnapped to Gaza," they were told. "He's alive and okay. We're going to use him to bargain with." That was a week after the massacre. Several weeks later, Israeli authorities contacted

Sergio to officially confirm that Orión was indeed alive and being held by Hamas in Gaza.

Keshet

Natalia Casarotti initially thought her son Keshet was simply unreachable, as was often the case.

She posted his picture online, soliciting information: Keshet's long blond hair made him easily recognizable. Was he dead? Injured? A hostage? And which would be worse? She searched every hospital, thinking her son might be unconscious and unidentified.

ZAKA's Haim Utmazgin returned to the party site near Kibbutz Re'im on the morning of October 8.

En route, a group standing by the road flagged down his ambulance once again on Road 234. As he exited the vehicle, people in the crowd pointed him toward a car parked by the roadside. Haim approached. A young man with a gunshot wound to the head was still seated in the driver's seat; the car's other doors hung open, facing the orchard across the road. Believing there might be more victims who fled into the fields, Haim ventured into the orchard.

There, in a short span, he discovered three bodies—two women and one man.

One of the women, who appeared to be in her thirties, lay face down in the partial shade of a tree. Her jeans had been cut off with a knife and she'd been shot in the vagina. The other woman, whose jean shorts had been pulled off, had been bruised heavily around her vagina, and her bra had been ripped. Her telephone still lay in her hand and her purse was on her shoulder.

Haim and his teams would continue to uncover bodies daily for a period of weeks.

All told, 364 people were murdered at the Nova music festival site and another forty were kidnapped, in what turned out to be the largest terrorist attack in the history of the state of Israel. Scores of rapes and sexual violence were reported by survivors and surviving eyewitnesses, but it was ZAKA's fast response that made the collection of hard evidence impossible.

On the fourth day after the attack, Natalia Casarotti received the announcement that a DNA sample she had provided from Keshet had matched one of the hundreds of anonymous bodies awaiting identification in a former military camp, now serving as a center for the identification of massacre victims. She laid him to rest in the desert kibbutz, requesting that the mourning assembly sing and dance at the funeral. It took an additional two months before she uncovered the circumstances and location of his murder, piecing together the details independently.

On the ninth day after the attack, Celine's body was also recovered. She'd suffered a gunshot wound to her stomach in the shelter by Kibbutz Mefalsim. Ido was preparing for a meeting with French authorities when the IDF soldiers knocked on his door. He asked to see her head—to see her curly hair—before the funeral, just to be sure.

Shortly after the funeral, he started feeding Ellie with baby formula.

Some of the victims' remains were so severely burned that it took weeks to identify them. As a result, some bodies were accidentally buried together, including a few of the bodies retrieved from the location where Matan's remains were ultimately found.

The remains of five bodies were discovered under the burned-out ambulance from which Matan called Alex for the final time. They'd been completely incinerated by the RPG that'd exploded the vehicle. Only a large purple ring, one that Matan hadn't taken off his hand for years, remained intact.

For three weeks, the Louk family was left without answers.

They received help from the leftist organization Women Wage Peace, which deputized a trusted elderly Palestinian man in Gaza to search hospitals for Shani's whereabouts. He came back with a message: "She is alive but has a head wound." However, the man confessed that he hadn't personally seen her and was only relaying the information he'd gathered.

As the IDF intensified its attacks on Gaza, Ricarda and Nissim were increasingly concerned. Could Shani receive proper medical treatment in a hospital without electricity or water? And if Shani died, what would happen to her body?

A midnight knock on their door brought clarity; a fragment of Shani's skull had been found. She had likely died instantly from a gunshot wound to her head. The terrorists who'd taken her to Gaza had been parading around a dead woman.

Raz Cohen was uninjured. Alex was uninjured. Physically, that is.

Shani Hadar underwent several surgeries to save her hand. Maayan and Adi went through long months of hospitalizations.

Raz Perry survived the gunshots to his stomach and returned to his routine of treatments, in the fight to survive lymphoma.

To Kibbutz Be'eri
and Back

1

Twelve hours before he was murdered, Roni Levy prepared to kick off an important celebration. Cheeks flushed, the spry eighty-year-old adjusted his glasses and shuffled forward onto the stage of the community hall at Kibbutz Be'eri to read from a creased sheet of paper.

An audience of hundreds had gathered that Friday evening to celebrate a holiday—not the religious holiday of Simchat Torah but a determinedly secular holiday commemorating the day that Kibbutz Be'eri was founded on October 6, 1946.

Friday was the kibbutz's seventy-seventh anniversary, and a party had been organized.

As one of its oldest residents, Levy had been asked to share some of his memories from the 1950s, when he'd arrived alone from Algeria, speaking only Arabic:

"I had no language in common; I was unable to communicate with the other children. I was informed that a private teacher would tutor me in the language until I was ready to join the class with the others. It was then that I encountered a kibbutz member, a woman with striking green eyes and the glow of pregnancy, who sat me down and introduced me to Hebrew. Her teaching was exceptional, and enabled me to join the school with a decent grasp of Hebrew after just three months. She and her husband extended an offer to adopt me—and we became a family."

Following Levy, other kibbutz members took turns onstage to offer their memories—of their childhoods, of the harvest seasons, of the profound sense of belonging they'd found at Be'eri, which at 1,200 members strong was the largest kibbutz on the Gaza border, a community that often functioned like an extended family.

Wine flowed freely, candles flickered on tables draped with checkered tablecloths, while a singer and guitarist onstage regaled the audience with songs chosen by the kibbutz members, serenading them with "Here It All Began" and "We Venture into the Unknown / Oblivious of Our Destiny or What Lies Ahead."

For eight decades, Be'eri thrived as a socialist cooperative kibbutz, where all members—be they executives or cleaners—received equal pay, "from each according to their abilities, to each according to their needs," as the phrase goes, which in the kibbutz was not a Marxist allusion but a hallowed practice.

Unlike many of the other 264 Israeli kibbutzim, which over the past decades have faced privatization and the departure of many residents, Kibbutz Be'eri remained stable, standing as one of the last bastions of the old authentic kibbutz movement advocating for a fully cooperative model. Its members succeeded in building a financially prosperous community, evidenced by the long list of children born there who wish to return to the kibbutz. For much of Be'eri's history, children had slept communally, apart from their parents, fostering bonds among classmates that were often stronger than those between siblings. However, responding to the growing desire among many families to raise their children at home, the kibbutz abolished this practice in the 1980s.

The key to Be'eri's success was its proud traditionalism and its economic diversification. The bulk of the kibbutz's income derived from a printing house established in the 1950s, which handled a lot of government contracts, including the printing of driver's licenses.

The kibbutz also cultivated field crops and citrus and maintained avocado and mango orchards. Be'eri's cooperative spirit extended beyond the socioeconomic and into the cultural and political: the kibbutz published a newsletter and maintained its own historical archives; over 94 percent of its members voted for left and center parties in the last round of elections. Despite two decades of frequent Hamas rocket fire, Kibbutz Be'eri—located just four kilometers from the border—donated thousands of shekels each month to Gazan families. This fundraiser was a community effort, which harkened back to the 1970s, when the kibbutz hired Palestinian workers in an age when movement between Gaza and Israeli kibbutzim was unrestricted. When the terror attacks of the Second Intifada caused the Israeli government to stop issuing Palestinian work permits, the kibbutz members started annually pooling their funds to support their former employees. Some also volunteered for an NGO called On the Way to Recovery, founded by an Israeli who lost his brother to a Hamas kidnapping and murder in 1993. On the Way to Recovery transports Palestinian patients from Gaza to Israeli hospitals for chemotherapy, surgery, and other lifesaving treatments.

At the anniversary celebration, many of these volunteers sat together, singing and drinking. Among them were the Dagans, Hadas and Adi.

Adi's parents were the first couple to get married in Be'eri—
the founding parents of the kibbutz. Hadas was the daughter of
the founders of a smaller, failed kibbutz that disbanded, and they
moved to Be'eri carrying a sense of loss. Despite growing up in
the same community, Hadas and Adi only met in their twenties
while leading a school trip to Sinai. She was a few classes above
him, a petite young woman, with blond hair falling to her shoulders, while he was an athlete—tall and broad, with deep dimples
in his cheeks.

They married and chose to stay in Be'eri to raise their four
children. Hadas became the kibbutz's education coordinator,
while Adi became its financial manager, guiding the kibbutz
through its most prosperous years. Upon retirement, he rein-
vented himself and devoted considerable time to his grandchildren and to landscape painting: trying to put on the canvas his
vision of the beautiful fields that surrounded his home.

Every Thursday, Adi and Hadas drove Palestinian patients to
Israeli hospitals. They'd gotten involved with the initiative thanks
to their good friend, fellow kibbutz member Vivian Silver.

Silver, a svelte septuagenarian with a piercing gaze and a Canadian accent, arrived at the anniversary celebration shortly after wrapping up a peace rally she'd organized in Jerusalem, which
had brought together thousands of Israeli and Palestinian women
from the Gaza Strip and the West Bank. Together, the women
had declared, "Israeli and Palestinian women are determined to
change the reality of the conflict! We refuse to bear witness to
more casualties. It's time for women's voices to be heard! We must
end this cycle of violence." Vivian had left the conference optimis-
tic, but then optimism was her usual mood.

Vivian had already reached middle age when she joined the
kibbutz. Born in Winnipeg and raised in an observant Jewish

family, she received a scholarship to study for a year at the Hebrew University in Jerusalem, where she found her sympathies
shifting from Judaism to Zionism.

She met a group of fellow students from the New York branch
of the Habonim Dror movement, joined them, and eventually
married another member named Marty. They officially emigrated to Israel in 1974, and became part of the founding generation of Kibbutz Gezer. Marty soon left but Vivian stayed and
became something of a maverick, taking on roles in the kibbutz
that traditionally had been held by men. In the early 1980s, she
established an official department within the greater Israeli kibbutz movement to advocate for gender equality. It was through
this activism that she met Louis Zeigan, with whom she started a
family. They moved to Be'eri in 1990, shortly after which Vivian
was offered the job of co-director of the Negev Institute, an Israeli
peace and education nonprofit. Furthering her commitment to
Israeli-Palestinian coexistence, she went on to co-found Women
Wage Peace and served on the board of B'Tselem, a leading
Israeli human rights organization. She identified as a "conditional
Zionist"—passionately supporting a Jewish national home only if
it also ensured the rights and dignity of Palestinians.

In the front row, near the stage of the anniversary celebration,
sat the parents of the Tzemach family. Shlomit and Doron were
children of the founders of the kibbutz—a community of Jews
deported from Baghdad, part of the massive influx of Arab Jews
who found refuge in Israel around the time of the founding of
the state.

Until 1941, nine-year-old Carmela Tzemach lived with her
family in the Iraqi capital, in a mixed neighborhood of Jews
and Arabs. The infamous Farhud pogrom changed her life. In
the span of a few days in June, more than 180 Baghdadi Jews

were murdered and thousands more were injured. This atrocity involved the abuse of infants, the desecration of bodies, widespread rape, and the looting and vandalism of synagogues and other Jewish infrastructure. A Muslim mob attacked Carmela's family's house, where the doors were locked and barricaded with heavy furniture.

Carmela arrived in Israel in 1950 as an eighteen-year-old. There she met Yaakov, another Baghdadi Jew, whose parents had roots in Hebron. He, too, had been persecuted as a child; his family was almost murdered in the same Farhud pogrom. At age fifteen, he joined the underground. Every morning he'd walk to school and pass a gibbet with a body dangling from the noose: usually the body of a Jew, often the body of a communist, sometimes the body of a Jewish communist.

Carmela and Yaakov's grandson, Shachar Tzemach, now thirty-nine years old, was born and raised in Be'eri. He was the young and brilliant financial manager of the kibbutz's printing press; he'd replaced Adi Dagan when he retired. Lanky bearded Shachar was also well-known as a left-wing activist; he had served in the IDF and later provided testimony to the Breaking the Silence organization about unlawful IDF actions against Palestinians in the Occupied Territories. He volunteered to give educational tours of Hebron to those wanting to deepen their understanding of the conflict.

Toward the back of the room, at one of the side tables, sat the Hetzroni family.

The grandfather, Avia Hetzroni, distinguished by his handsome cleft chin, grew up in the kibbutz and was in the same class as Adi Dagan, back in the days when the kibbutz children learned and ate and slept together.

Avia requested that the musicians play a song that their

kindergarten teacher used to sing to them, a song by Peña Berg-stein: "You have planted melodies in me, my mother and father, melodies from forgotten hymns. . . . Seeds, seeds . . . my heart is silent . . . until they grow and rise."

Avia's parents, Margalit and Yair, were Israeli-born Jews of the founding generation. Three of their children continued their legacy: Ayala, Nitza, and Avia himself.

Nitza had three sons, Avia had one daughter, and Ayala had no children.

Avia also had two grandchildren, the fraternal twins Liel and Yanai, during whose birth Avia's daughter, Shira, suffered complications that caused her to go into a coma. When she emerged, she was severely disabled, both physically and mentally.

From that day on, Avia Hetzroni devoted himself to caring for his daughter, Shira, while his sister, Ayala, stepped in to raise the twins. She lived with the children in the house opposite the Dagans, who'd give the kids fresh oranges and homemade cookies. Ayala accepted this help reluctantly, but willingly availed herself of the assistance of two of Nitza's children, Omri and Shagi Shafroni. In this mixed family, the boundaries between parents and uncles were blurred: all pitched in to raise the twins.

At one of the last tables in the room, the siblings Raya and Yair Rotem sat next to their friend Narkis Hand. Twelve years separated Raya from her younger brother. Yair was a commercial photographer and editor; Raya practiced Chinese medicine, acupuncture, and reflexology before moving to the printing house. Raya was the single mother of a twelve-year-old girl, Hila; Yair was newly married. They'd just returned a few days before from Yair's wedding to a Chinese woman; the ceremony had taken place in Thailand.

"Thailand is so beautiful, why not actually live there? There

are no terrorists or rockets here," Hila remarked to her uncle
during the trip.

Raya Rotem and Narkis Hand had grown up together in the
shared dormitory as members of the class of 1969. Narkis, a
dancer and kindergarten teacher, fell in love with Thomas Hand,
an Irishman who came to volunteer at the kibbutz. They married
when she was only twenty-four; she gave birth to Eden soon afterward and to Natalie two and a half years later. About three
years after that, the couple divorced. Tom met a woman named
Liat, and the two had a daughter, Emily Hand. When Liat died
of cancer, Narkis took in the two-year-old Emily and raised her
as one of her own.

That evening, the mothers left their daughters home alone.
While the adults sang and drank, twelve-year-old Hila Rotem
and eight-year-old Emily Hand had a pajama party with movies
and candy; they had the house all to themselves with no parents
around.

2

Just after six in the morning, Hila Rotem was awakened by the
high-pitched siren that warned of falling rockets. She quietly
crept past Emily, who could sleep through anything, and ran to
her mother's room.

"Should I wake up Emily because of the missiles, or will they
stop in a few minutes?" Hila wondered. She shared her mother's
bright eyes and curly black hair.

"Yes, wake her up; you girls can go back to sleep in the safe
room," Raya said and hurried to secure the house's always-open
front door.

Like most members of the kibbutz, Raya didn't have a lock on the safe-room door itself, so for additional protection she piled two armchairs—her late father's beloved armchairs—and stuck a flower pot atop them and placed them against the door: a make-shift tower of the heaviest items she had.

At 6:37 A.M., the kibbutz residents received their first alert by text message: "Remain in a protected area until further notice." At 6:48, another message read, "Dear residents, good morning and Shabbat Shalom. Heavy gunfire has targeted areas nationwide. Stay in protected areas until we update you further." At 7:14, a neighbor wrote to the kibbutz group, "A terrorist is on the stairs of the house." At 7:15, the official warning came: "Due to suspected terrorist infiltration, residents are advised to lock themselves in-side their homes, secure their doors, and stay away from windows until further notice." At 7:16, a neighbor asked, "Where is the army?" At 7:34, another wrote, "We hear a lot of gunshots; please update," and at 7:35, a concerned mother pleaded, "Someone is outside here; please come."

Emily didn't have a phone with her, but Hila did. Her class-mates exchanged blunter messages than the adults. One wrote, "My house is burning down," and another, "they are shooting at us!!!" a third, "goodbye, I love you all, I don't know what to do."

Raya didn't want to alarm her daughter's friend—it was one of the first times that Emily had been allowed to sleep over at a friend's house—but the girl had sensed something was amiss when she overheard Narkis Hand and Thomas Hand calling Raya. The adults agreed the situation was too perilous for any-one to try to pick up Emily and bring her home.

In another part of the kibbutz, Raya's brother, Yair Rotem, a sturdy man in his early forties, was panicking.

He tried to convince himself that it was normal to feel terri-fied, knowing that terrorists were lurking in nearby houses. He found himself alone; his wife was taking time after their Thai wedding to visit her parents in China. He began surveying his house, trying to find a spot to hide.

He emptied the linen drawer under his bed, thinking he could crawl inside it. Then he neatly made the bed, hoping to give the impression that his was just a tidy home vacated for the holiday. He decided to lock the house's main door but to leave the shelter door conspicuously open—terrorists wouldn't suspect that arrangement if someone in the house was hiding.

He became fixated on urination—would he be able to pee? Flushing the toilet might alert the terrorists that someone was home, but not flushing could give away his presence if they noticed the fresh urine in the bowl. Thus, he resorted to peeing in the sink. He regretted not having brushed his teeth that morning.

He kept going back and forth over whether to hide under the bed now or wait until the terrorists came closer. He briefly left his hiding spot to grab a knife from the kitchen, but forgot to take water. He would dart out of his hiding spot to drink directly from the kitchen faucet every hour, forgetting to take a bottle each time.

He thought about messaging his wife, "If something happens to me, know that I love you," but he refrained, thinking that such a message might jinx him.

Every half hour, he exchanged brief messages with his sister, Raya; they reassured each other of their safety.

"What's going on?" she inquired.

He responded with a smiley emoji.

"What's going on?"

She replied with a smiley of her own.

Shortly after, she added, "At my place."

"What at your place?"

"I'm being kidnapped."

3

Adi and Hadas hurriedly drew the curtains over the windows of their house. They'd been awakened by phone calls from their children.

Their youngest son, Sahar Dagan, and their son-in-law, Dor Harari, were part of the kibbutz's emergency response squad, an all-volunteer group of local men responsible for securing the kibbutz in the event of an attack before the arrival of the police or army. Zohar, Dor's wife, requested Hadas's help with the children while her husband was out with the other fathers, trying to evaluate the scale of the threat. "Sure, I'll have my coffee and then come over." As she took her first sips, reports of terrorists entering the kibbutz arrived in the kibbutz chat, followed by a loud knock at their door.

Standing outside were the Porat-Katz couple.

They had knocked on many doors, but no one had answered.

"Who's there?" Hadas called out. She felt no fear, thinking that terrorists wouldn't bother to knock.

"I'm Yasmin and he's Tal. We're from up north. We were at a party near Kibbutz Re'im and are looking for shelter; there are terrorists outside."

Hadas welcomed the couple into their living room. It was evident they'd been partying all night. Tal Katz was dressed in a red athletic shirt and jeans, Yasmin Porat in a black tank top and short skirt. Adi hastily made some sandwiches and coffee, suggesting that sustenance was more crucial than refuge, at least for the moment. The young couple was arguing; Tal, visibly shaken, was struggling to calm down, while Yasmin attempted to lighten the mood with jokes. They recounted their ordeal: escaping the party as rockets began to fall, being shot at by the roadside, and how the emergency response squad had directed them to find shelter inside the kibbutz.

The two couples were together in the Dagans' safe room as the shooting and smoke from the fires drew closer. Hadas called Vivian, who was alone, to check on her. "They're at my door, Hadas," Vivian whispered.

"Take care" was all Hadas managed to say before she ended the call.

4

Vivian Silver had been living alone for seven years, since her husband, Louis, died. Her children had also left home long ago.

Her many friends on both sides of the border, her work promoting peace, and her grandchildren filled the silence.

Her younger son, Yonatan Zeigen, was born when she was forty. For decades, she'd devoted all her time to her work but took time off to raise him and his brother. When the Palestinian construction workers whom Vivian had managed as the kibbutz construction coordinator stopped showing up to work from Gaza, Yonatan—just a small child—had wanted to know what happened. Vivian explained to him, "There's a conflict over land."

Yonatan filled a bucket with earth and asked his mother, "So will you give this land to Khaled so we can make peace?"

That morning, before Vivian realized a disaster was unfolding, one of her old friends from Gaza, a Palestinian man, was among the first to get in touch: "Vivian, what's going on? What's happening? We hear civilians and soldiers have been kidnapped and they're already in Gaza. The pictures look horrible. Where is your army?"

Vivian didn't know how to respond; she just shut her front door and took shelter in her safe room. She messaged her friends in the Women Wage Peace group: "The irony of the timing"—a reference to the fact that just three days before, they'd been together with their Gaza friends at the Jerusalem peace rally.

In the midst of her preparations, a major Israeli radio station reached out to Vivian for an interview. "I'm sitting in the safe room, the blinds down and door shut. They're saying there are casualties from the kibbutz. It's terrifying."

"Can you hear gunshots outside?" the radio interviewer asked.

"Yes, I can hear them very clearly."

"Is your house secure? Are you in a safe place?"

"As much as possible, yes," Vivian responded.

The broadcast was intermittently interrupted by radio announcements of incoming rockets, yet Vivian urged the interviewer to convey a message advocating for peace and calling for rational voices on both sides of the conflict.

"The time has come, the time has come," she kept repeating.

The interviewer, however, interjected: "It seems there's only one sane side this morning. Discussing both sides might not be pertinent now—we're under attack."

"Well," Vivian said, "then I suggest we continue this conversation after the crisis."

"Of course, the priority is your safety. Take care," the interviewer said, ending the conversation.

The last time explosions were heard so close to her home was during the 2014 Gaza war, a transformative year for Vivian. She became a grandmother, retired from her role in a Jewish-Arab coexistence organization in the Negev, and reflected on how she

should best invest her time in the active years she still had ahead
of her.

She didn't like to sugarcoat things: a sense of missed opportunities and regret surrounded her; she was haunted by goals still
unachieved. She hoped that Women Wage Peace might change
things. Fifty thousand women had joined the grassroots movement in its first decade of existence, both Israelis and Palestinians, demanding two states and equality from the Jordan to the
Mediterranean.

Vivian was on the phone with her son Yonatan when the shots
and gunfire seemed to get closer to the house. They decided to
hang up, so no terrorist would hear her.

Vivian went to hide in her safe room's closet.

After a while, Yonatan texted, asking how she was: "Just write
something."

She answered, "Something . . . Sorry, I'm trying to keep my
sense of humor."

"A sense of humor is great. What about the kibbutz? Is there
still shooting?"

"Up until a minute ago. Now there's a strange silence. If I get
out of here alive, I'll buy adult diapers so I have them on hand
for next time."

"Do you know if there are any soldiers on the kibbutz? Is anyone hurt?"

"I still don't know anything. I can't even tell if the yelling outside is in Arabic or Hebrew."

They were texting in English. She'd been living in Israel for
decades, but English remained her first language. "We may be
witnessing a massacre . . ." she wrote and then continued in Hebrew: "Without any joking let me say how much I love each of
you, and how blessed I am to have had you in my life."

"I love you, Mom."

"They're in the house now."

5

The Tzemach family was scattered across six different houses throughout the kibbutz: the parents, Shlomit and Doron, resided in one; the younger brothers, Ido and Shai, lived in two separate apartments for young adults; Uri, who has special needs, was in the fourth; Yarden in the fifth; and the eldest, Shachar, along with his wife, Ofri, and their children in the sixth.

Immediately after the initial sirens, Shachar and Ofri decided to leave for her family's home near Jerusalem, sparing the kids a day of anxiety. They'd barely started packing when Arik Kraunic, the emergency security coordinator, informed Shachar that he and the other squad members needed to report for duty immediately. Yarden Tzemach also received the call to action but was outside the kibbutz that morning, in the waning hours of a friend's bachelor party that had started the night before.

This sudden call to arms was the realization of a trend that Shachar had seen coming a decade earlier, writing in an article published in a small independent magazine called *The Hottest Place in Hell*," "The citizens of Israel stand—or are stationed—as the first line of defense against terrorist attacks when the political and military establishment instructs them to defend themselves privately, not relying on the security provided by the army and police. The Israeli security system is undergoing the same privatization that has affected the education and health systems." Shachar concluded his article with a warning: "The continuation of security privatization will claim many more victims."

He, the tall, slender, left-wing activist opposed to the occupation, was the first to arm himself in defense of his kibbutz when the army was absent. By seven o'clock, he was already on his way to the meeting point.

Arik, the emergency security coordinator, though, was nowhere to be found.

Another squad member, Elam Maor, soon provided the reason: while attempting to lock the kibbutz gate, Elam had found Arik shot dead. Another squad member, Yair Avital, then reported witnessing two terrorists shoot Gil Boym on his bicycle. Shachar was the first to find Gil, who was injured and bleeding from gunshot wounds. He called Nirit Hunwald-Kornfeld, the beloved kibbutz nurse, who lived nearby. Nirit rushed to the scene but realized the wounds were too severe and called Amit Man, the kibbutz's new twenty-two-year-old paramedic.

The blond, outgoing Amit, the youngest of five sisters, woke that morning alongside her partner, Ofir Peretz, also a paramedic at the national emergency medical service. As the rockets began, Ofir was called to duty at the local station in Netivot, close to Amit's mother's house, and he urged Amit to come with him for safety. A dedicated professional, she refused: "I need to stay here, especially if it's dangerous. I'm on call."

En route to assist Gil, Amit reached out to the national emergency medical service, where she'd volunteered since her youth: "There's a terrorist infiltration at the kibbutz. We urgently need an ambulance or police." She was among the first to make the report. "We have wounded here, hurry up." They assured her help would arrive promptly.

Shachar Tzemach took charge of securing the area while Amit and Nirit attended to Gil on the sidewalk. As the sound of gunfire neared, Shachar forced open the door of the nearby dental clinic and helped move Gil inside.

The clinic, set within an old house repurposed into an office and a modest dental practice, lacked sufficient medical supplies. The paramedics Amit and Nirit resorted to improvising tourniquets from gauze, clothing, and other available fabric.

Before eight o'clock, another injured man arrived, with a gunshot wound in his back. The team divided their efforts: Nirit focused on Gil, while Amit attended to the newly arrived patient.

Within minutes, a third wounded person arrived. Yair Avital, a member of the emergency squad, had heard a scream from the vicinity of a friend's parents' house and attempted to run toward it when a grenade was thrown at him. He managed to drag himself, bleeding heavily, to the clinic.

Now there were three seriously wounded people and two medical professionals on site in a facility intended for dentistry.

Amit reached out to the national emergency medical service again, inquiring about "the nearest location that an ambulance could access."

The response was empathetic yet firm: "Don't go anywhere; we're really making the effort. We know where you are. Don't worry, we won't abandon you."

They next called Dr. Daniel Levy, a physician from Soroka Hospital who'd moved to the kibbutz a year prior with his wife and two young children, having immigrated to Israel from Peru. "*Te amo*," he told his wife before rushing to the clinic.

His arrival was not quick enough for Gil Boym, who succumbed to his injuries. He died without knowing that his eldest son, Inbar Boym, age twenty-three, had been murdered on Route 34 while trying to return to the kibbutz upon hearing of the terrorist intrusion.

Nirit's phone buzzed incessantly with calls from wounded friends unable to get medical attention. Among them was Sandra

Cohen, a nurse herself, who reported the murder of her baby, Mila, not yet a year old. Her husband was severely injured, as was she; the terrorists had also tied up her mother-in-law, Yona, and murdered her. Three generations of the Cohen family were erased.

Shachar stood guard outside the clinic, facing barrages of shooting. Eitan Hadad, another member of the squad and the sales associate of the kibbutz's printing house, joined him, taking up an injured man's weapon and vest.

Amit continued to try to evacuate the clinic, but all her attempts were frustrated or met with silence, even from Avia Hatzroni, who'd worked as a paramedic and an ambulance driver at the national emergency medical service for decades.

The sixty-nine-year-old Avia gave first aid to kibbutz members when needed, drove to the hospital for emergencies, and more than once had delivered a baby. In addition, he volunteered at a nearby medical station in Netivot, a small, poor city near the kibbutz.

He had trained all the young volunteers in the medical organization, but was especially attached to one of them, Amit Man. Amit Man's father had died of cancer when she was fourteen, and the following year she began volunteering at the rescue organization service until she became a senior paramedic and the youngest instructor in the training course. Avia Hetzroni was her mentor and like a second father to her. When Kibbutz Be'eri needed a full-time paramedic, Avia Hetzroni knew whom to recommend. He persuaded the twenty-two-year-old to seize the opportunity to leave her mother's house for the first time.

Dozens of injured residents sought help from Avia Hetzroni that morning. But he was alone, bleeding to death after being shot by terrorists through his door.

He managed to take one call, from his sister's son, Sagi Sha-froni: "I ran through fire, my legs are completely burned, ev-erything's burning, and the skin's peeling open, my hands are burned too, what should I do?"

The Hetzroni-Shafroni family was also dispersed across dif-ferent houses in the kibbutz that morning. Ayala Hetzroni, Avia's sister, and his twin grandsons, Liel and Yanai, took shelter in one house. Sagi Shafroni, with his wife, Efrat, and their five-year-old daughter, Dror, were in a second. Their son, Tzur, who'd just celebrated his eighth birthday, stayed at his grandfather Ar-non's house with his uncle Omri Shafroni, who was visiting the kibbutz for the holiday and the boy's birthday. As the rockets started, Efrat decided in the heat of the moment to drive to be with Tzur, while Sagi would stay with their daughter, Dror.

"Dad, are they trying to kill us?" the five-year-old Dror whis-pered.

"Yes, but they won't succeed," Sagi answered as he bundled her up and went to hide with her under the bed.

Suddenly, bullets riddled the door to the children's room. Dror covered her ears to block out the shouts of "*Allah-hu Akbar.*"

Protected by a locked door that Efrat had insisted on install-ing years earlier—theirs might have been the only house with a proper lock—they thought they were safe.

They were still huddled under the bed when they smelled smoke and realized the house was on fire—the terrorists were intent on burning them alive.

"How will we escape, Dad?" Dror asked as her father stood up and opened the door to a wave of fire.

From the window Sagi saw the conflagration in the yard, but the flames were of a lesser intensity.

Wrapping Dror in a blanket, protecting her face with a pillow, he decided it was better to attempt escape than await their fate. "One, two, three—are you ready?"

"Ready."

Tearing out the window screens, he jumped through the window and remembered nothing of the fiery escape except Dror's words, "Your feet are on fire, Dad."

They dashed to the garden hose, only to find the water scalding. Ignoring his smoldering feet upon hearing shots, Sagi carried Dror to seek shelter in a neighbor's house. They eventually found a hiding place at another house, where Sagi concealed the diminutive Dror with laundry baskets and wrapped himself in laundry for camouflage.

As gunfire neared once more, Sagi was unable to run. He spotted a friend's bicycle with a child seat. Pedaling east, the father and daughter encountered some emergency squad members who directed them to the dental clinic where the injured were being treated.

As he started pedaling to the clinic, Dror warned him from the back seat, "Dad, Gazans," her term for Gazan Palestinians.

He glanced to the left of the clinic and saw a terrorist's motorcycle lying on its side.

As he pedaled in the opposite direction, Dror began to cry, "They told us to go to the clinic. Why aren't we going there?"

"This isn't the place for us. I'm taking us to a safer place," he responded. "We're going to see Mom and Tzur," thinking that if they were going to die, it would be better to die all together.

"Dad, are those the Gazans again?" Dror pointed out another group of terrorists, mere meters away.

He quickly veered right, toward his aunt Ayala Hatzroni's house, and briefly considered seeking refuge with her and the twelve-year-old twins, though ultimately he decided against it.

Meanwhile, inside the Hatzronis' house, the twins, Liel and Yanai, were terrified.

"What should we do? We hear Arabic," Liel said.

They reached out to their second uncle, Omri, Sagi's brother, who was sheltering with Efrat and Tzur at Omri and Sagi's father's house.

"Are they outside or inside? If they're outside, they've moved on," Omri attempted to reassure them.

"But what should we do?" Liel persisted.

"Hold the door handle tightly and don't let anyone in—but don't stand directly in front of the door," he advised. "Actually, stay under the window."

"We're on the bed; is that okay?"

"It's fine," he said.

"Call for help," Yanai suddenly blurted out.

"Sure," Omri promised, though he knew there was no one to call to save the children.

Ten minutes later, the twins called again.

"People with guns are still outside. Did you call for help? Did you make the call?"

"Yes, Yanai, help is on the way. Just hold on," he reassured them.

Sagi, having decided to head to his wife and son, kept pedaling; they managed to make it to his father's house without further incident.

Efrat quickly ushered him and Dror inside.

Five-year-old Dror told her eight-year-old brother, Tzur, about their house burning down: "The toys, too! They burned the toys!"

Ten minutes later, the twins tried to contact Omri again, but he didn't pick up—terrorists had already entered their house.

7

The children and Ayala were unable to defend themselves. Terrorists had taken them prisoner and brought them to a large nearby house belonging to their sixty-eight-year-old neighbor Pessy Cohen, who'd been hosting her sister Hana Siton and her family for the holiday.

The children passed the corpse of Yitzhak Siton, Hana's husband, who'd been murdered by the terrorists when they'd broken in.

The captives were brought to the dining room of Pessy's house and made to sit at an oversized dining table alongside their neighbors: seventy-five-year-old Chava Ben Ami, seventy-one-year-old Zeev Hakar, and sixty-eight-year-old Zehava Hakar, and the pair of thirteen-year-old twins, Liel and Yanai Hetzroni.

Several dozen terrorists walked around with weapons drawn, making phone calls, discussing plans.

8

For a whole hour Adi Dagan had managed to hold the door while the terrorists tried to open it. The terrorists knew their names and called out to them: "Adi and Hadas, come out, come out, don't be afraid."

Adi gripped the door handle tightly, and Hadas gripped Adi's arm; they were almost seventy years old but they still had their strength. Yasmin and Tal were hiding next to them in the wardrobe.

Suddenly there was an explosion, which blew the door straight off its hinges. Adi and Hadas, hurled backward, raised their hands in fear. In front of them were armed columns of

Hamas fighters with their guns drawn. Adi and Hadas were led outside, at gunpoint, from which vantage they surveyed the ruins of their home. Yasmin and Tal were found in the wardrobe and brought out after them. The Hamas fighters stripped Tal, searching him for weapons, and tied him up. They ordered Yasmin, who was wearing a miniskirt and halter top, to put on some of Adi's clothes, to cover her body. Speaking in Arabic and using hand gestures, the terrorists ordered the four of them to the tree-lined yard of Pessy Cohen's house. Gathered on the patio were their neighbors.

9

Dor Harari, the Dagans' son-in-law, a member of the kibbutz's emergency response squad, received a call from a friend of a friend, an air force pilot. The pilot put him on speaker in front of his squadron commander and asked him to describe the situation. Dor shouted into the phone, "Where's the army? Don't just send special units, send thousands of soldiers! There are hundreds of terrorists and we're just a few civilians with weapons!"

Elam Maor, another member of the kibbutz's emergency response squad, was moving from house to house at the same time, trying to save whoever he could.

He received a phone call from his cousin, who worked in the office of the prime minister. His cousin said, "I'm here with Prime Minister Benjamin Netanyahu and others. He wants a report from the ground. Can you speak?"

Elam spoke quickly, out of such a feeling of frustration that he was almost screaming: "Mr. Prime Minister, Kibbutz Be'eri is under attack by hundreds of terrorists. Hundreds. We are just a few people fighting, an emergency response squad, and some of our members have already been killed. Hundreds of terrorists are now attacking Be'eri and there's no one around to help. You need to send forces immediately."

"I understand," Netanyahu said. "Stand by."

10

Around noon, Raya Rotem heard shouts in Arabic coming from inside her house.

The girls, Hila Rotem and Emily Hand, were still in their pajamas and trying to hide under the couch when five terrorists entered the room with guns drawn: "You're going to Gaza!" they yelled in Arabic.

"Car! Car!" they kept saying in Arabic. Raya tried to explain that she didn't have a car, that most people in the kibbutz went on foot or by bike.

While the terrorists were searching the house for car keys, Raya managed to write to her brother, Yair, "We're being kidnapped."

Hila had time to take a small doll and Emily put on Hila's old flip-flops—she'd come for the sleepover barefoot.

"Go fast! Go fast!" the terrorists yelled. "You're our prisoners now."

The terrorists led Raya and the two girls on a circuitous route through the kibbutz, Raya going first, the girls behind her holding hands.

11

Eli Chresenti, a ninety-three-year-old kibbutz member, and Namisha Kolforat, his thirty-eight-year-old home-health aid, had been trying to fend off an attack, holding the door shut against the efforts of five terrorists. Finally, the terrorists broke in.

Namisha, a native of India, pleaded with them in English, "Don't shoot me, please don't shoot me. I'm not Israeli, I'm just a caregiver," and she showed them the cross she wore around her neck.

"Are you a Christian Jew?"

"Just a Christian."

"Go back to India," they told her and took her gold jewelry and the gold statues she had in her Hindu shrine, and then tied her up to her employer.

"Where is your army?" they asked. "Where is your Bibi?"

The elderly Eli remained calm. He reminded himself that he'd always had bad luck with this date, the seventh of October—a date he'd always associated with captivity. Fifty years prior, on October 7, 1973, the day after the outbreak of the Yom Kippur War, he was serving as an Israeli liaison officer to the United Nations at an observation post when he was taken prisoner by the Egyptians.

When the terrorists told him, "We're going to Gaza," he said, "Okay, no problem."

He didn't yet know that in the nearby houses, his ex-wife, Shoshana Chresenti, their daughter, Maayana Hershkovitz, and her husband, Noah Hershkovitz, had all already been murdered.

12

Raya Rotem and the girls Hila and Emily were brought into Eli Chresenti's house. One of the terrorists noticed that Hila was holding a doll and snatched it from her.

"Why do that?" Raya suddenly exploded, as if the taking of

the doll upset her more than their own abduction. "It's just a doll, a girl's doll, why do that?"

The terrorist pointed his gun at her. "Don't talk."

Eli Chresenti, Namisha Kolforat, Raya Rotem, Hila, and Emily sat in tense silence until the terrorists called them outside: the cars had arrived to take them to Gaza.

But there was a problem: there weren't enough seats, so the terrorists cut Eli and Namisha loose and loaded Raya, Hila, and Emily into a vehicle.

Raya and the girls were seated in the back, with one terrorist sitting on Raya's lap and another atop Emily, guns in their hands. The car started to move before the doors were shut.

They passed the bodies of kibbutz members, strewn along the roadside. The girls kept looking even though Raya told them not to.

They passed kibbutz buildings on fire and houses being looted of televisions and computers.

"Are you okay?" Hila whispered to Emily.

"Are they going to kill us?" Emily asked.

Hila said, "I think if they wanted to kill us we'd be dead by now."

Raya had hoped that upon leaving the kibbutz, or approaching the border fence, they'd be stopped by military forces. But there was no one at the border. They passed through the breached fence without hindrance. The terrorists covered their heads with a blanket, to prevent them from seeing where they were going, though it occasionally seemed that even the terrorists themselves didn't know, as Raya heard them arguing about their destination.

A mere fifteen minutes after they'd left the kibbutz, they were already hostages in Gaza.

13

Shachar Tzemach and Eitan Hadad of the kibbutz's emergency response squad had already killed a few dozen terrorists trying to infiltrate the clinic, yet more continued to approach. They'd been guarding the clinic for six hours and were starting to realize the army wasn't coming: they were the kibbutz's sole line of defense.

Shachar called his wife, Ofri, instructing her to barricade the entrance to their safe room with their refrigerator.

"Are you okay? Who's protecting you?" Dr. Daniel Levy's wife, Lehi, was getting concerned.

He assured her that he was safe "for now," protected by Shachar and Eitan.

"I love you," he wrote. "Hoping to survive this."

From the kibbutz mothers' group chat, Nirit learned that terrorists had broken into the home of her son's friend, where her son had been sleeping over. "They're at the door," the friend's mother wrote. "They're in the house." Nirit could only hope the woman would defend her son as if he were her own.

"What's going on there, Amit? Please update," wrote Haviva Man.

There were five sisters in the group chat: Haviva, Mery, Ruth, Lior, and Amit.

"They killed 2 more terrorists. I want to get out of here," replied the twenty-two-year-old paramedic.

"What about the injured?" asked Haviva.

"No good, there's no way to evacuate them. They're bleeding out here."

Yair Avital, suffering from his grenade wound, was bleeding and feeling cold, and there was nothing available to cover him; his condition was rapidly deteriorating. Nirit lay atop him for warmth and held his hands, encouraging him to talk about his family.

Gil's corpse remained on the floor and his phone kept buzzing with texts from worried friends and relatives.

14

The Tzemach and Shafroni families lived in the same building—a house subdivided to accommodate both families.

Doron and Shlomit Tzemach took refuge in their home, while the Shafroni brothers, along with their wives and children, hid in their father's house adjacent.

Doron and Shlomit Tzemach had secured their safe room using a walking stick to prevent entry: they didn't know how they managed to wedge the stick so well, but when the terrorists ransacked their home, the door held; the terrorists couldn't enter.

In the safe room of their home, the Shafroni family listened to the terrorists trying to break in; it seemed like they'd been firing at the door for hours. "I don't want to die young," eight-year-old Tzur was crying. "It's not fair, I just had my birthday."

His five-year-old sister, Dror, was already used to the shooting. Sagi found some sandals for his burned feet, in case they had to once again flee through the flames.

15

One block away, in Pessy Cohen's house, the twelve hostages were milling around the patio, watching one another, afraid to speak.

Yasmin Porat made eye contact with one of the terrorists—a man named Hassan who seemed to be their commander, or at least the oldest and most authoritative among them. She told him that if he intended to take all of them to Gaza, she had connections in the police and army; she could assist him in negotiations to allow him to take them to the Gaza Strip safely, without official interference.

The terrorists argued among themselves for a few minutes and then led Yasmin back to the Dagans' house, to the closet where she'd been hiding, to retrieve her phone, a Galaxy 22. Yasmin and the terrorists searched together but couldn't find it among all the rubble.

Back at Pessy Cohen's, the terrorists allowed Yasmin to dial 100 from a fellow hostage's phone.

"Police, shalom, Shiraz." A woman picked up at general police headquarters.

"Hello, Shiraz, this is Yasmin. I'm here at Kibbutz Be'eri with with fifty other hostages," Yasmin said, exaggerating the number of hostages, as the terrorists instructed her. "We're together with some friends of ours, Palestinians. And they want to free us . . . They want to get us out of here safely . . ."

Officer Shiraz tried to ask a few questions, but the terrorists became angry and demanded to speak with someone who spoke Arabic.

Once an Arabic-speaking officer came on the line, one of the terrorists took the phone and said, "I'm from the al-Qassam Brigade, Hamas. If you make trouble, I'll start killing hostages. I have fifty of them here."

"What's the problem?" the officer said. "You can tell me."

"The problem is that I want to take everyone to Gaza. Every time someone tries to shoot us on the way, I will kill one hostage. I'm leaving Be'eri. If you don't tell the army to allow us safe passage to Gaza, I'll kill all fifty of them."

16

A charged silence followed that phone call. Everyone seemed to be waiting for the army to arrive—the arrival was imminent, they thought. The hostages were hoping that the soldiers would free them, while the terrorists were hoping that the soldiers would allow them to return to Gaza. Hours passed, though, with no sign of any soldiers. It was only at 4:00 P.M. that jeeps began pulling up outside the house. Finally, the army was here, but they would satisfy the hopes of neither the captives nor the captors.

Hadas and Adi Dagan were standing in the yard of Pessy Cohen's house, next to a stone wall, when the shooting started. They ducked and tried to make themselves as small as possible as the bullets flew.

Tal writhed beside them on the ground, his hands still tied.

Yasmin went to hide behind the sofas against the wall as mortars crashed into the house.

Liel and Yanai shouted, "Please, save us, please."

The gunfire continued, with some terrorists returning the army's fire and others trying to hide.

After half an hour of heavy shooting, Hassan, the putative commander, called Yasmin over and told her he was going to surrender. He then undressed down to his underwear and tank top, grabbed Yasmin by the throat, and standing behind her and using her as a shield began pushing her and walking her out toward the soldiers who were shooting at the house.

As he pushed her and made her walk, he stripped off his tank top and underwear and stood behind Yasmin totally naked while she yelled to the soldier, "Stop. Stop shooting. I'm Israeli. I'm an Israeli citizen."

They reached the road and found twenty snipers. Hassan

shoved Yasmin toward them and was tackled and put in hand-cuffs.

17

Ohad Ben Ami, fifty-five, was a kibbutz accountant with a shock of gray hair who'd been taken from the safe room of his home; Itai Sabirsky, thirty-eight, had grown up at the kibbutz and returned for a holiday visit, only to be taken captive after his mother, Orit, was murdered in front of him; Noa Argamani, twenty-five, a strikingly beautiful young woman, was a stranger: she'd been kidnapped from the Nova party and brought here.

Into this small cramped room in a small cramped Gazan house came three more captives: Raya Rotem and the girls Hila and Emily, accompanied by six additional Hamas terrorists.

"I don't believe it," Ohad whispered to Raya. "They're taking children, too."

These newly arrived terrorists pointed guns at the gathered women and girls and ordered them to cover up: they didn't want to see any bare legs or arms.

The terrorists, who refused to reveal their names, asked their captives many questions:

"What's your name?"

"Raya."

"Where are you from?"

"From Kibbutz Be'eri."

"No, no—where are you from, really?"

"What do you mean?"

"Where were your parents born?"

"In Israel."

"So where were your grandparents born?"

"In Germany and Poland."

"We were in this country before you, understand? My grandfather is from Jaffa, so you will return to Poland and Germany and we will return to Jaffa. We will take this land back from you, and you Jews will return to the countries you came from. You do not belong here and you will not stay here."

In every room of the house they were in, there was a map of a Palestinian state stretching from the river to the sea: it was as if Israel didn't exist.

18

The gun battle at the clinic had been going on for seven hours.

Yair Avital's condition had momentarily stabilized, but Nirit, who'd been administering to him, felt that she was about to pass out.

She told Amit Man that she had to find a place, a bloodless spot, to rest for just a moment.

She stretched herself out on the bathroom floor.

A fighter jet flew over the kibbutz at that moment, and Shachar Tzemach told everyone in the clinic that they'd be rescued soon. He was able to get through to the jet's command center and asked them to order the jet to bomb the kindergarten in front of the clinic, which approximately fifty terrorists were using as cover. They had been firing from the kindergarten at the clinic all day. Shachar explained that no civilians were in danger; all residents of the kibbutz were hiding in their safe rooms, and at the clinic, the squad was running low on ammunition.

The commander replied that fighter jets did not have permission to operate inside a kibbutz. He said he was sorry and ended the call.

A few moments later, Shachar and Eitan ran out of bullets. Shachar had just written a text—"I need the army right now"— when his phone battery gave out.

He and Eitan retreated inside the clinic to inform the staff that the squad could no longer protect them. They told the staff to hide and keep quiet.

Amit hid in the clinic's kitchen, clutching a knife as the shots came closer and closer.

She wrote to her family, "They're back, they're attacking us. Please pray."

"Who's back? Who's attacking?"

"The terrorists, they're here."

"Hide, Amitush," wrote her sister Lior.

"Play dead, Amitush," her sister Haviva wrote. "Put some blood on yourself and play dead."

Six or seven grenades were tossed into the clinic. After they exploded, the terrorists followed.

"*Itbach al Yehud*"—"Kill the Jews"—was yelled again and again between the bursts of gunfire.

Shachar told Amit they should try to surrender. He stood up, raised his hands, and said in English, "I am not your enemy. Please, let's all just go back home."

He died in a storm of bullets.

Amit was hit in the leg. She managed to apply a tourniquet to herself, but the terrorists returned. She was shot in the head.

Nirit sent her partner, Einat, a farewell message from the bathroom floor: "It's all over for me. I love you. You're my whole life."

Einat answered, "You made my life the best it could be."

Nirit closed her eyes and waited.

Yair Avital hid inside a kitchen cupboard, soaked in his own blood, trying not to breathe.

From their hiding places, the surviving staff of the clinic heard the terrorists dragging the bodies of their companions down the halls, stabbing them repeatedly, cutting off body parts, making phone calls and laughing.

Shachar Tzemach, Eitan Hadad, Dr. Daniel Levy, Amit Man— all murdered.

19

Israeli troops gathered in front of Pessy Cohen's house. They gave Hassan a megaphone and forced him to call on his fellow terrorists to surrender. Hassan addressed the terrorists by name, asking them to leave with the hostages. The terrorists did not respond but merely continued to shoot and throw grenades.

Yasmin, who was standing with the soldiers, noticed that they were bringing a tank.

"Won't that put the hostages in danger?" she asked one of the soldiers, who told her, "No. It'll just take down the walls on the side."

The Israeli tank fired two shells toward the house.

In the aftermath of the impacts, Hadas Dagan got the idea that she was injured, but she soon realized that the blood covering her was not her own—it was her husband, Adi's. She didn't know if it was caused by the tank fire or by earlier shooting, but there appeared to be a hole in Adi's main artery, which she tried to block with her thumb. But too much blood was gushing and soon her husband was dead. Flashlights were shining and her husband was dead. Soldiers were swarming and her husband was dead. She was being lifted and taken away shrieking and her husband was dead: the man she'd loved more than life.

Adi Dagan; Pessy Cohen and her sister Hana Siton; Hana's

husband, Yitzhak Siton; Hana and Yitzchak's son Tal Siton; Tal Katz; Ayala Hetzroni and the children of her niece, Liel Hetzroni and Yanai Hetzroni; Chava ben Ami; Ze'ev and Zaveh Heker; and Sohib Abu Amar (an Arab Israeli taken by Hamas from the Nova party and forced to serve as an interpreter)—all of the hostages at Pessy Cohen's house save Hadas Dagan and Yasmin Porat were killed along with all the terrorists, though it's impossible to know who killed who.

20

"IDF! IDF! Is anyone here?"

In the afternoon, voices in Hebrew were finally heard inside the clinic.

Nirit, still sitting on the bathroom floor, did not respond; she almost didn't believe it.

"Paratroopers 890, is anyone here?"

Nirit slowly opened the bathroom door and called out, "Don't shoot! I'm an Israeli!"

In the clinic's kitchen, Yair emerged from the blood-soaked cupboard. They were the clinic's only survivors.

21

At the same time, early evening, the house of Shlomit and Doron Tzemach had been commandeered for use as a rescue headquarters by the army. Officers asked Doron to call his neighbors, to inform them that the army had arrived.

One by one, he called his neighbors. Noa Levy came over to the house, but without her husband, Roni.

"Where is he?" Doron asked.

She didn't have to answer.

Behind Noa Levy came an old man, Yitzchak Becher.

"And where's your wife?" Doron asked.

"In Gaza or in the sky."

22

During the first three days of captivity, the hostages were moved nightly, from one falling-down house to another. The terrorists dressed them in hijabs that covered their bodies and hair, and led them by foot through dark alleys. At the third house, a dilapidated two-floor building, they stayed.

They were told a Palestinian family lived upstairs. The hostages stayed downstairs, locked in a single room.

There were five remaining: Raya Rotem, Hila Rotem, Emily Hand, Itai Sabirsky, and Noa Argamani. Ohad Ben Ami had been taken somewhere else; they didn't know where.

Five Hamas fighters guarded them around the clock, with their weapons drawn. Two of them were regulars, the other three rotated.

The regulars told them to call them Abu Khaled and Abu Al Walid, but the hostages called them "the religious one" and "the fat one" among themselves.

They all shared one tiny room, pitch-black.

Five thin mattresses lay on the floor, without any bedding. The hostages could sit or lie down, as they wished.

It was hot, very hot.

Food was pita, a dwindling supply. They often had to split two cucumbers or a single orange among five people. Rarely there were canned beans and cheese. The hostages called the man who arrived every few days to deliver this food "Santa Claus" and "Uncle Sam": he was their sole link to the outside world.

There was almost no drinking water, and sometimes the water they had was dirty, as if from a polluted well. The hostages waited until evening to drink, afraid to finish the day's supply too soon.

Once a week they could take a bath in a tub that was sometimes filled with boiling water from a kettle, and at other times was freezing.

There was no water in the toilet, so it couldn't be flushed. The smell was unbearable. The girls were afraid to go to the bathroom alone.

Everyone suffered from lice and fleas but tried to hide their itching from the terrorists.

Sometimes the terrorists would call the girls into the next room alone.

They made the girls sit in front of them and look them in the eyes while they held guns or knives in front of their faces.

Occasionally, they spoke sentences in Arabic and ordered the girls to repeat them back.

After the girls obeyed, saying words they did not understand, the terrorists informed them that they'd converted to Islam. They were Muslims now.

Back in the room with the rest of the hostages, Raya had to explain that the men were lying, that changing your religion wasn't as easy as that.

Raya told the girls to keep their pajamas on, under their clothes, so they had another layer atop their underwear. She kept asking herself whether the terrorists would prefer to rape an eight-year-old girl or a thirteen-year-old girl, soon to be a teenager?

The girls competed for Raya's attention. Hila kept asking for hugs. Afraid that Emily would feel left out, Raya kept her daughter at a distance. After a few days of this, Hila asked, "Mom, why won't you hug me anymore?"

Raya then decided to share her hugs equally, spending a few minutes holding Hila and then a few minutes holding Emily.

23

On the day after the massacre, in a hotel on the Dead Sea to which the survivors of Kibbutz Be'eri had been evacuated, Thomas Hand and Yair Rotem were told: Emily's body was found in the kibbutz.

Hila's body was found in the kibbutz.

There was still no official identification, they were told, but people from the kibbutz had recognized the bodies of the girls.

Thomas Hand was interviewed on CNN about Emily's death, and he tearfully recounted the moment he learned his daughter was killed. "They said: 'We found Emily, she's dead,' and I said, 'Yes, yes,' and I smiled, because that was the best news of the possibilities I knew. It's either she's dead or she's been kidnapped to Gaza. And if you know what they do to people in Gaza—it's worse than death. So death was a blessing."

Unlike Thomas Hand, Yair Rotem kept the news of his niece's death to himself. A part of him refused to believe it.

After Vivian Silver's body wasn't found in her burned house, her relatives and friends, both Israeli and Palestinian, led an international campaign seeking her release from captivity. They hoped that her long record of service to the people of Gaza might earn her some reprieve.

24

They weren't allowed to listen to the radio or watch television; they didn't know if anyone was looking for them, or even if there was anyone left to look for them. They knew nothing. Neither Emily nor Hila knew they were dead.

There was a single window of frosted glass set into the middle of the wall of the small room. Through it, they could see when the sun rose and when it set, but little else. Between the hours of dawn and dusk, they slept, being unable to sleep at night: they were too terrified.

The most important thing was to stay still. Quiet and still. This was easier for adults, harder for children.

Emily and Hila invented games: ladders and snakes, a game with dice made from crumpled paper, alphabet city (name a city that begins with A, the next person has to name a city that begins with B . . .).

If the terrorists caught the girls laughing or talking loudly they'd be called to the living room and punished.

The terrorists would hold a knife to them and say, "You'll be quiet from now on or else."

They'd be punished even if they cried.

Emily asked every few days, "Is my father dead or alive?"

Her fellow hostages shushed her.

Noa Argamani and Itai Sabirsky were tired, insomniac. They told the girls to stop the noise: they were going to get everyone killed.

Itai spoke to Noa about his father, who'd been hiding in another house. Itai was afraid he was dead. He kept having flashbacks to his mother's murder.

Noa, an only child, told Itai about her own mother, who had

terminal cancer. She also spoke about her boyfriend, who'd been kidnapped from the Nova festival alongside her but was separated from her by the kidnappers.

Sometimes the terrorists separated Itai and Noa—they didn't like seeing a young man sitting next to a young woman.

25

Toward the end of October, representatives from IDF intelligence summoned Yair Rotem to a meeting. He was told that a mistake had been made, and new intelligence gathered from multiple sources indicated that Raya, Hila, and Emily were still alive in Gaza.

In fact, this "new intelligence" came from Namisha Kolforat, the Indian caregiver of ninety-three-year-old Eli Chresenti who, after being spared by the terrorists, spread the news that she'd witnessed the kidnapping of three females with her own eyes: one older woman and two girls. It was Thomas Hand himself who relayed this information to the authorities.

26

At the end of October, the noises changed: the hostages started hearing more and more explosions, and they were getting closer.

The IDF had entered Gaza.

Soon after the start of the ground operation, the terrorists found a television and connected it to a car battery. Soon they were watching homes destroyed by the IDF, the images of dead children and mourning mothers.

"What do you say to that?" the terrorists asked their hostages.

"We apologize."

"We are sorry."

"We don't want anyone to die."

What they didn't say was that they were often more terrified by the IDF bombing than by their captors.

There were bombs and mortar fire—the worst of it at night. With each major explosion, the girls would jump to their mattresses; they'd try to hide under their mattresses, and the terrorists would laugh: "That mattress won't help. A direct hit makes a crater up to ten meters underground."

One day, the window in the room, their only source of light through its frosted glass, shattered in the aftershock of a blast. The terrorists covered the empty window frame with a plastic tarp and blocked it with three sofas, cutting off all light and forcing the hostages to remain even quieter so no one on the street could hear them.

After one particularly heavy stretch of bombing, the food distributor "Santa Claus" (or "Uncle Sam") didn't show up for a few days. The hostages went hungry. When he finally arrived, in bloodstained clothes, he said that his family had been killed in a bombing.

Another day, the terrorists shaved Itai's beard and dressed him in their clothes, perhaps planning to use him as a decoy.

Itai told Raya that if Israeli soldiers came, she had to vouch for him and yell that he was an Israeli so that he wouldn't be killed. He reminded her of this daily.

27

Massive protests, in which tens of thousands of Israelis demanded the immediate return of all the hostages held in Gaza, unfolded throughout Israel. Tel Aviv Museum square was renamed "Square of the Hostages," and every Sabbath it was packed with protestors, speakers, Israeli and international celebrities, all challenging the government to bring the hostages home.

In London, Thomas Hand held a press conference at which he expressed deep concern for his daughter's well-being: "I don't know what condition she's going to be in, but she's going to be very broken mentally and physically, and we'll have to address that. She must be asking every day: 'Where's my daddy? Why didn't he come to save me?'"

28

The terrorists told their hostages that negotiations with the Qataris and the Americans were faltering, all due to Netanyahu, who didn't care whether they lived or died. Every time the terrorists said "Netanyahu" or "Ben Gvir" (the minister of national security), they spit. And yet they constantly wanted to talk politics with their hostages. They explained that they were angry with Netanyahu and Ben Gvir—"the crazy people," they called them—and that every time they'd get angry with "the crazy people" again, they'd return to Be'eri, until they finished what they started.

Sometimes the captives were asked to sit in front of a blank wall and a camera, or a phone on camera mode; they were told to make a *V* sign with their fingers and tell the world that they were being treated well and that it was up to Netanyahu to release them.

Emily was occasionally told that because she also had Irish citizenship, she would be released alone before everyone else. The terrorists seemed to enjoy how every time they said this,

Emily started crying: she wanted to stay; she didn't want to be alone. Raya would cradle her in her arms, promising her that they'd stay together. "If you make it out of here," the terrorists kept warning them, "don't ever go back to Be'eri. If you do, we'll return."

29

On November 13, the remains of Vivian Silver's body were identified in the safe room where she'd been hiding. She hadn't been kidnapped after all, but murdered that day in her home.

Her funeral was the largest gathering of Jews and Arabs since the outbreak of the war.

Hundreds showed up and heard Yonatan deliver a eulogy that addressed his mother directly, promising her that "now we'll try even harder to bring about the tomorrow you always talked about. . . . With your passing, I fell in love all over again with the words *peace*, *equality*, and *brotherhood*."

Before he recited the kaddish prayer, he read a statement from a friend in the Gaza Strip—the very friend who was the first to call Vivian to warn her of the attacks:

"Vivian was like a sister to me. I'm very sorry that on that occasion I didn't tell her how much I loved her."

A week later, the remains of Liel Hetzroni were found in the same place where the remains of his twin, Yanai, had previously been found—nearby where the body of their grandfather's sister, Ayala, was also recovered.

Both Vivian's and Liel's bodies were identified by archaeologists employed by the Antiquities Authority, who'd been recruited for their expertise at locating human remains.

30

October 8, Sunday
October 9, Monday
October 10, Tuesday

Each morning, the five abductees together said the date and the day of the week to themselves and to one another, so as not to lose track of time.

October 11, Wednesday
October 12, Thursday
October 13, Friday
October 14, Saturday
October 15, Sunday
October 16, Monday
October 17, Tuesday

The hostages celebrated Noa's twenty-sixth birthday, whispering, "Happy birthday, Noa."

"I should be in class at Ben Gurion University right now," she said.

October 18, Wednesday
October 19, Thursday
October 20, Friday
October 21, Saturday
October 22, Sunday
October 23, Monday
October 24, Tuesday

October 25, Wednesday
October 26, Thursday
October 27, Friday
October 28, Saturday
October 29, Sunday
October 30, Monday
October 31, Tuesday
November 1, Wednesday
November 2, Thursday
November 3, Friday
November 4, Saturday
November 5, Sunday
November 6, Monday
November 7, Tuesday
November 8, Wednesday
November 9, Thursday
November 10, Friday
November 11, Saturday
November 12, Sunday
November 13, Monday
November 14, Tuesday
November 15, Wednesday
November 16, Thursday

31

November 17, Friday: after forty-two days of captivity the hostages celebrated Emily's ninth birthday. Hila made a "Mazel Tov" sign out of letters she'd managed to make out of hoarded modeling putty. The terrorists gave Emily the crumbs of a *sfenj*, a type of donut they'd fried for themselves.

In Tel Aviv, pink balloons were released into the sky to mark the occasion.

In New York, a demonstration had formed in front of the private residence of UN secretary general António Guterres. When he left for work, the crowd yelled and sang "Happy Birthday" to Emily in Hebrew and English.

In London, a table was set up with cupcakes.

Elsewhere in London, and around the world, massive demonstrations were erupting, calling to "Liberate Palestine" and "Decolonize the Zionist Entity."

November 18, Saturday
November 19, Sunday
November 20, Monday
November 21, Tuesday
November 22, Wednesday

A cease-fire agreement between Israel and Hamas was reached after negotiations mediated by Qatar, with Hamas pledging to release ten hostages per day.

November 23, Thursday
November 24, Friday

32

On Saturday, November 25, Raya Rotem sensed that something was about to happen. She detected a change in her captors' behavior. The men kept looking through the girls' clothing and talking among themselves in worried tones.

Though it wasn't the usual bath time, they asked her to wash the girls in the tub.

"What about me?" she asked.

"You don't need to bathe, just them."

"I think they're going to take the girls," she whispered to Noa Argamani.

"Why?" Noa said. "There's no way they're going to separate you."

Raya felt tense all day. At noon, she reminded Hila about the half sister she had through her father; she made Hila remember and repeat the half sister's name and address, wanting to prepare her daughter for a situation in which her father was dead.

At nine in the evening, when Raya returned from a quick trip to the bathroom, she found Noa helping the girls put on sandals.

"What's going on here?"

"We're taking the girls now," the terrorists answered.

"But what about me?"

"You stay."

She was allowed to give the girls a quick hug.

"Don't worry, I'm fine," Hila reassured her. Hila also reassured Emily, who was afraid to be with the terrorists without an adult. The terrorists took the girls and left.

The girls left in their pajamas, holding hands, and boarded Red Cross vehicles.

This was the first time, after nearly two months in captivity, that Raya Rotem broke down in tears.

Thomas Hand and Yair Rotem were waiting for the girls at the Kerem Shalom border crossing.

As part of its agreement with Israel, Hamas had pledged not to separate children from their mothers. When they were criticized for leaving Raya in captivity, they claimed that they hadn't been able to find her.

33

On the day after the release of Hila Rotem and Emily Hand, the terrorists split up the remaining hostages, taking Noa to one place and Raya and Itai to another.

Raya and Itai were put inside a small asbestos shed, dark and cold. All night they heard bombing, shooting, sirens.

In the days of their original captivity, they hadn't talked much. She'd spent most of her time with the girls, while he had latched on to Noa. Now they had time to get to know each other. Raya and Itai spoke about the kibbutz, about its families, about death.

Itai asked Raya, if she were released before him, to tell his sister, Merav, that he was alive. He was sure Merav would do whatever she could to get him home. She was his only close relative who he was sure was alive.

After several sleepless nights together, a few terrorists came and took Raya, leaving Itai alone. They brought Raya to an abandoned building and sat her on a chair against a wall. She was sure she was about to be executed, but then another hostage was put in the room with her, and they were moved again, together.

In another building, they were joined by at least ten other hostages: children, mothers, a few non-Israelis. A strangely happy mood descended on the gathering. Everyone was giddy, including the terrorists, who handed out food and water and played cards with the hostages, taking photos and videos of them eating and drinking.

Once the terrorists announced that a deal had come through,

Raya was incredulous. She experienced no relief, no waning of fear. She was still surrounded by terrorists with guns. Gazans along the route swarmed the ambulance in which she was traveling: they jumped on its back; they shook its sides. She only managed to get control over her breathing once the ambulance stopped at the crossing at Kerem Shalom: back to Israel, back to life, neither the same as she'd left it.

34

Hila waited for her mother at Kerem Shalom, alongside doctors and psychologists.

Food, drink, clothes, phones, Hebrew—it was overwhelming.

Raya was afraid to ask the question she'd been preparing to ask for fifty-three days: "Is my brother Yair alive?"

The answer was yes. "He's alive. He's healthy."

35

In mid-January 2024, Hamas published a video of Itai Sabirsky, in which he was made to beg Netanyahu to stop the war: "Netanyahu, please stop the war. Bring us home."

At the end of the video, Hamas announced that in the next video, it would provide an update on Itai's fate.

The following day, that video came—a video in which Noa Argamani was made to announce Itai's death:

"I was in a building. It was bombed by an IDF airstrike, an F16 fighter jet. Three rockets were fired. Two of the rockets exploded; the other didn't. We were in the building with al-Qassam soldiers and three hostages: I, Noa Argamani, along with Itai Sabirsky, and Yossef Sharabi.

"After the building we were in was hit, we were all buried under the rubble. Al-Qassam soldiers saved my life, and Itai's, too;
unfortunately, we were not able to save Yossi's. . . . After many
days . . . after two nights, Itai and I were relocated to another
place. While we were being transported, Itai was hit by an IDF
airstrike. He did not survive."

IDF spokesman Daniel Hagari accused Hamas of lying: "Itai
was not exposed to fire from our forces—that is a lie. The building they were in was not targeted, nor was it ever bombed by our
forces."

The army informed Itai's sister, Merav Sabirsky, that as Israeli soldiers approached the building where he was being held,
Itai tried to escape and was shot by one of his captors. Merav
had already lost her mother and father in the attacks of 10/7, and
now she'd lost her brother, too, on the eve of his hundredth day
in captivity.

36

At the funeral of Adi Dagan, in the temporary cemetery at Kibbutz Revivim, where Be'eri's victims were provisionally buried
until the cemetery of Be'eri could be reopened and the kibbutz
once again made habitable, Hadas Dagan paid tribute to her
husband:

"The love of my life was murdered in my arms, my home was
burned to the ground, and everything I ever believed in, cham-
pioned, and lived for, had its light trampled by unimaginable
evil and inhuman cruelty. But I have four children and eleven
grandchildren who managed to survive the inferno, and I have a
strong community . . ."

At the end of the ceremony, Hadas met Yael Noy, CEO of On

the Way to Recovery, the volunteer group that transports Palestinians to and from hospital treatment in Israel.

"I apologize," Hadas told her. "I'm not really in a position to volunteer anytime soon. I hope you understand. But please, keep making those drives; it's important."

Kathmandu
to Kibbutz Alumim

Interrogation cell of the IDF Intelligence Corps, Unit 504 | October 15

The young man answered the investigators' questions in a calm tone, gesturing with his hands for emphasis.

He had short black hair and a beard, and was wearing a white jumpsuit issued by the Israeli authorities. He appeared to be in his late twenties, just a few years older than his victims. Born in Gaza, he'd worked as a self-proclaimed "combat engineer" and soldier in one of Hamas's ground battalions. On October 7, he was commanded, along with more than twenty others, to "infiltrate Kibbutz Alumim" with explicit orders to "kill everyone you encounter." He'd carried out his orders.

The operation was called Al-Aqsa Flood—a name honoring the Al-Aqsa mosque built atop the ruins of what Jews call the Temple Mount in Jerusalem. The protection of this site—and the eradication of Jewish claims to it—is a prime tenet of Hamas's ideology. The young man being interrogated had been prepared to die in defense of a mosque he had never visited.

A week after Al-Aqsa Flood, he sat in a wooden chair facing an investigator and recounted the operation in his own words:

Prisoner: "All the battalions were to take part in the raid. The plan was for jeeps to attack the kibbutz. We were on the jeeps and we disembarked—there were people [from Hamas] who went in advance to open the gates. Everything was coordinated. We arrived at the kibbutzim in the jeeps, we opened the rooms, the houses, and started to raid them, going room by room, one after the other, until we finished."

Investigator: "But what did you do in those rooms?"

Prisoner: [pantomiming firing a gun] "Threw grenades and opened fire."

Investigator: "But what was the goal?"

Prisoner: "To kill."

Investigator: "To kill whom?"

Prisoner: "Everyone who was in the room."

Investigator: "What does that mean?"

Prisoner: "Women, children, everyone. Anyone who was in the house."

Investigator: "You told me there was someone [a fellow Hamas terrorist] who asked how you were supposed to get back to Gaza?"

Prisoner: "Right."

Investigator: "And what was he told?"

Prisoner: "Figure it out yourself. Meaning you're going and there's no coming back."

Investigator: "Your sheikh gave you a sermon telling you that you have to kill everyone?"

Prisoner: "The battalion commander told us to kill, stomp on their heads, chop off their legs, whatever."

These orders were not only in words but also in writing. They were concise and clear, printed on a white page with colored section headings in green and orange. Detailed maps of Kibbutz Alumim were attached. The mission statement read: "Attack Kibbutz Alumim with the goal of inflicting as many casualties as possible, taking hostages, and holding ground within the kibbutz until further instructions are received." The assigned tasks included: "Liquidate and secure the department's area of responsibility, and collect the hostages. Ensure external security and protect the perimeter of the kibbutz against any IDF forces' attempts to breach it."

Kibbutz Alumim, Kitchen | October 7

When the thirst became stronger than the pain, they drank one another's urine.

They were just horribly, desperately thirsty.

"Prabin, how bad is your leg?"

"It's bad. I can't feel much of it. And you, Himanchal?"

"You see the holes in my chest and shoulder, right? It's getting harder to breathe."

"We need water. I can't bear this."

Struggling, Himanchal rose from their hiding spot under a cheap wooden table to fetch water. As he moved, he aggravated his chest wound and lost more blood. He managed to collect some water in a shallow plate, but half of it spilled on the kitchen floor as he returned to Prabin.

It wasn't enough. Prabin's throat was parched and he was writhing in agony.

"Pramod, do you have any water to give me? I beg you."

Pramod didn't respond. Hidden under the sink in a small plumbing cabinet, he was the only student unharmed, having avoided being seen by the Hamas shooters.

"Pramod, there's water in the sink above you. I beg you, I can't move to get it. I'm so thirsty I might scream, and they'll come again and finish us off."

He pleaded again and again, until Pramod made a small hole in the sink pipe and collected some murky water in a pot. Extending his hand from the cabinet, Pramod whispered, "Here, this is all we have."

Prabin lapped up the mixture of water and urine from the pot like a dog.

His roommates, Rajan and Prabesh, lay dead under the table. They'd been killed immediately. Padam, a fourth roommate, took longer to die. "I am dying, *bhauju*," he had managed to send in a short text message to his sister-in-law, then pleaded with his friends to help him: "Kill me. I can't stand this anymore. Kill me with a knife if you can."

"Please, friend, bear this pain. The police will come for us," Himanchal said, though he, too, believed they were doomed. Beneath the table, he noticed his own breathing growing heavier and heavier, matching the heavy breathing of Padam and Prabin.

In the moment he was shot, Himanchal felt nothing—he went numb. He watched the bullets tear his flesh, but there was a disconnect between what his eyes saw and what his body felt. It took a long minute until the pain hit him. It crept up on him, gradually intensifying, until it suffused his entire body.

Covered in blood and sweat, Prabin recorded a short video of himself: "My mother is very sick. Please save her. I think I'm going to die."

They were among the only students left alive from their cohort, 4,500 kilometers from their home in Nepal.

Tribhuvan International Airport, Kathmandu | September 13

Himanchal Kattel, a twenty-five-year-old from a small village in the mountains of Gorkha, sported a large red *tika* on his forehead when he arrived at the Tribhuvan International Airport in Kathmandu. This was a blessing from his older sister, Niruta. He was the youngest of four siblings.

All seventeen students awaiting their midnight flight were adorned with *tikas*, tokens of pride and blessings from their families. In Nepali culture, they serve as good-luck charms and vouchsafes for significant journeys. Many parents had come to the airport, some in tears, many bearing gifts. It was a long goodbye—their children were leaving for eleven months.

These students were part of a labor force of guest workers in Israeli agriculture, replacing the Palestinian laborers who for decades themselves replaced the initial Israeli farmers. In the first two decades of Israel's existence, when an ethos of back-to-the-land self-reliance played a crucial role in shaping a new identity, 15 percent of Israel's population were proud young farmers cultivating their own crops.

The disappearance of Israelis from Israeli agriculture started after the Six-Day War, when local farmers began employing Palestinians from Gaza and the occupied territories of the West Bank and East Jerusalem. The government itself partially encouraged this influx, hoping to prevent uprisings by providing economic incentives. By the mid-1980s, more than one hundred thousand Palestinians were employed within the borders of Israel, many of them in agriculture. The twenty years of Palestinian presence in Israeli agriculture changed with the First Intifada, when Israel began restricting the entry of Palestinian workers due to security concerns about terror attacks and began seeking an inexpensive workforce sourced from countries uninvolved in the local conflict. Approximately twenty thousand Palestinians still received work permits in agriculture, but Thais, and other foreigners like Himanchal and Prabin, were the main solution—young people who were willing to make the trip for the money, as well as for the education: they were supposed to earn more in one year in Israel than they'd earn in several in Nepal, as well as gain skills that would advance their careers.

The group of seventeen students had all been accepted into what they thought to be a desirable and exclusive university program called Learn and Earn, combining high wages (by Nepalese standards) with classes in high-tech agriculture. Aged between twenty-two and twenty-five, most of the students had been raised in poverty. Prabin Dangi, twenty-four, was hoping to support his chronically ill mother but found that despite his education, good jobs in Nepal were scarce. This was a common dilemma in his family—one of his brothers was working in Dubai and another in Saudi Arabia for the same reason. His mother pleaded with him, her youngest son, not to leave, but he was determined to provide her with the best possible care. Prabesh Bhandari, twenty-four, aimed to save enough money to build a house and a farm in Nepal and employ his entire family. Rajan Phulara, twenty-three, wanted to use the money he'd earn and the experience he'd acquire to take the civil service exam in Nepal. Ashish Chaudhary, twenty-five, wanted to become an agriculturist and open his own farm. Ananda Sah, twenty-five, had promised his grandmother that he'd build a house for her. Dipesh Raj Bista, twenty-four, was the sole supporter of his family after the death of his father, and planned to finance his brother's medical studies. Bipin Joshi, twenty-three, wanted to learn advanced agricultural techniques that he could apply back home. For months after he finished his undergraduate studies, he couldn't decide on the best next step. When he first enrolled in the Learn and Earn program, he wasn't supposed to be sent to the Gaza border, but he was relieved to be assigned there with Himanchal, his best friend and roommate from college.

The group was sent to a classic "old-style" kibbutz named Alumim, where they shared responsibilities and lived communally. The kibbutz population and founders were a mixture of religious Jewish immigrants from Arab countries, members of the UK's largest Orthodox Jewish youth movement, agricultural workers from Thailand—a community of five hundred people—and now, them as well.

They arrived in Israel in mid-September: warm, sunny days.

Kibbutz Alumim | September 14 to October 6

Soon after they arrived in Israel, the students' expectations collided with reality.

Their accommodations consisted of small cramped rooms equipped with bunk beds to maximize space. They ate separately from the rest of the kibbutz, preparing their own meals in a modest gray kitchen stocked with spices they'd brought from home: coriander, cumin, turmeric, various chilis, along with mango pickles, enough to last for several months. Their days began around 4 A.M., when they'd gather in the kitchen to cook the lunch they'd bring with them to the fields—making ample use of the kibbutz's industrial-sized sacks of Persian rice—before heading out to do arduous physical labor under the sun, which typically lasted until approximately 4 P.M.

Prabin, Padam, and Rajan were responsible for managing the kibbutz's irrigation system. Their duties included carrying heavy pipes out to the fields, assembling and connecting them to the irrigation system, and fixing malfunctions.

Himanchal and Bipin worked together in the orchards, trimming trees and picking and packing pomelos and oranges. The work was simple, not technically advanced; it was difficult for them to ignore their growing sense of disappointment.

Foreign workers and students working in Israeli agriculture years before them had already raised complaints about exploitative labor practices and living conditions. Despite this, many did not seek legal redress, because they were still earning several times what they could earn at home. Each evening of the three weeks the Nepalese cohort spent in Israel, many students called home, reassuring their families that their time in Israel, though draining, was a wise investment in their futures.

They clung to the hope that their situation would improve once the university opened in October—the "learn" portion of the program, which involved attending classes at Ben Gurion University of the Negev once a week.

On October 3, an earthquake struck Nepal. Padam Thapa was anxious when he called home on October 6. His sister-in-law, Mekhu Adhikari, told him about the frightening aftershocks. Ganesh Nepali urged his elder brother to look after their parents and stay safe, as their family home had sustained structural damage.

Kibbutz Alumim,
the Foreign Workers Zone | October 7

Himanchal had stayed up until 3 A.M., engrossed in the final season of *Vikings* on Netflix. Saturdays offered the only chance for sleeping in.

Drifting off with his earphones in, he didn't hear the sirens.

At 6:30 A.M., Bipin woke Himanchal, urging, "We need to get to the shelter quickly."

In the other room, Prabin, still half-dressed, rushed to the bunker, witnessing rockets slicing through the sky.

The seventeen students were confined in the open-door shelter for more than an hour, waiting for instructions. This was the first missile attack they'd ever experienced. They'd been reassured before that rocket attacks from Gaza were common but rarely harmful and told that staying inside a shelter would keep them safe. To pass the time, they divided into teams, playing Ludo on their phones.

Meanwhile, Rafi, a kibbutz member and the security officer of the Sdot Negev Regional Council, was worried: the sheer number of missiles being fired was unusual. He headed to the council's headquarters to activate the emergency center. En route, he was warned at the Re'im intersection about the presence of terrorists nearby and soon after received an alert about terrorists approaching the gate of his home, Kibbutz Alumim. He set about notifying the dozen young men who composed the kibbutz's emergency response squad. Some of these men—kibbutz members and civilians all—were roused from their beds; others were pulled away from morning coffee and breakfast. By 6:45, they were armed and ready. At 7:00, about twenty Hamas terrorists were at the kibbutz gate.

Kibbutz emergency response squads are all-volunteer groups

tasked with securing and protecting kibbutzim in the event of emergencies before the arrival of the police or the army. In theory, a kibbutz's emergency response squad should never be left alone with an immediate threat for more than a few minutes, but that day the young men of the emergency response squad of Kibbutz Alumim were left alone for hours, trying to prevent the terrorists from reaching the kibbutz's residential area.

As some kibbutz members went to defend the gate and others went to hide, the Nepalese students remained unaware of the invasion. No one told them that terrorists riding motorcycles and mopeds were firing RPGs at the kibbutz. They assumed the noises they heard were from the missiles alone.

The terrorists, having been repelled from the gate, went looking for another target. They found the workers' quarters, near the cows and orchards.

From their shelter, the students heard loud Arabic being spoken by the approaching terrorists. Thinking the Arabic was Hebrew, they were relieved: someone had come to help them.

Dipesh Raj Bista stepped out of the shelter, followed by Ganesh Nepali, who just needed to use the restroom.

Outside the shelter, they were met by two men in black, pointing guns at them.

Realizing these weren't kibbutz members, Dipesh Raj Bista yelled, "We are Nepalese!"

They were killed on the spot.

Soon after, a grenade was thrown into the shelter where the fifteen other students were hiding. Bipin immediately realized what happened and threw the grenade back out. However, he couldn't catch another grenade that followed, and five of the students were injured. Ananda Sah, severely bleeding, clutched a pillow to stifle his screams. Lokendra Singh Dhami, also bleeding, whispered his love for his wife, his five-year-old daughter, and his two-year-old son.

Prabin, Himanchal, and Bipin weren't hurt. They had huddled in a corner of the room, squeezing together so tightly that it was hard to breathe.

Together, they called one of their bosses, pleading, "Please help us, we're in trouble."

The response was short: "I'm so sorry, I can't help you. There are terrorists attacking all over. I'm hiding, too."

Narayan Prasad Neupane wasn't as gravely injured as the others: despite having lost three toes, he could still walk. He happened to have remembered the number of the Israeli emergency medical services and now called for an ambulance. The operator, speaking English, assured him that help would arrive.

Soon after, two men in blue uniforms entered the shelter.

"Please don't hurt us," the few students still alive begged.

"We're the police, the Israeli police," the men assured them.

"Please, take us to a hospital. . . . These people are dying. . . . Get us out of here."

"There are still terrorists outside," the police said. "It's impossible to move you now, but we'll be back. Everyone who can walk, you need to move to a different place; it's not safe in the shelter. Go to the kitchen or to your room."

"And leave the wounded here?"

They had no choice.

Bipin, Himanchal, Rajan, Prabin, Prabesh, and Padam, leaping over the corpses and injured bodies of their friends, made their way into the dining room.

There, a few Thai workers were also hiding. Others had been murdered while sleeping in their beds.

Narayan, Lokendra, and Dhanbahadur Chaudhari decided

to make the hundred-meter sprint to the residency area. Upon hearing a car outside, Narayan went out to check if it was the ambulance he was waiting for.

He was shot twice by a passing terrorist.

Crawling back into the room, covered in blood, water was his last request.

Kibbutz Alumim, Kitchen | October 7

A wall of Persian rice sacks.

That's what they constructed to shield themselves from further grenade attacks. Prabin came up with the idea, and they quickly arranged a defensive perimeter out of the kibbutz's supply of industrial-sized burlap bags.

Most of the Nepalese and Thai workers crouched behind this "rice wall," under the wooden table, with Pramod hiding under the sink. Bipin, positioned in the middle and not shielded at all, grew increasingly worried about the friends they'd left stranded in the shelter.

As time passed without any sign of rescue, Bipin considered going back to help them. "We need to think about our next steps. Will you come with me and help bring our friends here?" he asked Himanchal.

They sought the opinion of a Thai worker who'd been hiding in the kitchen before them. His name was Phonsawan Pinakalo, a thirty-year-old tractor driver who'd arrived in Israel four years earlier, to earn a salary that was four times what he would've earned in Thailand. They communicated using Google Translate, going back and forth between Nepali and Thai. Phonsawan's response was unequivocal: "Don't do it. If you do it, you'll die. We've heard the terrorists walking around here for hours."

On the other side of the table, Rajan tried to reassure his roommates Prabin, Prabesh, and Padam. "Don't worry, nothing will happen. Help will come soon."

Exhausted by their ordeal in Israel, Prabesh declared, "If we survive, we're heading back to Nepal as soon as possible."

An hour and a half later, Hamas terrorists broke down the kitchen door, shouting *"Allah-hu Akbar"* and shooting indiscriminately. The makeshift wall of rice sacks offered no protection.

The bullets pierced the sacks and hit the young men. Blood and rice were spilled on the floor.

All of the students were killed except for Prabin, Himanchal, Pramod, and Dhanbahadur, who were hiding in another corner.

Bipin remained alive but was taken hostage. The terrorists captured him and Phonsawan, who was bleeding from his head, and dragged them out of the kitchen at gunpoint.

From their hiding spot in the kitchen, Himanchal and Prabin overheard one of the terrorists questioning the hostages about their religion, to which Phonsawan responded, "Buddhist, Buddhist, Thailand, Thailand."

Two hours later, Bipin and Phonsawan were seen with their captors being pushed into al-Shifa Hospital in Gaza City.

Himanchal and Prabin, wounded and bleeding, waited seven more hours until the Israeli army transported them to the hospital. The other students in the shelter no longer needed rescue.

Interrogation cell of the Shabak, Israeli Security Service | November 20

One month and one week later, Adham Hawwas, who identified himself as a member of the "Hamas military police," and Ismail

Hawwas, who identified himself as part of the movement's "military police and public relations" division, were apprehended in Gaza on suspicion of involvement in the massacre at Kibbutz Alumim.

They'd been captured on the kibbutz's cameras during the kidnapping of Bipin Joshi and Phonsawan Pinakalo, and then again in footage shot hours later at al-Shifa Hospital in Gaza City, where Adham could be seen holding Bipin by the head, covering his eyes and face. Beside him, other Hamas members placed Phonsawan, shirtless and bleeding from his head and hand, on a gurney, which was wheeled into one of the rooms.

The two captured terrorists were taken in for investigation by the Security Service.

Investigator: "Tell me what happened on the seventh of October from the moment you crossed the fence, okay?"

Adham Hawwas: "We drove up to the gate of the kibbutz, which was closed. We climbed over the gate and went inside. Everyone went into the area of the farmers' residences. Two people I was with took someone and left with him."

Investigator: "He was kidnapped?"

Adham Hawwas: "Yes, he was kidnapped. He had a head wound. They took him first. . . . We went out with two hostages and continued to the fence, where there was an [Hamas-commandeered] ambulance. . . . In the ambulance, a guy bandaged the wounded hostage's head."

Investigator: "The hostages taken were Thai?"

Adham Hawwas: "When we were in the ambulance, they asked him: 'What is your name?' but he didn't understand what he was being asked. The second hostage said, 'Thailand.' We

realized that they both had the same nationality and were
most likely guest workers."

Investigator: "Where did the ambulance drive?"

Adham Hawwas: "We were told to go with the ambulance to
al-Shifa Hospital."

Ismail Hawwas: "[In the hospital] the first hostage [Bipin
Joshi] was able to walk by himself. They took him walking
into the elevator. . . . The second [Phonsawan Pinakalo]
was carried on a gurney. . . . They put him in the room—
there was one al-Qassam armed member inside . . . and
two outside the room. They took the guy who could
walk. . . . They covered his head and put a hood over him
so that he would not be recognized."

Those who arrived in Israel as "neutral" replacements for Palestinian workers with the escalation of the conflict returned to
their home countries either empty-handed or in coffins.

Of the seventeen Nepalese students, ten were killed, four injured, two survived—and Bipin was taken hostage. While other
Thai citizens who'd been taken hostage, including Phonsawan,
were released by Hamas after a few weeks, Bipin remained in
captivity for months. His family organized demonstrations
pleading for his release in Nepal, but he has not been seen or
heard from at the time of this writing.

Padam's father, Tikaram, who suffers from hypertension, was
hospitalized immediately upon hearing the news of his son's death.

Rajan's father, Ghyanshyam, fainted when he learned about
his son's fate. In addition to losing his son, he'd gone deep into
debt to finance Rajan's education.

Ashish's grandfather Kanaiyalal wished aloud that God had
taken him instead of his grandson.

As Israel went to war, thousands of Thai and Nepalese guest workers left the country, while Palestinians who still worked in Israel had their work permits canceled. Some of Israel's most important crops—including 70 percent of its tomato crop, 60 percent of its potato crop, and about 40 percent of the cabbage and carrot crops—were in dire need of harvesting, along with a crucial belt of fields, orchards, and greenhouses that provided fruits, vegetables, and grains to a wide swath of Israeli cities. The agricultural sector was on the edge of collapse, and the volunteer harvesting effort was insufficient.

Israel desperately sought out a new workforce, changing its existing policies and allowing in new workers from India, Malawi, and Sri Lanka, among other countries—young people who put aside safety concerns in the hopes of earning higher salaries. One of these workers was Patnibin Maxwell, a thirty-one-year-old Indian citizen, who came to Israel in December 2023 to work on a farm in the northern village of Margaliot. In March 2024, he was killed in an attack by the Iran-backed militia Hezbollah, struck dead while harvesting an orchard.

Himanchal and Prabin spent several months in Israeli hospitals, lonely, unable to communicate adequately, facing a range of complex surgeries and medical procedures. Israelis, many of whom they'd never met, donated money and supplies toward their rehabilitation. The medical treatment they received in Israel was free, yet their families could not afford to travel and be by their side.

At night, the two students often had nightmares about their murdered friends. When they woke up, they both reported a burning thirst—desperately dry throats.

Warning

A HISTORY OF GAZA

Gaza is a toponym that refers both to a city and to the narrow strip of land where Asia and Africa meet. A dusty stretch of Mediterranean coastline occupying a strategic position on one of the most important and lucrative trade routes between Egypt, Lebanon, and Syria, it has known practically every Levantine regime and developed as a mixture of all of them.

The "official" history of Gaza has always competed with, and been informed by, the scriptural accounts, from the Old Testament books of Chronicles and Judges, and the prophetic books of Jeremiah, Amos, and Zephaniah, and the New Testament Book of Acts. The territory's name is derived from the Semitic root *az*, meaning "strength," a fitting appellation for a site so associated with the heroics and martyrdom of the biblical Samson, the strongman of Israel who waged a war against the Philistines that for many religious Jews has become a template for the seemingly unending cycle of violence involving Israel and Palestine, through an erroneous association of "Palestinians" with "Philistines." In the biblical telling, Gaza was a site of temptation: Samson repeatedly became entangled with its women and sought revenge for perceived betrayals by killing Philistines—most infamously killing one thousand of them with the jawbone of an ass. In another act of vengeance, Samson is said to have uprooted the gates of Gaza and carried them across what was then the land of Judah—forty kilometers or so—to Hebron, a feat that gains in symbolism from the fact that both locations, at opposite ends of Israel, beyond the official state borders, are frequent flashpoints of political strife: Hebron, which contains the Tomb of the Patriarchs, purportedly the burial place of Abraham, is a major Palestinian city in the Occupied West Bank.

It's Samson's demise, however, that provides the most compelling metaphor for the current situation: According to the Bible, Samson reveals to the Philistine woman Delilah that his hair is the source of his strength. She cuts it while he sleeps and arranges for the Philistines to abduct him. Samson is imprisoned by them in Gaza, set to work grinding grain, and is blinded. At a festival dedicated to the Philistine deity Dagon, the Philistines bring out their prisoner and force him to dance. Samson grips the columns of the temple and brings the entire edifice down upon his head: "So the dead which he slew at his death," says the Bible, "were more than they which he slew in his life"—a cautionary parable that has gone unheeded.

The archaeological record of Gaza (dating from 3000 BCE), and the written record of Gaza (dating from the fourteenth century BCE) contain the same warning, but in historical form, comprising a saga of constant invasion, occupation, and bloody conquest by multiple empires, including the armies of all three Abrahamic religions. Egypt was the first major kingdom to rule the waterfront in the territory the Egyptians referred to as Canaan. In the twelfth century BCE, the Philistines conquered the area and it became the southernmost outpost of the Philistine Pentapolis; in the eleventh century BCE, the region passed into Jewish hands,

under David; the Assyrian Tiglath-Pileser III ruled the territory thereafter, followed by the Persians. Alexander the Great
besieged the Persian garrisons in 332 BCE and was reputed to
have sold the entire population into slavery. Under the Greeks,
Jewish life returned to the region, which experienced tenuous
self-rule through the Roman conquest, when Gaza prospered: a
school of rhetoric was founded, and a temple was erected to the
local god Marnas, who some scholars believe was a syncretized
incarnation of the Philistine Dagon. Worship of Marnas/Dagon
extended even through the Christian period, and Christianity
reigned as the dominant religious force until the campaigns of
Amr ibn al-As in 637 CE, which resulted in most of Gaza's population converting to Islam and Arabic becoming the primary
language. In the twelfth century CE, possession of Gaza passed
back and forth between Crusaders and the armies of Saladin,
until the Crusader Knights Templar effectively decimated the
city, leaving it a ruined backwater for much of the Mamluk-
governed Middle Ages. In 1799, Napoleon Bonaparte briefly
occupied Gaza en route to the port of Acre, following which the
territory passed through the hands of successive empires, both
in their twilight: the Ottoman and the British.

After the official cessation of hostilities in 1948, Gaza was left
part of Egypt, and its population—almost entirely made up of
Palestinians who'd been deported from their homes or fled—
were left subject to Egyptian military governorship. In 1956,
during Israel's Sinai campaign, Israeli forces briefly occupied the
strip only to return it to Egypt, which still would not consider
the area part of Egypt proper or grant its denizens Egyptian citizenship. (At the same time as Egypt was denying equal status
to Palestinians, it was tacitly expelling its Jews: in 1956, nearly

twenty-five thousand Egyptian Jews left for Israel as part of a mass exodus of Jews from Arab countries.)

In the 1967 war, Israel once again seized control of Gaza, but this time soldiers remained, initiating a military occupation of the territory until 1993. Israeli authorities imposed restrictions on political activity inside Gaza, which was left with no electoral process, and no right of public assembly. At the same time, Jewish settlement of the strip was tacitly encouraged, with twenty-one settlements appearing over this period, whose aim was to create a buffer zone for terror attacks originating in Gaza and to tactically control communications between the more populous Arab sections of the strip.

Those years, many Gazan workers took jobs in the agriculture, construction, and service industries in Israel. In 1968, 6 percent of the Palestinian workforce was working in Israel, but by 1974, that number had increased to 33 percent. According to a UN report in 1980, the average daily wage in Gaza increased by 50 percent between 1970 and 1974 and by another 18.4 percent in the period between 1974 and 1979.

This trend was broken in 1987, after a funeral for four residents of the Jabalia refugee camp, who were killed in a car accident. The taxi in which they were traveling had collided with an Israeli truck near the Erez border checkpoint. However, following the accident, a rumor spread in Gaza that the collision was a deliberate Israeli act of revenge for the murder of an Israeli citizen by a Palestinian a few days earlier. The rage that radiated from the strip soon acquired a name: Intifada, the term for a popular uprising that at the time consisted mainly of labor strikes and swiftly escalated to terror attacks. Stones, knives, guns, and improvised explosives were the weapons of choice, and would continue to be, until the strip passed from Palestinian Authority control to Hamas control and more sophisticated technology and weaponry, including stock-piles of rockets, started arriving courtesy of Hamas's sponsors in Iran.

Israel's withdrawal from Gaza, just two decades after the withdrawal from Sinai, was the country's first government-sanctioned evacuation of Jewish settlements in the history of the state. Under Prime Minister Ariel Sharon, the country undertook the controversial step of disengaging completely from Gaza—evacuating Israelis from their homes in the strip and handing over the entire territory to Palestinian control, without making any demands or seeking compensation.

It's significant that this disengagement—known in Hebrew by the single now-infamous word *Ha-Hitnatkut*—was initiated and implemented by a coalition government led by Likud, Netanyahu's party, under the leadership of the ex-general Sharon, the so-called father of the settlements.

Against the backdrop of the Second Intifada, which started in autumn 2000, Sharon began arguing for this severance, with the logic that it would minimize friction—it would minimize contact—with Palestinians, "in order to bring about a better security reality at least in the long term."

Following his declaration, the Israeli settlers of the strip began an intensive campaign to reverse the decision. The period between the announcement of the plan and its implementation, one year and eight months later, was one of the most turbulent in Israeli society, as settlers clashed with Israeli police and military.

Despite their resistance, the settlers' efforts failed, and in 2005, Israel withdrew itself to its 1967 borders to the east and ceded internal control of Gaza to its Palestinian population, which then numbered approximately 1.7 million people. With this action, a precedent was set: it was "land for peace," presented as a fait accompli.

Sharon's hopes for "a better security reality" would soon be quashed, however. In 2006, Palestinian parliamentary elections were held, and Hamas—which was already internationally recognized as a terror organization—won 42.9 percent of the total vote and 74 out of 132 seats.

Following the election, intense clashes between Hamas and supporters of the Palestinian Authority and its Fatah movement commenced—fighting that claimed the lives of more than six hundred Palestinians. Though Hamas set about forming a national unity government with Fatah, the group soon seized total control of Gaza through intimidation and violence; in the words of Human Rights Watch, Hamas "conducted arbitrary arrests of political opponents, tortured detainees, clamped down on freedom of expression and assembly, and violated due process rights enshrined in Palestinian law."

In response, Palestinian president Mahmoud Abbas declared Hamas's tactics an "armed mutiny," and formed a new government excluding Hamas, which, though its seat of power was located in the West Bank, was eventually recognized by the international community, including by Egypt, Jordan, and Saudi Arabia, as the sole legitimate Palestinian government.

After Hamas's takeover, both Israel and Egypt sealed their borders with Gaza, with Israel asserting control over the border crossings. This control evolved into a blockade, preventing most Palestinians from leaving the territory and miring them in poverty amid periodic shortages of water, food, and medical supplies, and severe restrictions on the importation of fuel and consumer electronics, on the pretext that they might be repurposed for weaponry. Together, the measures taken by Hamas, Israel, and Egypt were catastrophic for the people of Gaza, radicalizing some and immiserating all.

The tunnels of Gaza, which achieved infamy during the war that followed the October 7 attacks, were originally utilized as a means of circumventing this blockade, providing pipelines for goods, including weaponry. The primary smuggling occurred along the so-called Philadelphi corridor on the Gaza-Egypt border, and the primary provider of the weaponry was Iran, which according to a 2010 report of the US Department of Defense supplied "funding, weapons, and training to oppose Israel and disrupt the Middle East Peace Process." Israel seemed to be one of the only issues that could unite the Muslim *ummah*, bringing unprecedented cooperation between the Sunni-aligned Hamas and the Shia-aligned Iran. With Iranian support, as well as significant infusions of money that came through Hamas's political wing headquartered in Qatar, Hamas grew wealthy, but Gaza didn't. The money seemed to be invested in armaments and on infrastructure underground, in the vast tunnel network that eventually grew into a Gaza-under-Gaza, a subterranean maze sheltering a virulent regime that didn't govern and develop its above-ground population so much as use it as a political, and often as a physical, shield.

In the minds of many Israelis, including leading politicians, disengagement from Gaza was the original sin, and a direct line connects Israel's 2005 withdrawal from the strip and the far-right Judicial Reform and massacre eighteen years later.

Hayim Katsman, a young and promising Israeli American sociologist with a PhD from the University of Washington, studied the effects of the disengagement from Gaza on the West Bank–based Religious Zionist movement—the movement in which he was raised and which he left. Katsman's dissertation pointed out that Religious Zionists experienced the disengagement as a collective trauma, a "personal," "political," and "theological" betrayal: "The uprooting of Jewish settlements, which were perceived as a redemptive fulfillment of God's promise to Abraham, seemed incomprehensible," he wrote, noting that this betrayal caused Religious Zionists to become more involved politically in order to prevent such a tragedy from ever happening again. These members of religious settlements understood that it wouldn't be possible to prevent future evictions—from the West Bank, or, as they referred to it, Judea and Samaria—without creating a foothold not only in the Knesset but in every branch of the Israeli establishment: the courts, the army, the police, and the media.

Disengagement in Gaza led to their engagement in Israel: for nearly two decades, they set about increasing their power, culminating in their historic victory in the most recent elections, in 2022, when their coalition with Netanyahu won them high ministerial positions, superintending everything from the national budget to law enforcement and even war policy. On October 7, the thirty-two-year-old Katsman, who was not merely a respected academic but also a well-known peace activist and an avid opponent of the occupation, was murdered by Hamas terrorists who'd invaded Kibbutz Holit.

The Religious Zionists who were the subject of his research had an expectable reaction: in the wake of the massacre, they called for the reversal of the disengagement and the return of Jewish settlements to Gaza, which would involve the reannexation of the strip and the imposition of a one-state solution from the river to the sea.

Simchat Torah 5702/1941 – Simchat Torah 5784/2023

1

On Simchat Torah, October 1941, Moshe Ridler was deported from his home in Herta, on the border between Romania and Ukraine.

The youngest child of Pearl and Zelig Ridler, Moshe was a third-grade student, age ten.

The family's persecution began a year earlier, when the Soviets invaded the city. At first, it was only the bourgeois Jews who were deprived of their property and deported. But when Romanian troops took over, the repercussions for all Jews were immediate. On July 5, 1941, a new mayor and a civil guard were established with a clear mission: to get rid of the Jews of Herta.

Nearly the entire Jewish population was herded into a square in the city center. Men, women, children, and the elderly were separated from one another, stripped naked, beaten, and tortured. Dozens were forced to dig their own mass grave before being shot.

Three weeks into the Romanian occupation, most of the sixteen hundred surviving Jews of the town were deported to the Edintz transit camp. The very last group, including the Ridler family of five, was sent on a three-hundred-kilometer death march to transit ghettos and camps in Transnistria.

Pearl Ridler, the forty-six-year-old mother of three, succumbed to typhus during this death march. The rest of the family made it to the Romanchi ghetto, but fifteen-year-old Mina Ridler died of exhaustion shortly thereafter. From Romanchi, Moshe's father, Zelig, was sent to a labor camp in Odessa, while his eldest sister, Feige, was sent to another labor camp in Tulchin. Moshe Ridler, not yet eleven years old, found himself alone in the ghetto.

2

The name Ridler was the bane of Tel Aviv criminals in the 1960s.

Thieves, drug dealers, sexual predators—one by one, Master Sergeant Moshe Ridler from the city police central investigation unit led the denizens of Tel Aviv's underworld into the district courthouse.

Two men attempting to molest schoolgirls by seducing them with marijuana—Ridler found the substance hidden in a flower vase during a surprise search and arrested them; four masked men broke into a diamond polisher's premises, stealing $50,000 worth of diamonds at gunpoint from an elderly couple—Ridler acted on a tip from an informant and didn't just find the loot, he found other stolen diamonds worth well over $100,000; in 1965, the same year he busted a hotel owner for tobacco smuggling, he won a citation as the Best Police Driver—which came with a certificate personally signed by the police commissioner.

Master Sergeant Moshe Ridler was a slim young man with a thick mane of dark hair and a noticeable Romanian accent. He lived among the criminals he pursued, in a modest apartment in a police-only building with his wife, Pia—a fellow Romanian immigrant who fled to Israel after the war—their son, and two daughters.

He named his first daughter Pnina, the Hebrew translation of Pearl, his mother's name.

Neither the criminals nor the policemen of Tel Aviv, not even his own children, knew the origins of Master Sergeant Moshe Ridler.

3

After a few months alone in the Romanchi ghetto, eleven-year-old Ridler threatened a group of older boys he overheard planning an escape: if they didn't include him in their escape plans, he'd report them to the camp commander.

In the ghetto's informal justice code, being a "moser"—a Jew who informs the authorities about a fellow Jew's suspected crimes—was a transgression punishable by death. That the boy would risk this punishment was proof that he was serious, so after initially rebuffing him, they eventually included him. A few days later, under the cover of darkness, the group made a small hole in the ghetto fence and started running, without any intended destination.

The next day, Ridler awoke atop a stove in an unfamiliar house. He'd been discovered, nearly frozen, by a couple in a Ukrainian village about thirty kilometers from the ghetto.

The family welcomed him as a member of their household.

He worked alongside the family's children, tending to the land and milking cows. He was there for a year and a half, until he heard that Jews were returning to Herta.

Out of the 1,940 Jews who lived in Herta before the war, only 450 were still alive.

Moshe visited the synagogue he'd gone to with his family, sitting on the stairs, waiting and hoping. One of those times, his father, Zelig, was there. They managed to reunite with his sister, Feige, as well. They were now a family of three.

4

Moshe emigrated to Israel in 1951, and Zelig and Feige joined him a decade later.

At the beginning, the family resided in Neve Yarak, a moshav in central Israel established and settled by Holocaust survivors from Romania. The founders petitioned the first president of Israel, Dr. Chaim Weizmann, arguing that they could build a new community and "serve as an example for middle-aged and older immigrants" (the typical moshav at the time was populated by people in their late teens and twenties).

It was one of the only kibbutzim or moshavim founded by Holocaust survivors.

After retiring from the police, Moshe opened a private investigation office in Tel Aviv, where he specialized in financial crimes. He also conducted extensive investigations on behalf of the Jewish Agency, focusing on individuals who'd defrauded the country's immigration services.

All those years, he never talked about the past.

5

At the age of ninety, after the deaths of his sister and wife, Moshe
Ridler moved to Kibbutz Holit, to live near his daughter, Pnina.

For years, Pnina had implored her father to join her at the kibbutz, asserting that there was no finer place to grow old than in
its tranquil and serene surroundings. Pnina taught English in the
local school and also volunteered to direct the kibbutz's command
center, where she was responsible for updating members during
emergencies—which, fortunately, were rare, despite the kibbutz's
proximity to the Gaza border. In 2019, Moshe finally agreed. Thus,
he became the senior-most member of Kibbutz Holit, a physically
vigorous though increasingly senile grandfather emeritus. His
new home was an even smaller Jewish community than the one in
which he'd grown up in Eastern Europe.

Originally established in the Sinai, Holit was relocated following Israel's territorial concession to Egypt as part of its peace
treaty. Although still named after the desert terrain of its original
Sinai location (*hol* means "sand" in Hebrew), the kibbutz saw
most of its founding members depart. At times, its population
dwindled to a mere twenty-five members, as it struggled to attract new residents.

Finally, a group of young urban idealists, inspired by the
communal spirit of the original kibbutzim, stepped in to save
Kibbutz Holit from decline in the first decade of the 2000s. Moving to the kibbutz, they helped to reinvigorate its orchards and
especially its dairy production, guided throughout by their mission statement: to create "a cooperative community that engages
in regular joint study and social work, and fosters a connection
to the land and agriculture."

At Holit, Moshe found himself speaking Romanian again

in order to communicate with his nurse-attendant, who hailed from Moldova and helped him arrange his meals and dress and accomplish daily tasks.

Petro Bushkov, thirty-five years old, left his wife, Aliona, and their three young daughters in Moldova, moving to Israel to earn money. He'd paid thousands of dollars to middlemen in order to secure a work permit, confident that his earnings from eldercare would more than cover the investment.

Everyone in the kibbutz knew the strange duo: the elderly but energetic Ridler, walking with a walker, and the calm Bushkov, always at his side, trying to slow the old man down.

They made a daily trip together, a regular route: first they would walk to the post office, then to the grocery store, and finally—the highlight of the day—they'd walk to the pool.

Each evening, he'd see Pnina, who lived in the house across the way.

It was a graceful way to age.

6

The Jewish holiday of Simchat Torah, October 2023, was the day Moshe Ridler was murdered in his house in Kibbutz Holit, at age ninety-two.

In the days preceding the holiday, his daughter, Pnina, had told him she'd be celebrating by visiting her eldest child and grandchildren in Tiberias. Moshe decided to stay home rather than accompany her for two reasons. First, he preferred the comfort of his own bed. Second, October 7 was the last day his beloved local pool would be open before being closed for the winter. Moshe went to bed on Friday, October 6, planning to take a nice long swim when he woke up.

In Tiberias, at half past six the next morning, Pnina Ridler was startled by urgent calls informing her that a massive rocket attack had begun on the kibbutz.

"Heavy volleys of gunfire have targeted our kibbutz and others. Please enter a shelter and secure your doors," she alerted the residents in her role as the kibbutz's command center director.

Her father was still sleeping in Holit, oblivious to the sirens and incoming missiles.

Pnina called him to ensure he knew what was going on and had moved to their safe room.

Petro Bushkov, who was already awake, reassured her that they were fine, but their next-door neighbor, sixty-two-year-old Lily Keisman, was convinced that the noises she heard were unlike any rocket attacks she'd previously experienced.

Lily shared her concerns in the kibbutz group chat again and again—until her texts stopped.

From the house adjacent to Lily's, owned by Shahar and Shlomi Mathias, forty-seven-year-old musicians and educators, came reports of gunfire.

Their sixteen-year-old son, Rotem, managed to write to the group chat that he was wounded and his parents had been murdered.

Next to the Mathias residence was the house of Ronit and Roland Sultan.

Ronit, a fifty-six-year-old art PhD from Argentina, and Roland, the sixty-eight-year-old Tunisian-born community director of the kibbutz, were murdered—Ronit inside the house and Roland on the balcony.

One block on was the Elharar household, whose only survivor was a seven-year-old girl, Adi, who hid in the closet.

Judy Torgman, a professional photographer and mother of two, wrote into the kibbutz group chat that terrorists were burning her home with her family inside: "Help—the house is on fire—Help."

Anani Kaploun, a manager of the citrus and tropical fruit groves, and his wife, Adi Vital-Kaploun, a cybersecurity expert, were among the more prominent young professionals of the kibbutz, along with Anani's brother, Ahuvia, and Ahuvia's girlfriend, Tahila Katbi.

That morning Anani and Ahuvia set out from the kibbutz early for a brothers' trip, while the women stayed home.

When the gunshots started, Adi called her husband, asking for instructions on how to use their rifle. She was murdered in front of their young sons: four-month-old Eshel and four-year-old Negev. The terrorists rigged her corpse with explosives, then filmed themselves feeding her two boys milk.

The next house belonged to Hayim Katsman, the young doctor of sociology who studied the effects of the disengagement from the Gaza Strip on the Religious Zionist movement.

In the living room he had a broken TV set, which had been sprayed in red graffiti: "the revolution will not be televised." He was a DJ specializing in Arabic electronic music and a peace activist—as well as the bartender, the car mechanic, and the gardener of the kibbutz. The night before the massacre, Katsman fell asleep reading a monograph called *Hamas: From Religious Ideology to Terrorism*.

Woken by sirens the next morning, he went out to check on his neighbors and found Tahila Katbi shot to death. He ran to his other neighbor's house, a Pilates and yoga instructor named Avital Aldjem, and hid with her in her closet. When the Hamas terrorists entered Avital's house, Katsman shielded her with his body, and was shot dead.

The Hamas terrorist then pulled Avital out of the closet, dressed her in three skirts, and kidnapped her and the two Kaploun children to Gaza. After they crossed the border on foot, a terrorist suddenly ordered Avital and the children to turn around and return to Israel and filmed the "pardon" for Hamas social media. Avital escorted the Kaploun children home—carrying the youngest, an infant, in her arms, while the oldest child had to crawl over the pebbly wasteland due to the shrapnel lodged in his leg.

Fifteen members of Kibbutz Holit were murdered. Fourteen children became orphans. A number of Pnina's students from nearby Kibbutz Be'eri had been killed; some had been kidnapped: third-grader Emily Hand, seventh-grader Hila Rotem, sixth-grade twins Liel and Yanai Hetzroni.

It was only around midnight that Pnina received the news about her father:

Hamas terrorists had launched an RPG at the safe room where Moshe Ridler and Petro Bushkov were taking cover. Afterward, the terrorists threw grenades at the house and then broke through the door. Petro was shot multiple times and died of his injuries. Moshe was later found dead in his bed: as if he hadn't yet woken up, as if it was all just a dream.

Victims of Grief

1

Route 1:
Kings of Israel Square,
Tel Aviv to Neve Dekalim, Gaza |
March 1993

Haim Ben Aryeh closed the door of his bus just before midnight.

"We'll be home in about two hours," he announced. Home was Neve Dekalim, Gaza's largest Jewish settlement.

The bus was packed; not a single seat was left empty. For most of Haim's passengers, Tel Aviv was unfamiliar territory, the sin city of the secular left. Yet, they'd had a good reason to be there that evening: a protest against the upcoming signing of the Oslo Accords by Israeli prime minister Yitzhak Rabin and Palestine Liberation Organization leader Yasser Arafat.

As part of the peace process, Israel consented to withdraw from Gaza and Jericho, and to recognize the establishment of a Palestinian Authority. The Palestinians, in turn, agreed to recognize Israel's right to exist. Not everyone was in favor, to say the least. Slogans like "It's not peace, it's terror," "Don't give them guns," and "Rabin is a traitor" resonated through Kings of Israel Square late into the evening.

As Haim started the bus's engine, he heard knocks on the bus door.

A breathless black-haired young woman was tapping on the glass.

He opened the door for her.

"Is there room for one more to Gaza?" she asked.

"No, but you're welcome to sit here on the steps next to my seat."

She nodded and boarded, apologizing for the inconvenience. "I'd been protesting with my friends and lost track of time; yours is the last bus home."

Her name was Irit Cohen Yonatan. She was a nineteen-year-old teacher.

Haim was twenty-six years old, the twinkle-eyed, soft-spoken son of immigrants from Iraq and Turkey. Irit came from a family of Algerian *kohanim* (Jews descended from the priestly class) who'd lived in Djerba, Tunisia. He was the third of six siblings; she was the ninth of ten. They discovered that they were almost neighbors. He lived in Moshav Katif in Gush Katif, in one of the American suburban-style detached houses situated between Rafah and Khan Yunis; she had grown up in Neve Dekalim, the "capital" of the Jewish settlement in Gaza, built on virgin dunes along the seashore by newcomers from France and India. Their political views were closely aligned: "There was peace before we started talking about peace," Haim commented as he drove; Irit nodded in agreement. That month was called "the month of blood," following the murder of fourteen Israelis in Palestinian terrorist acts. Though both of them had lived alongside Palestinians, they still believed that the Oslo Accords were not a pathway to peace so much as a prelude to war.

After a month, they were engaged. Seven months later, in October 1993, they were married.

Route 2:
Moshav Katif to Moshav Ganei Tal |
May 2, 2004

Irit and Haim Ben Aryeh, along with their four children, were planning to drive from their home, Moshav Katif, to the polling station in the city of Be'er Sheva, to persuade Likud voters to reconsider their stance.

It was an important morning—the Likud party was holding a referendum on the disengagement plan. It was the last chance to convince Prime Minister Ariel Sharon to abandon his plan of withdrawing Israeli settlements from Gaza and ceding the land to the Palestinians.

Sharon argued that the withdrawal would bring peace: "I am willing to make painful compromises in order to put an end to this ongoing and malignant conflict between those who struggle over this land, and that I would do my utmost in order to bring peace. . . . The disengagement plan holds the potential to usher in a different reality."

The residents of the Israeli settlements in Gaza along with many from the political right argued that Sharon's plan would lead to a catastrophe—violence and more wars. They believed terrorist organizations would interpret the plan as evidence that Israel could be coerced into relinquishing territory through terror. They also emphasized that Gaza was an integral part of the Jewish people's historical heritage, and no secular law should have the authority to confiscate land that was traditionally—biblically—theirs.

For months, Haim and Irit had traveled across Israel, encouraging voters to reject the plan. They even painted their house and Haim's bus orange—the color of the protest movement (borrowed from Ukraine's contemporaneous Orange Revolution).

Haim, now the official bus driver for the Gaza Coast Regional Council, had become a well-known figure in the twenty-one Jewish settlements of the area. He was recognized for his long beard, broad smile, and an orange bus adorned with Israeli flags and decals of Torah scrolls. It wasn't just his appearance that made him stand out; he also cultivated a few eccentricities. He didn't like cell phones (too distracting), he'd never held a credit card (but always carried cash), and he knew every child he took to school by name and family background. Some considered him more of a teacher than their teachers.

The night before the referendum, Haim and Irit's eldest daughters, eleven-year-old Lior and ten-year-old Maytal, proudly showed an article about their parents' political efforts to their friends and next-door neighbors, eleven-year-old Hila Hatuel and ten-year-old Hadar Hatuel. The families were close: Tali Hatuel and Irit Ben Aryeh had synchronized pregnancies and helped each other raise the kids. That morning, the Hatuel family left for a polling station in Ashkelon shortly before the Ben Aryeh family did.

The Ben Aryehs were delayed, waiting for Haim to return from his morning school route. Ever since meeting Irit, he had made it a habit to wait an extra minute or two at each stop, ensuring no late-running children were left behind.

Just as they set off, Irit's brother, a police officer, called. "There was a terror attack on the main road," he said. "Go home and stay there."

Heeding his advice, they returned to Moshav Katif, only to be informed that the dead were their neighbors.

Tali Hatuel, her four daughters, and her unborn boy had been traveling in a white Citroen station wagon heading out of the Kissufim Crossing east of Khan Yunis when they were ambushed by gunmen affiliated with Palestinian Islamic Jihad and Fatah. The initial barrage of gunfire sent the car spinning off the road, following which the attackers approached the vehicle and opened fire on the family from close range.

Someone needed to identify the bodies. Haim's bus had been bulletproof for a few years now, a necessity since the start of the Second Intifada in the fall of 2000. The Kissufim route, the road where the Hatuel family was murdered, was part of his daily route. He himself had survived shootings and a bombing. Yet, at the morgue in Moshav Ganei Tal, Haim found the sight of the bullet-riddled bodies unbearable.

Upon hearing that David Hatuel insisted on seeing the bodies of his wife and children, Haim pleaded with him, "There are some memories you don't want to have. Trust me. Spare yourself."

The following day, the day of the funerals of the Hatuel family, the results of the Likud referendum were made public, with 65 percent voting against what came to be called "the Disengagement." Despite these results, Prime Minister Sharon decided he had the political capital to go forward with the plan.

Two decades after the withdrawal from Sinai, Israel was again making the gamble of trading land for peace, this time unilaterally, without any prior concessions from the Palestinians. In August 2005, Prime Minister Sharon deployed twenty-five thousand soldiers to evacuate all Israeli citizens from Gaza, whether they wanted to go or not.

Route 3:
Moshav Katif, Gaza to Kfar Pines, Israel |
August 21, 2005

Haim was holding a fishbowl with three goldfish, Irit was cradling their newborn boy, and the other four Ben Aryeh children were carrying the bags that contained most of their worldly possessions.

The family had just been forcibly evacuated from their home in Moshav Katif and were boarding a bus driving them out of Gaza. They were being resettled on the orders of the Israeli Defense Forces.

"We don't even throw fish out of their homes. We're not like Sharon," Haim told the soldiers. Up until the moment he was ushered onto a bus that wasn't his and forced to take a passenger seat, he had refused to believe that he would become homeless. Now, he was watching his home disappear over the horizon.

Their driver sped erratically out of Gaza. It was already afternoon, and they were among the last Israelis to leave. During one of the driver's abrupt stops, Haim dropped the fishbowl, which shattered, and the fish flopped onto the floor and died.

In the middle of the night, the Ben Aryehs were dropped off at a religious girls' school in Central Israel, sharing bunk beds with other displaced families. They stayed there for two months. Next they were moved to a caravan complex in the south, squeezed into a forty-five-square-meter trailer, lacking even a door. Six months later, they were relocated yet again to a trailer park on the western slopes of Mount Hebron; their belongings, expected within two weeks, only arrived ten months later.

Haim changed after the deportation from Gaza. He struggled with unemployment. He became quieter, more introverted, bitter.

For thirteen years the Ben Aryehs waited, until the state of

Israel fulfilled its promise of providing them with a new home within the state's 1967 borders.

It was only in 2019 that fifty families from Moshav Katif in Gaza were resettled together in the new moshav built for them— Karmi Katif.

Haim managed to find work once again as a children's bus driver in their new community; Irit was relieved to see her husband smiling again.

David Hatuel remained their neighbor. He'd remarried and had six more children.

Route 4:
Karmi Katif to Kibbutz Be'eri |
October 7, 2023

Haim received an urgent call from the bus company.

They needed him to transport children who had survived the Kibbutz Be'eri massacre to safety at hotels near the Dead Sea. His boss knew Haim's experience in handling delicate situations, especially with children.

Around 4 A.M., Irit heard the sound of a key turning in the door.

Haim stood at the entrance to their house, crying in a manner Irit hadn't witnessed before.

"What happened? Tell me what happened," she said.

"I couldn't help them." Haim struggled to speak, his words choked by tears.

"I'm sure you did help them, Haim. Tell me everything, what did you see?"

He struggled to form the sentences, and Irit remembered that so many of his statements sounded like questions: "I couldn't help. . . . People boarded my bus half-naked. . . . They were wrapped in blankets? In towels? . . . The blood . . . People were covered in blood? Children covered in blood? Children without socks or shoes? Fathers in their underwear? They ran for their lives? These people saw their families murdered, the most horrible images . . . and the silence . . . the entire two-hour drive to the Dead Sea was totally silent. . . . My bus was full and no one said a word? Even the babies weren't crying? Not a single child said a single word and what could I do? I couldn't do anything? I couldn't help them?"

Last Ride:
Karmi Katif to Moshav Neta |
October 25, 2023

Haim had withdrawn into himself. He'd been spending days lying in bed watching the news on the right-wing Channel 14, fixated on every detail of each murder and massacre reported.

"Your son killed Jews, Dad! Look how many I killed with my own hands!"—that recording of a Hamas terrorist deeply troubled Haim. He kept playing that clip and trying to show it to his wife and children. Irit refused. "I need to stay sane, for you and the kids. I can't watch all this, I can't bear it." Even the children stepped in, expressing concern over their father's news obsession. Haim insisted, "It's under control."

But as days passed, with the rising numbers of victims and endless news coverage, Haim's distress grew. Unbeknownst to Irit, he sought help, reaching out to a rabbi.

He told the rabbi everything: the blood, the silent children, the bodies on the roads. He admitted he took another drive to the front, on October 9, driving roads clouded with smoke, passing countless bodies lying by the side. He didn't tell Irit or their children about this trip, which he made at the behest of the IDF, transporting soldiers to the front.

On October 20, Haim and Irit celebrated their thirtieth wedding anniversary with their eight children. Haim had seemed happy, thankful.

On Wednesday morning, October 25, Irit lay in bed, listening to the familiar sounds of Haim's morning routine. The creak of the door as he quietly left their room, the shuffle of his feet across the floor, washing up.

Haim found Irit in the kitchen, sipping coffee and reading a news article—which surprised him. She'd been purposefully avoiding the news so far. "I'm trying to catch up," she told him, "little by little, at my own pace." Haim rested his chin on her head, reading the news along with her, before going out to his bus.

Haim turned right instead of left at the moshav's main square, heading toward a local kindergarten. He visited the kindergarten for a few minutes, greeting some of the children he knew from the synagogue, and then he got back into his bus and drove a few minutes to nearby Moshav Neta.

He sent Irit a brief message:

"I apologize."

Then another one:

"I apologize to my parents, I apologize to our kids."

A few minutes later, Irit heard breaking news of a shooting in Moshav Neta.

Fearing a terror attack, Irit instructed her children to lock the house. Then her brother, the police officer, called.

Haim Ben Aryeh, fifty-six, had shot himself to death in the driver's seat of his bus.

2

Three to six funerals a day.

Sivan Sekeli Benzekry wasn't a professional mortician. She wasn't even a professional funeral planner—a niche occupation almost as lucrative as wedding planner—but she learned on the job. She learned quickly.

She was a manager at an insurance company, selling health and life insurance policies. She was also a mother of three, whose military service in the reserves and later as a volunteer had been with the Casualty Unit of the Israel Defense Forces. Twice a year for the past twenty years, she'd volunteered for this duty, which was how she—a thin forty-year-old woman, half-Polish, half-Iraqi with green eyes and black hair—found herself responsible for organizing nearly thirty funerals in the span of a week.

Most of the deceased were young adults, just a few years older than her eldest, a twelve-year-old daughter. Sivan managed every logistical aspect of the ceremonies: making sure the grave was dug, ordering the flower arrangements, setting up the plastic chairs, installing the speakers for the eulogies, providing catering for the mourners, and—most stressfully—asking the cemetery employees to please refrain from digging the next grave until the currently mourning family had completed their funeral. For each interment, she was the first to arrive and the last to leave.

Sivan's role with the Casualty Unit entailed notifying families about the deaths of their loved ones. She embraced a task that nobody else wanted. She developed her own personal coping mechanisms for the funerals, teaching herself to tune out the despairing cries and gun salutes, to look away from the flag-draped caskets being lowered into the ground. She tried not to remember any names.

It was during her twenty-ninth funeral, at the military cemetery in Kiryat Shaul, Tel Aviv, that Sivan reached her breaking point. As she watched the gravediggers preparing another seventeen graves for the next day, she felt herself falter. Her legs went weak and a sharp pain gripped her chest, but she managed to stay upright.

Her twenty-ninth funeral that week was for Sagi Golan, a thirty-year-old high-tech worker from the beachfront city of Herzliya, who had been due to marry his partner of six years, Omer Ohana, just thirteen days after Sagi was murdered.

A few days prior, Sagi and Omer woke up in Herzliya and lingered in bed discussing the vows they were intending to write and the design of their wedding canopy. They'd just received their suits back from the tailor—Sagi's in light green to match his eyes, Omer's in cream. They'd planned a wedding in the Judean Desert, between the Judean Mountains and the Dead Sea.

But that morning brought a change of plans—with Sagi checking the news on his phone and jumping out of bed. He was a reserve officer in the IDF, and though he hadn't been called up yet he knew it was only a matter of time: civilians were being murdered in their homes.

"Just a few days until the wedding," Sagi told Omer, kissing him goodbye at the door.

"Don't be a hero," Omer replied.

The following night, Sagi was killed by Hamas terrorists while rescuing families from Kibbutz Be'eri.

The cotton flowers carefully selected for their wedding were transformed into a wreath for Sagi's grave. The famous Israeli singer Ivri Lider, whose song they had chosen for their walk up the aisle, ended up performing the same song live at the funeral instead. Omer utilized the wedding reservation system, which sends messages to all invited guests, to inform them of the time and place of Sagi's funeral.

Not everyone in the Casualty Unit was as touched by Omer's grief as Sivan. In the time between the announcement of Sagi's death and the funeral, another Casualty Unit officer dismissed all of Omer's questions regarding Sagi's death and all his requests regarding the funeral, stating that Omer, as a gay unmarried partner of the deceased, had no official status.

Ultimately, this problem of status would've been the same had Sagi lived. Despite their event being a "wedding" in name, it wasn't a legal wedding, as Israeli civil law subjects official marriage to Jewish religious law, which forbids homosexual unions. In the absence of a governmental solution, Israeli courts have acknowledged same-sex relationships as legal marriages only if the couples were married abroad. For that reason, Omer and Sagi had an appointment for a Utah-based virtual wedding to be held via Zoom on October 12.

Sivan returned home from Sagi's funeral around midnight and went straight to sleep. The next morning, a Friday, she was called to another funeral, for a young woman. Throughout the ceremony, Sivan again felt dizzy; she left for home immediately after the interment.

Sivan awoke at 4:30 A.M. on Saturday morning with intense chest pains. Her husband, Haim, called an ambulance. Although the initial EKG performed by the paramedics returned normal results, Sivan insisted on being taken to the hospital. There she had another EKG and blood tests, along with a chest X-ray, which indicated that everything was normal.

A few minutes after the X-ray, Sivan suffered cardiac arrest.

For the next four days, Sivan would be on life support suffering from what was alternately diagnosed as spontaneous coronary artery dissection (a tear in the arterial wall) and so-called broken heart syndrome (when the heart suddenly becomes stunned and weakened). On the fourth day, which was also her fortieth birthday, her husband, Haim, asked the doctors to try to wake her up. Sivan slowly regained consciousness, and while she was found to have no permanent neurological or cognitive damage, her memory was missing. Almost all of the memories related to the war seemed to be erased, and she could recall the name of only one of the deceased she had buried—Sagi Golan.

During the week that was now missing from Sivan's memory, Omer had publicly protested for the right to claim official status as Sagi's fiancé. Three weeks after Sagi's death, the Israeli Knesset unanimously passed an amendment officially recognizing LGBTQ victims' spouses as IDF widows or widowers. Omer Ohana, who hadn't been able to legally marry, became the first recognized LGBTQ widower in Israeli history.

3

OCTOBER 7

Seventeen sirens. The Torpiashvili family, father Avi; mother Manana; daughter Tamar, age nine; son Itzik, age eleven; and daughter Eden, age twenty, had to run to their missile-proof safe room seventeen times. In Ashdod, they had about forty-five seconds from the start of a siren to get to shelter: the missiles would come in that quickly. Their safe room doubled as the bedroom of Manana's mother, who'd left Georgia after the Abkhazia War in 1993 only to find herself in the perpetual wartime atmosphere of Ashdod.

OCTOBER 8

Manana spent the day crying in front of the television, explaining to Tamar that another war had officially started. Tamar asked Manana if the children and mothers in Gaza were as afraid as they were. Siren at 12:30 P.M., four missiles struck central Ashdod. A fifty-year-old woman was seriously injured. A few hours later, a nine-year-old boy in the neighboring city of Ashkelon was wounded when a rocket hit a four-story building. Tamar was worried about her friend Adele, who had moved to Ashkelon with her family the year before and sent her a message on WhatsApp: "Adele, I listened to the news; the missile didn't fall near your house. It hit the main road, that's why you heard it."

That evening, Tamar had her first menstruation. The only people she told were her mother and Adele. A gynecologist had told Manana that early menstruation was often the result of increased anxiety and stress.

OCTOBER 9

Siren 3:23 P.M., after which Tamar and her fifth-grade classmates returned to their remote-learning class. They were accustomed to doing school online: for two years during the pandemic, they hadn't attended school in person.

Tamar and Adele texted after the lesson.

Adele: "How are you?"
Tamar: "Okay, but a little anxious because I heard an explosion right next to me. For a second, I went crazy. I'm also having a hard time with my period."

OCTOBER 10

The news reported suspected terror activity in Ashdod; gunshots were heard from the direction of the beach; soldiers were being deployed to search the area. Following this report, Tamar went to the kitchen and took out two knives, the sharpest and largest she could find, and placed them in the safe room. Having earlier seen a television news segment about civilians who'd saved themselves from Hamas terrorists on October 7 by locking their safe-room doors with an iron bar, she went to the bathroom and found a broom and mop, thinking that these cleaning supplies might serve a similar purpose. She told her mother, who was sitting in front of the television, that though her father was at work and unable to protect them, she would defend them if terrorists came. When Ashkelon was again mentioned on the news broadcast, Tamar's concern shifted to Adele, and messages went back and forth:

> Tamar: "Are you okay?"
> Adele: "Yes, you?"
> Tamar: "Okay . . . I got really worried when I heard about the rockets in Ashkelon. Is the situation calming down?"
> Adele: "No, there was another siren two minutes ago."
> Tamar: "Be safe."
> Adele: "Thank you, be safe too."
> Tamar: "I worry about you a lot."

OCTOBER 11

Siren at 1:29 P.M. Siren at 2:08 P.M. Siren at 4:00 P.M. Siren at 4:26 P.M. Siren at 6:01 P.M.

Tamar: "Adele, are you all right?"

Adele: "Yes, you?"

Tamar: "I'm OK, I guess."

OCTOBER 12

Siren at 4:28 P.M. Siren at 5:30 P.M.

OCTOBER 13

A series of three sirens, sounding one after the other, from 9:00 P.M. Siren at 10:00 P.M. Tamar asked to sleep in the safe room, telling her mother that she felt calmer there.

OCTOBER 14

Siren at 5:04 P.M. Siren at 8:42 P.M. Manana called Tamar's teacher for advice on how to help with her daughter's anxiety and was directed to call a public hotline.

OCTOBER 15

Siren at 9:32 P.M.

OCTOBER 16

Siren at 11:41 A.M. Siren at 1:32 P.M. Siren at 9:02 P.M. Siren at 10:12 P.M. When Avi returned from work, he tried to calm his daughter. "You're too dramatic, girl. Maybe you'll be a famous actress when you grow up. There's no need to make a big drama out of missiles; you're used to it, sweetie. We're all safe in the safe room. We're here with you."

OCTOBER 17

Siren at 7:00 P.M. Siren at 7:29 P.M.

OCTOBER 18

No sirens.

OCTOBER 19

No sirens.

OCTOBER 20

Siren at 12:02 P.M. Tamar ran to the safe room while Manana called Avi at work to check that he'd managed to find shelter. She cut off the call when she saw Tamar writhing on the floor, writhing and then unconscious. Manana yelled for help and one of the neighbors came and performed CPR. An ambulance that was already in the vicinity, due to the sirens, showed up immediately, staffed by a Canadian doctor who'd just arrived in Israel as a wartime volunteer.

OCTOBER 21

Tamar remained under sedation at Assuta Hospital. "Please help us by reading psalms for Tamar's healing," her father, Avi, told the media. "We need a miracle."

OCTOBER 22

Tamar remained sedated and on a ventilator.

OCTOBER 23

A CT scan revealed a severe cerebral edema.

OCTOBER 26

The medical committee of Assuta Hospital determined brain death. Treatment was stopped.

OCTOBER 28

Tamar Torpiashvili, age nine, was declared dead from cardiac arrest—a heart attack—suffered during a warning siren. The state of Israel officially categorized her death as having been caused by "hostile action."

OCTOBER 29–NOVEMBER 2

Hundreds gathered around Tamar's corpse, draped in a red sheet with gold embroidery, at the Ashdod municipal cemetery. Rabbi Aharon Mor, who delivered the eulogy, said, "I have accompanied many families in their difficult times, but I've never had a case like this."

The Torpiashvili family home couldn't accommodate the large number of mourners for the shiva, prompting the observance to be held at the Shazar School of Arts and Sciences, where Tamar had been a student in the fifth grade.

Avi Torpiashvili found himself puzzled.

From the moment he passed through the iron gate of the school, he'd had a nagging feeling that he'd forgotten something—or someone. Why was he at his daughter's school? Why was he speaking with her teachers for so long? And Tamar—where is Tamar? He knew what had happened to her, and yet every few minutes he was gripped by the impulse to check on her, to pick her up. Why had he left his child alone in a cemetery and walked to her school without her?

Manana Torpiashvili remained silent. She didn't blame Hamas but herself. She felt guilty for leaving the news on the TV for days, guilty for not hugging Tamar more, guilty for not taking her to see a psychologist, guilty for letting Avi tell Tamar she was "exaggerating." All they were left with was guilt and regret.

Kites and Eulogies

1

Testimony of Ayelet Shachar-Epstein, fifty,
Kibbutz Kfar Aza:

On the seventh of October my world collapsed.

The evening before Simchat Torah, we celebrated, all of us: grandfather Amos and grandmother Bilha, founders of Kibbutz Kfar Aza; my husband, Uri Epstein, and our three children, Rona, Alma, and Neta, together with Neta's girlfriend, Iran; my husband's sister, Vered Liebstein, her husband, Ofir Liebstein, head of the Sha'ar HaNegev Regional Council, and their four children, Aviv, Nitzan, Idan, and Uri. We parted with kisses and hugs with the plan to all meet in the morning at Amos and Bilha's house and make kites for the Afifoniada—a festival of kite flying, where we fly kites over the border of the Gaza as a gesture, a sign that we wish to live in peace.

6:25 A.M.

I was still tossing and turning in bed. I think I dreamed about our last evening in Lucerne ... we were eating at a restaurant, drinking excellent wine from Italy that the owner was pouring and everything was on the house. . . . I don't remember the exact details, but I remember the feeling: happiness.

The dream shattered into a sequence of events that I have a hard time grasping.

6:30 A.M.

Code Red, rocket barrages, and lots of gunfire. We ran to the safe room and closed the door. After five minutes, my father-in-law called and said that Bilha, my mother-in-law, was unreachable. "I call and she doesn't answer." I ran to their house in pajamas. I heard gunshots on the way and found Bilha lying on the balcony. I thought it was a heart attack or stroke. She lay face down on the floor. I checked for a pulse and turned her over. Only then did I realize she was shot.

6:40 A.M.

I went to my father-in-law's house and stayed with him in the safe room.

Leaving Amos alone was not an option, and in any case, it was too dangerous to go back home.

9:00 A.M.

The members of the kibbutz's emergency response squad left the moment they were summoned. Among them were my two brothers-in-law, Uri Russo and Ofir Liebstein.

Uri left his house on his bicycle, carrying his gun. He fought courageously and was found shot dead with six dead terrorists lying around him and six bullets missing from the magazine of his gun. He was a loving partner to my sister Dafna, who to-gether with her raised three daughters in a colorful house where there was always something going on: a walk with the dog, Peanut, a mandala workshop, a gourmet meal being cooked.

Ofir Liebstein, the head of the Sha'ar HaNegev Regional Council for the past five years, was no longer an official member of the emergency response squad. He didn't have to go out to fight, but it was clear to him that it was his responsibility. He was shot and killed while trying to return fire and died in the garden of our home, under an olive tree.

Ofir was my brother-in-law, my neighbor, my friend. He was a beautiful soul, a peace-seeking soul. He believed in co-existence. He had just founded a new industrial complex designed to create jobs for thousands of Palestinians from Gaza alongside Israelis. He believed that once we decided to work together—Israelis and Palestinians—there was no limit to the future we could build. He also initiated the Red South festival, which brought people from all over to the Gaza border to see the anemones bloom. At one of those events, he was asked to describe himself in a single sentence and he said, "I see everything twice—once when I dream it and the second time when it happens."

10:00 A.M.

We received notifications about break-ins in the youth neighborhood, where Nitzan, my nineteen-year-old nephew, lives alongside my eldest son, Neta, and his girlfriend, Iran.

There were a lot of terrorists in the neighborhood, moving from apartment to apartment, murdering the residents.

Nitzan, who already knew that his father and grandmother were murdered, wrote to me: "they're trying to break in" and later, "I just want to live." Murderers entered his apartment and shot at his safe room. Nitzan was hit in the thigh and lost a lot of blood. With his last strength and the guidance of his doctor cousin, he used his own clothing as a tourniquet.

Iran had to use her body to stop Neta from going to his cousin's house under fire—she physically restrained him, held him back.

11:00 A.M.

Neta messaged me about hearing shouting in Arabic and bursts of shooting. A car alarm. "Is Iran afraid?" I asked him, and he answered, "We both are." I told him to hug her tight.

Three terrorists broke into their apartment and then into the safe room. They threw a grenade that didn't explode and then two more.

1:00 P.M.

I asked if Neta was still breathing and Iran wrote:

"No."

"Iran? Is he breathing?" I asked again.

"No."

Neta had shouted "grenade" and leapt onto it. They'd also fired numerous shots at him.

I felt as if the sky had fallen on me.

I cannot come to grips with you being gone, Neta.

My child, my dear child, where are you?

I long to have you beside me, to hold you close, to gaze into your eyes, to rise up on my tiptoes just to match your height.

My Neta, my firstborn, a beautiful boy who grew up into a beautiful man both inside and out. A volunteer for children and young people with special needs.

Just last Thursday, you couldn't bear to see me sitting alone in the dining hall. You slammed your tray down in front of me, declaring, "The person who eats alone dies alone," so we dined together. How can it be that you're the one dead now?

Your goodness knew no bounds.

3:00 P.M.

It was a slaughter. The shooting was nonstop.

Grandfather and I had been holding out for eight hours by then. Stuck in the safe room. No electricity, no phones.

The both of us were crying.

His stomach hurt.

I felt a sharp ache in my womb.

4:00 P.M.

Iran was rescued—she was the first to be rescued from Kfar Aza. You made a choice, my son—one that can't be ignored—you saved Iran. This was your victory.

5:20 P.M.

Shouting in Arabic. The terrorists were outside in Amir's sukkah.

8:30 P.M.

Thirteen hours of a siege. I began to understand we wouldn't be rescued and we made ready to sleep in the safe room. Except Grandfather Amos refused to sleep there—he wanted to go back to his bed. "Everyone's already dead," he said. "What does it matter if we die too?"

OCTOBER 8, 2023

7:13 A.M.

Twenty-four hours into the fighting, it didn't look like it was going to end. During the night, they shot at the house and shattered all the windows in the living room.

I had a dream of you as a newborn, gazing at me for the first
time, blue-eyed and beautiful. Then, images from our family trip
to Mount Pilatus, bathed in Swiss sunlight, flashed through my
mind, followed by an image of you, your curls bouncing, as we
walked hand in hand to school under the "Hello First Grade" arch.

7:39 A.M.

More shooting than before. Shouting in Arabic.

How did you feel when the bullet hit you, my boy? I want
to see you and hug you one last time. To kiss those eyes and
then—to close them.

I'm thinking about Iran and what she went through in those
moments. She hid under the bed for so many hours. I sense her
love for you is strong and pure.

9:00 A.M.

A car stopped outside and I wasn't sure whether it was the army
or not. I decided to take the chance and check: it was an IDF
soldier, who told me to get back inside—"we're coming to rescue
you."

11:00 A.M.

Grandfather and I were rescued after twenty-seven hours.

And after us: Uri and Alma, Vered, Aviv, Idan, and Uri.

We left four family members dead in Kfar Aza—and then
there was Nitzan, whose fate was unknown.

Iran told us about your heroism, my son—how you saved her—and we took comfort in knowing that you didn't die in vain. We hugged her—for ourselves, but also for you, Neta.

OCTOBER 20, 2023

For a few long days there were conflicting reports regarding Nitzan's fate. When IDF soldiers entered his apartment in the afternoon, they found no trace of him. In all our hearts, there was hope that they'd find him alive. Today, we laid him to rest in the same cemetery where his father was buried just two days earlier.

Vered, his mother, paid tribute to him at his grave: "Your intelligence, courage, and willpower were endless. . . . You were always the first to offer a helping hand. . . . Forgive us for leaving you alone to face the murderers. We pleaded for your rescue, but help never arrived. . . . Take care of Dad up in heaven."

OCTOBER 21, 2023—MATAN VILLAGE

Two weeks after you died and I still couldn't sleep, my son.

I wanted to hug you, smell you, feel the stubble of your beard against my cheek.

Today, we visited a house in Matan Village. We've been resettled here, in this vast place so different from our 110 square meters in Kfar Aza. What would you think of it? Will we be able to find happiness here? Is it possible to build a new home away from our home? Without you?

NOVEMBER 10, 2023—LONDON

Good morning to you, my now twenty-two-year-old boy.

Yesterday we celebrated your birthday with beers and tears in a neighborhood pub near the apartment we found in Kensington. You would have loved this place, which has an endless beer list, along with traditional English pies and burgers. In the afternoon we flew colorful balloons from the roof. The staff of the place joined in with a toast to your memory and the balloons rose up and brought a moment of color to the gray London street.

NOVEMBER 15, KFAR AZA

Today was the first time I returned to Kfar Aza since October 7.

Your and Iran's apartment is destroyed.

The bed is broken, everything's shattered, and tossed into the center of the room in a heap of everything you owned—burned and crushed.

I recognized the laundry basket I bought you, and the laundry that I'd washed and folded was scattered everywhere; the bed sheets were stained with blood. We managed to save a few of your items: a mix CD that Iran made for you for your anniversary, and a photo of you in your green goalie uniform jumping to make a save during the semifinals. There's also a pillow in the room, wrapped in Alma's sheets—it's so out of place with all the destruction and blood. She must've brought the pillow with her one of the times she came to your place to get pampered by you—you positively spoiled her. You were her beloved big brother and I can't tell you how much she misses you—the way you'd end an argument with her by tickling her . . . which somehow always calmed her down . . .

NOVEMBER 16, MATAN VILLAGE

The remnant of our family: Vered, Dafna, and their children moved into Matan Village with us.

No Ofir. No Uri. No Nitzan. No Bilha. No Neta.

A tiny kibbutz of mourners.

I'm looking at your photos, and angry that you're not here.

Angry that there is no "you" in all your size and height, no smell of your sweat after a workout, no sound of your voice calling me Mom, no warmth of your body when you hug me from behind and squeeze my shoulders.

I'm angry about what we've endured. About your grandfather crying with every announcement that someone from our family had died. About being abandoned to our fate that day in Kfar Aza, without any support from a country that suddenly seemed to not exist.

I don't know how to say goodbye to you, my child.

2

Five members of the Kotz family were murdered on October 7:

Aviv (fifty-three), Livnat (forty-nine), Rotem (eighteen), Yonatan (sixteen), and Yiftach (fourteen).

The surviving members of the Kotz family (Benny, Tamar, Talia, and Sharon), and of the Levy family (Yehuda, Paulette, Ashi, Ziv, and Adi), collaborated on the following eulogy:

One hundred years before the day of our disaster, the Kotz family fled the Russian Revolution in Ukraine and immigrated to Mandatory Palestine. They were seeking a refuge, a land where they would not be persecuted for being Jews. Thirty-three years later, the Levy family fled the riots and pogroms of their home outside Marrakech, Morocco, in search of the same haven in the young state of Israel.

In light of our disaster—in light of the murder of our children, our siblings, our grandchildren—we must ask: Did our ancestors make a mistake?

On that cursed Sabbath the family was supposed to gather

together with other members of Kibbutz Kfar Aza for a festival initiated by Aviv and Livnat—the Kite Parade, a festival featuring the flying of kites above the border fence as a symbol of peace to our neighbors in Gaza. For a decade and a half, on the holiday of Simchat Torah, this festival has occurred.

As the explosive-filled balloons sent over the border from Gaza multiplied, we merely multiplied the kites.

That Saturday, instead of flying kites for peace, however, we woke up to war.

Shelling and sirens woke us.

We weren't able to get in touch with everyone—and as our attempts at contact failed, it slowly dawned on us what a disaster this was, though at the time we had no idea of the scale. *There are terrorists in my house . . . we're being shot at . . . he's injured . . . she's bleeding . . .* As our neighbors' messages piled up, we realized no help was coming.

Aviv and Livnat's next-door neighbors were murdered: Roy and Smadar Idan. Two of their children survived by hiding in the closet. Their three-year-old, Abigail Idan, fled after seeing her parents murdered and was abducted and taken to Gaza, along with neighbors from the adjacent house, Hagar Brodach and her three young children, Ofri, age ten; Yuval, nine; and Oriya, four.

In another house, our eighteen-year-old Rotem's closest friend, Agam Goldstein-Almog, age seventeen, was kidnapped along with her mother, Chen, and her brothers, Gal, eleven, and Tal, nine.

The father of the Goldstein-Almog family, Nadav, and the eldest sister of the family, Yam, were murdered in front of everyone. We repeatedly called Agam to ask after Rotem, not knowing that she'd already been taken to Gaza. We found out only three days later.

A kibbutz member entered the house and found the five of you together, dead in bed, Aviv hugging Livnat and the children.

Tell us, how to bury five pure souls? How can two grandfathers and two grandmothers say Kaddish for their children and grandchildren? Whom to cry for first?

Aviv Kotz was born in Kibbutz Kfar Aza on the eve of Passover, 1970, to parents Beni and Tamar. In the kibbutz of those days, the children lived in communal housing—without their parents—and this taught them responsibility from the youngest age. They managed their own lives, driving the tractor through the orchards, running barefoot in the hills. Aviv was good with his hands. Like many of his friends, he built his own house in the kibbutz. He was an engineer, the manager of a consultancy company, and also an artist in a number of fields: photography, sculpture, and illustration.

Livnat was born in the city of Rehovot in 1973, in the midst of a ceasefire during the Yom Kippur War. Paulette, her mother, was in the hospital in labor while Yehuda, her father, was serving at the front, defending Israel against the attacking Arab armies. He was in his tank when he got the news: "Congratulations, Yehuda, you have a daughter!"

Livnat was educated at the Rehovot schools, but her mind was always elsewhere: she was a wanderer, a dreamer.

Aviv fell in love with her the moment he met her. This was in the late 1990s: she was working as a dispatcher, and he was a courier, which meant she told him where to go. But time and again, she refused his advances. Still, he never gave up. Superficially, they were quite different: Aviv laid-back, Livnat energetic, even stormy. But he found a fierceness in her, and she found a calmness in him, which helped her pursue her own artistic passions, as a graphic designer and art educator. Frequent collaborators, they lived together in Tel Aviv and then in the United States, but chose to return to the kibbutz to raise their children.

We have no other home, they said. *We have no other country.*

After Operation Protective Edge [the 2014 Gaza War], Livnat founded an after-school space for art activities and crafts—a place for kids to go to forget about the rockets. She'd noticed her own son Yonatan developing anxiety from the constant rocket fire and decided to dedicate herself to improving the lives of Israeli children at the border. She encouraged all of us to think more critically and to pursue a life of service: whenever she had an occasion that would warrant a gift, such as a birthday, she would ask people in lieu of presents to volunteer for a few hours in the community.

The children: how to eulogize them, who didn't have the time to grow up?

Rotem, eighteen, had just enlisted in the army, but she never lost her smile. Her friends report having never seen her sad, the same friends who cry over her today.

Yonatan, sixteen, was witty, sensitive. He dreamed of playing basketball professionally and was obsessed with his favorite team, Hapoel Tel Aviv, whose trainers chose him as their Discovery of the Year—a promising future draft pick.

Yiftach, fourteen, followed in his brother's footsteps, honing his basketball skills and unwilling to receive the compliments he deserved on his intelligence, his humility, and his work ethic.

A month after the disaster, we all met up in Tel Aviv to hold the Kite Festival there, flying kites for the hostages, calling for their immediate return.

As Aviv used to say, decorating the sky.

Afterword

The events of 10/7 had barely passed into history when story came to claim them, in a process that scholars call "homologizing," wherein new events are made "homologous" with past events, creating commonalities, similarities, templates, and patterns that turn the discipline of history into something religious, even mystical. "The deadliest day for Jews since the Holocaust" was the common description, a phrase that as it was repeated and repeated by heads of state, by the media, and by my own friends and family, seemed not merely to bind the two phenomena but even to propose one (the Holocaust) as the progenitor of the other (10/7).

Historians have long pointed to this relational, recapitulative process as fundamental to Judaism's survival, its tendency to associate each new event with preceding events, turning all occurrence into recurrence, the present into a concatenation of pasts, a semblance of premessianic lived eternity.

Jewish time is like a scroll, to be unrolled and rerolled yearly. The calendar of the holidays annually recurs, as does the calendar of the Torah reading. Every Sabbath, a certain portion of the Torah is read, so that every year the full cycle of the Torah reading is concluded and immediately begun again on the holiday of Simchat Torah, which this year fell on the secular date of Saturday, October 7.

As Yosef Hayim Yerushalmi explains in his masterpiece *Zakhor*, this reincarnation of the prior in the present is meant to be experienced personally but winds up expressing itself politically. Every year, when a Jew reads the story of the Exodus from Egypt, he is to think of himself as having been personally redeemed, brought out of slavery and through the split Red Sea. Every year, when a Jew reads the story of Moses receiving the Torah, he is to think of himself as having been personally present at Sinai, standing alongside the souls of all the generations before and since. Jewish history, which Yerushalmi considered something of an oxymoron, permits the destruction of the Second Temple and the Roman exile to be treated as a recurrence of the destruction of the First Temple and the Babylonian exile; both are said to have occurred on the same date, the ninth of Av, just half a millennium apart, and both are to be attributed not to political struggles but to divine punishment for Israel's sins. Accordingly, each enemy who arose in the Jewish diaspora was portrayed as an incarnation of prior enemies, in an iniquitous lineage that links Stalin and Hitler and the pogromist Khmelnitsky to Titus, Nebuchadnezzar, Haman, Pharaoh, and the warrior-nation of Amalek, which ambushed the wandering Israelites in the desert.

It was Prime Minister Netanyahu himself who invoked Amalek immediately following the Simchat Torah attacks, telling the Israeli and Jewish publics, telling the world, "You must remember what Amalek has done to you, says our Holy Torah, and we do remember, and we are fighting. Our brave troops in Gaza . . . are joining the chain of Jewish heroes, an unbroken chain that began three thousand years ago with Joshua ben Nun and that continues through the heroes of 1948, the Six-Day War, the '73 October War."

While the press was telling us that this massacre (and Israel's massive reaction) was "an epochal event," "a game changer," "a turning point in the crisis" (to quote a few major international news outlets), the prime minister of Israel refused to agree: to Netanyahu and not just to Netanyahu, the violence perpetrated by Hamas and Palestinian Islamic Jihad and others was the old Amalek violence returned, as ancient as recorded time, and just slightly younger than the Jew hatred that fomented it. This remains the primary interpretive challenge of 10/7—the challenge of whether to approach its slaughter as an era-defining tragedy or a theological recrudescence; as a man-made terror or a God-ordained horror, as Israeli history or Jewish story.

If the deaths of 10/7 can be treated historically, in terms modern and factual, then Israel, too, can be treated as modern and factual, and inquests can be made into its failures, and policy solutions to its problems can be found; fanaticism can be de-incentivized, and through compromise even the most intransigent of enemies can be turned into neighbors, even into neighboring states.

But if the deaths of 10/7 are to be regarded as just the latest iterations of the immemorial story of Jewish suffering, then Israel itself becomes party to that story—which was precisely the fate that Israel was founded to avoid; Israel's mission was to end Jewish victimhood, not to extend it.

"The deadliest day for Jews since the Holocaust" was also the day that Jewishness returned to Israel: Jewishness as an identity, regardless of belief or practice. At a time of rising nationalist religiosity and Jewish extremism, a massacre was perpetrated on the avowedly secular: Jews were killed for being Jews; not because they were wearing kippot, not because they were conspiring to raze Al-Aqsa and erect a Third Temple, but merely because they had the temerity to exist as Jews within the borders of a Jewish state; while the Arabs who were killed that day, the Christian Arabs and Muslim Arabs both, were killed because they had the gall to live among Jews as fellow citizens; and the Nepalese and Thai citizens who were killed that day were killed because they dared to work for Jews, toiling in Jewish fields, picking Jewish produce. It's tempting to take this even further and say that the dogs that were killed that day were killed because they were Jewish dogs, and that the cars that were burned that day were burned because they were Jewish cars . . .

Murder, rape, abduction, torture, mutilation, immolation—these are the acts by which history entered Judaism, in the very first books by Jewish communities that didn't attempt to relativize the past, just to record it accurately. *Sifrei ha zikhronot* ("memory books") appeared centuries after the sacred canon was closed but attained a type of sacral standardization in the Middle Ages. Communally composed summaries of archives, these books recorded the names of the community's rabbis and leaders, along with testimonials of persecutions and lists of victims to be read aloud in synagogues during memorial services for the dead. The most famous of these books might be the earliest that survives, that of the community of Nuremberg, which was kept between 1296 and 1392 and contains accounts of persecutions throughout Germany and France from the First Crusade in 1096 through the libel-sparked pogroms that attended the outbreak of plague in 1349.

Widespread throughout Ashkenazi Jewish life, and among certain Sephardi and Mizrahi communities, this tradition was given new urgency following the Holocaust, when survivors sought to reconstruct what had been taken from them, at least on the page. *Yizkor* books ("memorial books") are most notable for the dispersion of their authoring collective: the book memorializing the town of Bershad, for example, one of the Pale of Settlement towns from which my family hails, features contributions about Bershad written by Bershaders scattered to Jerusalem, Tel Aviv, New York, Mexico, Panama, and elsewhere, reminiscing about the town's inhabitants, its illustrious sages, its geography and industry, alongside descriptions of the inconceivable evils the town endured, from a Haydamak Cossack pogrom in which a bride and groom were slaughtered under their wedding canopy to the myriad butcheries committed by the Black Hundreds, Bolsheviks, Nazis, and Romanians.

10/7: One Hundred Human Stories is the heir to those *Yizkor* books, the first major *sefer ha zikhronot* since the spate that concerned the Holocaust—the necrology and martyrology of a single day that seeks to reclaim the dead, at least some of them, from numeric anonymity and political exploitation.

It is possible to read this book and finish it with a desire for revenge, and it is equally possible to read this book and finish it with a renewed commitment to peace. I have read this book multiple times, in a few languages, and have had both responses. I have witnessed the unflagging dedication of its author, my wife, who wrote this book in the winter after the massacre, even while mourning her own dead and comforting strangers who began as sources and ended as friends. It is my greatest hope that the friends and families of the victims portrayed here find a humanity they recognize, and that the memories of those they've lost transcend the injustice of victimhood and live on fully, within their communities and in a fairer, freer world.

—JOSHUA COHEN

Acknowledgments

Writing a book about such painful events can be painful itself, though in retrospect I can't imagine how else I would've spent the winter of 2023—a time of mourning for myself, my family, and my friends.

I count myself lucky to have had the support of many throughout this process, and I would like to acknowledge at least a few of them here: my research assistants Nurit Laxer, Merav Weiss, Tamar Peled, and Shani Alush, first-line interviewers and transcribers extraordinaire, who went to great lengths to track down and establish initial contact with families of the victims; another of my research assistants, Maayan Hirsch, also happens to be my sister-in-law, whose strength and intelligence have been a blessing; without these dedicated, sensitive women, this book simply would not exist. The same can be said for Joachim Schnerf, this book's commissioning editor, the man who first understood the importance of a work such as this and who guided me throughout its writing. Additionally, I would like to thank my US editors Tim Bartlett and Kevin Reilly at St. Martin's Press and my agent Gail Ross for their support; their belief in me helped instill some of the confidence necessary to write a book in what isn't my native language.

A great deal of thanks is also due to my family at *Haaretz*, the newspaper that fostered me, and to my actual family, my parents, Yoram and Rachel, and my brother, Shai; every day I try to live up to the values they've instilled in me. My husband, Joshua Cohen, provided invaluable assistance (and a beautiful afterword): the love he's shown me I can only hope to return.

Lastly, and most crucially, I would like to express my gratitude to the bereaved—to the family and friends whose mourning I interrupted with questions about their loved ones, who in the midst of their most difficult days found the time and the heart to share with me their stories, their histories, their communities, their lives. This book is subtitled *100 Human Stories*, but each victim of the October 7 massacre contained a world of stories—as do the indirect victims who survive them: the widow, the widower, the orphan, the parent without a child. For trusting me to tell at least a few of these stories, they have my deepest appreciation, admiration, and respect.